A Breed
Apart

By the same author

Adam's Farm: My Life on the Land
Like Farmer, Like Son
A Farmer and His Dog

ADAM HENSON

My Adventures with
BRITAIN'S RARE BREEDS

A Breed *Apart*

BOOKS

1 3 5 7 9 10 8 6 4 2

BBC Books, an imprint of Ebury Publishing
20 Vauxhall Bridge Road,
London SW1V 2SA

BBC Books is part of the Penguin Random House group of companies
whose addresses can be found at global.penguinrandomhouse.com

Penguin
Random House
UK

First published by BBC Books in 2019

www.penguin.co.uk

A CIP catalogue record for this book is available from the British Library

ISBN 9781785943751

Illustrations by Ella Mclean

Typeset in 12/18.4 pt ColdstyleRoman
by Integra Software Services Pvt. Ltd, Pondicherry

Printed and bound in Great Britain by Clays Ltd, Elcograf S.p.A.

Penguin Random House is committed to a sustainable future for
our business, our readers and our planet. This book is made
from Forest Stewardship Council® certified paper.

To my gorgeous partner Charlie and our wonderful children Ella and Alfie, for all their love and support.

Contents

Introduction

To everyone else, the place I call home looks just like any other farm. At its heart there's the yard, busy with the coming and going of people, vehicles and livestock. A well-used shovel is propped against a wall, there's an antique water trough by the gate and old milk churns stand in each corner. The farm sits alongside an old Roman road called Buckle Street, or *Bugghilde Street*, and the ancient track across this part of the Cotswolds might even have been a Neolithic trading route before then. So when I look at our wide-horned cattle and our flocks of Longwool sheep, I can see the same animals that lived on this land a thousand years ago; the ones that were herded and worked on the very same spot by our farming forebears. If I close my eyes I can sometimes imagine the sounds of Roman carts rattling over the rough, rutted earth and the faint, far-off thud of heavy hooves, carried on the breeze.

I was raised on this family farm along with my sisters, Elizabeth, Louise and Rebecca (known as Libby, Lolo and Becca) and it's where I live and work to this day. It was my dad, Joe Henson, who took on the tenancy of Bemborough Farm in 1962 with his old school friend, John Neave, and set our lives on a path to share this patch of the countryside with a host of unusual livestock.

Farming on thin Cotswold brash is always going to be hard work and, it was believed, only paid if you ran a large-scale arable enterprise. So that's exactly what they did, but it wasn't long before Dad's lifelong fascination with old breeds of livestock took a hold. Not just any sort of farm animal, his passion was for native breeds; in other words, ones that developed or were created over hundreds, and in some cases thousands, of years here in the British Isles.

'Traditional' is the word often used for the types of native sheep, cattle and pigs that fell out of favour in the post-war years, mainly on account of being considered non-commercial, as they tend to be slow to grow, all-purpose farm animals. The drive in the second half of the twentieth century was towards an intensive commercial food system which involved introducing highly productive, fast-maturing breeds dependent on winter feeding and housing, and on management and veterinary interventions. No room there for the Caithness cow or the Ulster White pig.

But the ones that really intrigued my dad were the rare breeds. That is, livestock that were now so few in number that they were in need of immediate help if they were to avoid extinction. These were the animals that came to the attention of the conservation charity, the Rare Breeds Survival Trust (RBST), when it carried out its inaugural livestock census in the 1970s and defined categories of rarity for the first time. These days, that tally of breeding stock, the Trust's Danger List, takes place every year in order to track the changing fortunes of Britain's farm breeds. Breeds that are enjoying a resurgence may drop off the list, while others that are struggling are added.

It wasn't a tool that was available to Dad nearly 60 years ago, though. He started gathering a livestock collection – some of them unloved, most of them unfashionable and all of them uneconomic in the modern world of post-Second World War agriculture. He didn't care though, because he knew these animals were uniquely British and had each played a role in our history. He believed they might carry genetic traits that could prove useful in the future. In short, he was a visionary with ideas that were decades ahead of his time.

With the constant support, and occasional bemusement of our mum, Gillie, he became the figurehead of a fledgling rare breeds movement, and before long the media started taking an interest in him and his unusual collection of livestock. He became a regular face on children's TV show *Animal Magic*, and then went on to appear on long-running shows such as *Tomorrow's World*, *Blue Peter* and *Any Questions?* He even fronted his own primetime BBC One series for the Natural History Unit and for several years he was one of the presenters on BBC Two's *In the Country*. Looking back at the old recordings now, after 40 years, it was clearly an early blueprint for today's high-profile BBC rural affairs programmes. And I know a bit about them!

Dad helped to set up and lead the RBST. Since it was launched in 1973, with J. Henson Esq. as its first chairman, I am very pleased to say that not a single breed of British farm livestock has died out – a dramatic about-turn when you consider that 26 breeds had been driven to extinction in the first 70-odd years of the twentieth century.

Dad also devised and created the Cotswold Farm Park. When it opened, on part of the tenanted farm near Guiting Power, it was the first farm park in the world. On launch day, in the spring of 1971, the initial, inquisitive visitors were treated to the sight of three local breeds: Cotswold sheep, Gloucester cows and Old Spots pigs. The other sheep breeds on display were Soays, Portlands and Jacobs, and one of the last surviving original Norfolk Horn rams. Meanwhile, in the main cattle pens they saw White Parks, Longhorns, Highlands, Belted Galloways and Dexters.

Today, I'm incredibly proud to continue Dad's work at Bemborough, alongside my friend and business partner, Duncan Andrews, and our team. The original livestock collection has grown over the years; we've now got hundreds of individual animals representing 60 different breeds from all six main species – cattle, sheep, pigs, goats, equines and poultry. I suppose you would call it the nation's home-grown menagerie and it really does include sheep whose diet is seaweed, pigs who gorged on windfall apples and a herd of goats whose relatives were part of the resistance movement against invading German troops. Some of the breeds can trace their ancestors back to the Iron Age, or even before, and they are as much a part of the British landscape as the dales of Yorkshire, the waterways of Norfolk and the moorland of the West Country.

I'm an enthusiastic promoter of rare, native and traditional breeds of unique and wonderfully British livestock. They're often called the county breeds because many of them originated in their own particular parts of the country, mostly in the shires or within very small geographical areas such as Exmoor, Wensleydale or Jersey. That's where they evolved, or in many cases were selectively bred over time, to suit the soil, landscape, weather, farming traditions or the food needs of a hungry population in that specific place. So lean, wiry, agile sheep grew up in the craggy, mountainous highlands and islands of Scotland, while much bigger, rounded flocks with plenty of lustrous wool lazily grazed the meadows of southern England to satisfy the meat and cloth-making industries.

There are 116 officially recognised rare and native farm breeds in the UK today, and that's before you count the numerous varieties of chickens, turkeys, ducks and geese which are listed. The number's even higher if you go back in time and add the breeds which were once popular but were allowed to die out over the last couple of centuries.

So where did these wonderful, varied breeds come from and why do they differ so much? All our domestic animals are descended from a small number of wild ancestors. Thanks to the insight of Charles Darwin we now understand that wild populations are moulded over time by natural selection. He observed that all plants and animals produce more offspring than survive in each generation and that, on balance, the offspring which survive to be parents themselves are those which best 'fit' their environment. That is, how well adapted they are to their surroundings. Hence the term 'survival of the fittest'. Darwin didn't know how traits were carried from parent to offspring because genes hadn't yet been discovered, but he understood that they were passed down the generations.

The wild ancestors of modern farm animals first came into close contact with humans when they raided their crops. This provided the opportunity for those early farmers to corral and capture small groups. Humans could provide winter feed, summer water supplies or protection from wild predators, so they lifted the natural selection pressures normally acting on the wild population and therefore more of the offspring survived. This allowed the humans to impose their own selection pressures. Those individuals which tolerated captivity would have thrived and had more offspring than those with a wilder temperament. So, humans created docile, manageable populations which became increasingly dependent upon humans, because they'd become less well adapted to a wild environment.

The farmers could then begin to favour those animals with traits they valued, keeping those to be the parents of the next generation while eating the ones which were less desirable. The result over generations were animals which grow more quickly, thrive on a particular diet or management system, or livestock which produce more milk than is needed by their own calves, kids or lambs.

Domestication was a first step carried out by our ancestors thousands of years ago, but the principle of animal breeding by replacing 'natural' selection in order to develop breeds and strains to 'fit' our manmade environments, remains exactly the same.

We think of mainland Britain as a secure, well-defended, democratic island today but that's really only been the case for the last thousand years or thereabouts. The victory of a French duke, William of Normandy, at the Battle of Hastings in 1066 was just the last in a long wave of visits, settlements, raids and invasions. Early Neolithic farmers, Celts, Angles, Saxons, Jutes, Vikings, Romans and others all came here, and every time new peoples landed they brought their culture, customs, language and very often their animals with them.

All the cattle we see today can be traced back to the great prehistoric wild Aurochs which migrated from Asia and arrived in Europe about 250,000 years ago. It's the Aurochs that appears in the famous primitive cave paintings discovered at Lascaux in France. These were creatures so big they've been called elephant-cattle and dino-cows and they would certainly have dwarfed our modern-day breeds. Standing at least seven feet tall with enormous forward-facing horns, this was a beast which roamed freely for thousands of years. But hunting, disease and habitat loss eventually led to their extinction. The last Aurochs, a female, died in the Jaktoro forest in Poland in 1627.

Although the story doesn't quite end there, because two attempts were made to recreate the extinct ancestors of modern cattle by 'breeding back' in German zoos between the 1920s and the 1950s. Using preserved skulls and original drawings as a guide, scientists selected old and unimproved cattle breeds from across Europe which shared certain characteristics with the Aurochs – similar shoulders, the correct skin type or the right sort of pointed horns.

They actually succeeded in creating something which not only looked like the extinct original but behaved like it too. The descendants of those recreated animals are on display in Munich, but their so-called de-extinction is still hotly disputed and even the zoo authorities now refer to the animals as look-alike or bred-back Aurochs.

We know that the Iron Age descendants of the ancient Aurochs were used as working animals in Britain. Two and a half thousand years ago, castrated bulls – the trusty and powerful ox – started being trained to haul basic implements and pull the first simple ploughs. But the earliest evidence that cows were being kept for their milk comes much earlier, about 7,000 years ago. Pots unearthed by archaeologists in the Sahara desert point to African peoples making rough types of cheese, butter and even yoghurt.

The story of British sheep also starts in prehistoric times with their wild ancestors, the magnificently-horned Mouflon – a reddish-brown animal with a short coat whose large curled horns are so long they almost form a full circle. Sheep were domesticated much earlier than cattle. Herders started favouring the animals that best suited their needs, preferring small hornless sheep, ones with more wool fibres than hair in their coats and choosing those with the whitest fleeces, which could be spun, felted and dyed. Unlike the Aurochs, the Mouflon is alive and well in the twenty-first century with flocks still running wild in Europe. The DNA of the Mouflon that forage on the mountainous islands of Sardinia and Corsica in the Mediterranean can be found in those gambolling lambs which so delightfully signal the start of spring in Britain.

The British sheep which differ most from the agile, short-haired Mouflon are the leisurely, flamboyant-looking long wool breeds. Instead of tight, white wool on their backs imagine long golden tresses hanging down in curls. It's the outstanding feature found in the county breeds of Lincolnshire, Leicestershire, Yorkshire and the West Country, and stems from the fleecy rams and ewes brought over by Emperor Claudius and his Roman legionnaries when they invaded in 43AD. The occupiers prized their long-fleeced sheep and used the wool for making their uniforms. Soft, cosy, long wool jumpers really should have been on the list when *Monty Python* asked the immortal question, 'What have the Romans ever done for us?'

There's one old livestock word that's hardly ever heard these days: 'swine' was used to describe the wide variety of farmed pigs, as well as feral hogs, that foraged all over Britain and the wild boars whose temper and tusks were feared and infamous. Until a couple of generations ago, 'swineherd' was the name given to anyone who bred or tended pigs – as in, a person who literally herded swine – but the word eventually fell to the wayside in favour of the much more workaday 'pig farmer'.

Most wild pigs were coarse, hairy beasts with cloven hooves, small 'piggy' eyes, long snouts, powerful jaws and lethal tusks. They lived in scrub, woodland and forests where they scavenged on plants, roots, fallen fruit, worms and fungi. That ability to sniff out food and eat just about anything lives on in the pigs that are farmed in the British Isles today.

The domestication of pigs happened in different places and from more than one wild species. Pigs can't be herded easily so they were of no use to nomadic (or semi nomadic) farmers, but they were quickly associated with settled farming all over the world. Orphaned piglets could be reared without too much trouble and the most docile ones were selected out of each litter to be the parents of the next generation. Pigs were an easy source of food and they were also used to prepare the ground for crops, rooting up the weeds and fertilising at the same time. Pigs can plough up a field with their snouts in no time at all and their excellent sense of smell was put to good use hunting for truffles.

In the New Forest, where people were forbidden from having dogs large enough to hunt, the foresters traditionally trained their pigs to seek out and even retrieve game. I can quite believe this, pigs are very intelligent and great opportunists. Years ago, one of our piglets discovered that she could sneak up on a sleeping Highland cow and steal a suckle of milk. Within days all the piglets had learned the same trick, and it persisted throughout the summer, learned knowledge passing from one litter to the next.

The first domesticated pigs arrived in Britain with the Romans and their lop ears and curled tails marked them out from the native prick-eared, straight-tailed, wild woodland boars. Between the prehistoric swine and the modern breeds we know today there was a big, floppy-eared hog called the Old English pig. In the centuries before the Industrial Revolution, when Britain was a pastoral nation, the Old English pig was popular with swineherds because it more or less looked after itself, rootling around for acorns, nuts, windfall fruit and anything it could find to eat in the woods, on common land and at village edges. It had strong legs and a docile nature so even walking it to market was easy.

The biggest change to our swine came when Asian pigs started to be imported to Britain in the late eighteenth and early nineteenth centuries. Chinese and Siamese boars were broad, short-legged, 'hammy' animals which had much larger litters, matured fast and fattened quickly. Soon breeders discovered that when they were crossed with their native sows the offspring were easy to keep, efficient and provided plenty of meat.

Right across the country, this influx of new blood changed the shape, colour and characteristics of local pig varieties, and in the 1800s most English counties had their own strain, most of which have long since disappeared. Pigs fitted into the lifestyles of the times. Three hundred years ago, when most working people did hard, manual labour, they found that eating fat pork gave them plenty of energy.

During the Second World War, people were encouraged to keep a pig which could be fed on household waste to increase meat production. Then, from the 1950s onwards, when the workforce was more sedentary and health conscious, the trend turned towards much leaner cuts and larger scale production of specialist breeds, leaving the local strains behind.

It's a similar story with poultry. The Red Jungle Fowl is the ancestor of all today's domestic chicken breeds, and it shows. Originally from India, Indonesia, Malaysia and the Philippines, the male Jungle Fowl is an unmistakable bird. Its gold, orange, red and green colouring makes it look at first glance like its cousin, the pheasant. The comb and wattle are bright red and it carries long, black arched tail feathers which shimmer green in sunlight. When you hear the sound of a cockerel crowing first thing in the morning, you're essentially listening to the same centuries-old call of the Red Jungle Fowl. It was domesticated more than 5,000 years ago, used for cock fighting, and then the popularity of keeping fowl for meat and eggs as well as 'sport' gradually spread west from Asia to Europe.

Here, we didn't get a taste for breeding chickens for the table until the Romans introduced the idea more than 2,000 years ago. The Dorking chicken is a big, beautiful bird and a living connection with the fowl that was popular with the Romans – though historians still can't agree if the Dorking was originally an Italian breed which the invaders brought with them, or one that was already here when they arrived. I've always signed up to the theory that when the armies landed on the south coast they had poultry with them, squeezed onto their ships alongside cargoes of weaponry and cavalry horses.

We know that the Romans were familiar with the quiet, dignified Dorking, because the Roman Empire's most celebrated writer on farming, Lucius Junius Moderatus Columella, wrote about his fascination with the fact that the bird has five toes instead of the usual four. In the first century, Columella produced an impressive 12 volumes covering all aspects of farming and food production at that time (it's a much harder read than *Farmers' Weekly* but it surely makes him the earliest known agricultural journalist). In his chapter on 'Common poultry yard hens and cocks', Columella identifies the Dorking as a good choice for a big, square-framed breeding hen: 'the largest that can be found, and not with an even number of claws, they are reckoned the most generous which have five toes.'

That extra hind toe showed up again in the 1970s when animal footprints left in Roman ceramic tiles were tested against the imprints of current breeds, almost as if an archaeologist had uncovered evidence of Cinderella's legendary glass slipper. The hoof marks of sheep, goats and pigs were all compared but the best match was between the preserved footprint of the Roman chicken and a modern Dorking hen. We were involved in that research and I can tell you that trying to get animals to walk across wet replica Roman tiles when you want them to is a challenge and a half.

Caesar's army wouldn't have known them as Dorkings of course. Only much, much later was the breed named after the charming market town in the Surrey Hills, a place that by the 1670s was being described as 'the greatest market for poultry in England'. Breeders in the town and the rest of the Mole Valley made a healthy living by supplying London's meat and poultry traders with table birds.

Catching, taming and domesticating the wild, roaming beasts and birds they found around them was a major step for the ancient farmers of Britain. But something more impressive was to come later, and it led to the transformation of many rough, old breeds into the type of farm animals we see in our fields and farmyards today. Selection truly was one of farming's greatest achievements.

Once early farmers had fought off the predators who threatened their animals and figured out how to deliberately choose the livestock that did the job they wanted them to do, they were of course used as the father, or the mother, of the next generation. So over time the population slowly adapted. The old wild and primitive sheep naturally shed their fleece each spring, so the first shepherds selected breeding animals whose wool didn't fall off, allowing it to be retained and collected as a crop. That done, they then picked out white sheep, as colourless wool can be dyed. Thus, over the centuries, we changed a wild species into a wool machine.

Right up until the 1700s though, breeding farm animals remained a haphazard business. Bulls were often kept with cows, rams ran with ewes and it was common for domesticated animals, especially pigs, to mate with the wild population. In different areas of the country, farmers would favour a type or a colour pattern that they felt was more productive – which may or may not have been based in fact. Any planned breeding was mostly done by sheer instinct and experiment, until one man stepped up with a revolutionary idea that changed farming forever.

Robert Bakewell was a Leicestershire farmer, and while he's far from being a household name today, we all owe him a huge debt of gratitude because his techniques in animal breeding and management changed the agricultural landscape and continue to influence modern day farming. He began to grow crops specifically to feed his animals, to house them over the winter and to carefully plan his breeding strategy – all of which was radical thinking in the eighteenth century.

His experiments began in 1760, when Bakewell inherited the tenancy of the family farm in Dishley near Loughborough. He was 35 years old at the time and, having travelled all over Britain and Europe studying farming methods, he saw it as the right moment to put his revolutionary ideas into practice. He separated male from female livestock and started deliberately selecting which bulls and rams should be mated with which cows and ewes. The choice might be based on how much milk the animal produces for instance, or how fast it runs or the speed at which it grows. The principles of this selective breeding technique are used to this day and are now based on measuring those characteristics we're interested in.

Before Bakewell, sheep were bred especially for wool, and cattle were bred for strength, but he started breeding for meat. His timing could not have been better. As he was transforming animal husbandry, another change was taking place in society. In cities across the country the Industrial Revolution was beginning and Bakewell's techniques would help feed the growing urban workforce in mills, foundries and factories everywhere.

By careful inbreeding of his animals – the mating of closely related males and females to concentrate 'good genes' – he was able to exaggerate the most desirable traits and 'fix' the breed, purifying the genetics to push through the attributes he'd chosen, whether that was a bigger fleece, longer body, meatier carcass, more muscle or stronger feet. Bakewell's breeds have survived into the twenty-first century and, despite a few close shaves with extinction, the results of his revolutionary techniques are still walking around on four legs, if you know where to look.

He improved an old Yorkshire breed of cattle called the Longhorn, refined the black working horses of England into the mighty Shire and developed a local breed of sheep from the Midlands to form the Leicester Longwool. Bakewell worked successfully on the main farmyard species with one obvious exception – there are no 'improved' pigs on his list of breeds. It is known that he was interested in breeding swine and intriguingly he might have had a go at developing a Bakewell baconer, but if he did he kept it under wraps and didn't leave any accounts or written records of his attempts. He wasn't a great one for documents and explanations, so much so that the Leicester Longwool breeders call Bakewell 'secretive and self-reliant'. Make of that what you will.

Thankfully breed societies are absolute sticklers for completing the paperwork, some almost to the point of obsession, as without them we'd be at a loss to know the full history of many really important and typically British livestock types. These societies started to be formed around 140 years ago when farmers with a shared interest in particular breeds started organising themselves into formal groups to create essential records of the breed. They continue to promote and champion the breeds, set the standards for organised breeding and establish the rules for showing, preserving the all-important gene pool and striving to improve production.

The societies can be a bit of a mystery to outsiders, but like any other club or organisation, they're a focal point for both enthusiasts and experts. Most members own or farm a specific breed, but it's not a requirement and there are plenty of armchair enthusiasts who are happy to support the cause by simply paying their annual subscription fee. There's a society for virtually every breed and I'm not exaggerating when I say they're crucial to the future of Britain's livestock, not just in terms of maintaining our native breeds but also continuing to develop our highly productive commercial strains.

The phrase 'pure breed' (or pedigree) crops up a lot and I'm often asked what it means. In simple terms it's a population of animals that are bred to one another, which all share the same genetic characteristics (perhaps short horns, long wool or large, lop ears) and have offspring which look the same. Farm breeds follow the same principle as dog breeds, where there are plenty of identifiable differences between Labradors, whippets and poodles for instance. By the same token, we all know what a mongrel looks like. If you ignore pure breeding and just randomly cross animals, you have no way of knowing what the offspring will be like.

A hybrid is a cross of two different pure breeds and usually the offspring grow faster and bigger than either of the parents. The improvement on the previous generation is called 'hybrid vigour' and it's what all commercial breeders want – but it's dependent on there being pure-bred strains to work with in the first place.

While cross-breeding is important to improve the traits of commercial flocks and herds, which chiefly means the most numerous animals that are bred for meat, it's crucial that the 'true' types are allowed to thrive and the original genetics maintained. It's all about genetic existence and excellence, making sure the gene pool of each breed stays undiluted. If the original DNA is preserved, and can be traced back, then a firm foundation has been created for livestock breeding and developing the breed far into the future.

If I was on *Top Gear* instead of *Countryfile* and looking for a handy example, I'd say while it's great to drive a new BMW-built five-door Mini Countryman Plug-in Hybrid, that doesn't mean we should send every surviving original 1959 vintage two-door Morris Mini-Minor to the breaker's yard. Equally, we may never drive a Formula One racing car, but the technologies used to create it filter down to the cars we all drive.

One of the most vital functions of the breed societies in the early days was to oversee the all-important herd books. I like to think of herd books, and flock or stud books for that matter, as the family tree of all pedigree animals. Published annually, these meticulously compiled volumes are the place to check out the ancestors of every registered bull, cow, boar, sow, ram, ewe, stallion, mare, billy or nanny in the breed. You'd be surprised how engrossed you can become in page after page of lineage and genetic history, but these books also have a very basic, practical role. If you're looking to buy or borrow a beefy bull or a vigorous stallion to produce the next generation of prize-winners, then the herd book is the go-to directory in your search for the most suitable, virile and potent males in the market. Think of it as an Argos catalogue of mating animals. *Love Island* for livestock, if you like.

The societies talk about bloodlines and by that they mean families within breeds which have particular characteristics. In the digital age, the bloodlines of Britain's pure-bred native livestock are just a mouse-click away, but many breed societies still produce physical herd books. Some of the oldest herd books are objects of beauty: leather bound, embossed with crests and emblems, decorated with gilt lettering and illus-trated with etchings or full-page plates. Collecting them is more than a hobby, it's a guilty pleasure, and getting a full set to display with pride on the bookshelf is the ultimate ambition for the most dedicated breed enthu-siasts. Tap the phrase 'herd book' into eBay and you'll see what I mean.

So if this genetic pool of distinct DNA is swirling around, why can't we just recreate a breed whenever we like? It sounds simple enough but ideally you'd need to cross back to another closely related surviving breed. The RBST has only ever been involved in resurrecting one breed, the Norfolk Horn sheep, and that was because only a handful of rams and some infertile ewes were left. That's why the expensive job of collecting and storing rare breed genetic material (semen and embryos) is an increasingly important role of the Trust. I think of the gene bank as a living insurance policy for the future, ready to be used to help bring back a breed if it's needed.

More than 30 years ago, a BBC Radio 4 programme visited our farm. The presenter was Cliff Morgan, the respected former Welsh rugby fly-half who had become a successful commentator and broadcaster in later life, and he asked my dad the ultimate question. After being shown a few of the breeds Dad was saving, and hearing about his efforts to get their numbers up, Cliff turned to my father and said, 'Why, for goodness sake, bother?' Wow, that really was a direct hit!

Dad had the answer of course. He bothered because the breeds are a vibrant, living slice of our national heritage, their sheer variety and individuality has aesthetic value, and finally they provide genetic diversity with the door left open for new roles in an ever-changing world.

All these years later, well into the twenty-first century, there are still plenty of people who share the passion, energy and expertise to keep these apparently unfashionable and uneconomic breeds going. So I decided to go out to meet them and find out for myself just what motivates them. Why, for goodness sake, do *they* bother? What drives a modern day farmer to spend valuable time and money on rearing livestock that most people consigned to the history books generations ago? With some of Britain's native farm breeds rarer than the Giant Panda, what's being done to make sure that no more go the way of the dodo and the dinosaurs? I'm curious about what farmers think the future might hold for their breeds.

I've always thought that our traditional farm livestock have a place in the landscape that's just as important and telling as the oldest oak or the river in the deepest valley. Their environment has a big role to play in which animals can survive and thrive in any specific area, determining their size, shape, behaviour and even how thick their coats are. Because the geography of Britain and Ireland is so diverse, we have more farm breeds than any other country in the world.

I believe the best way to really appreciate these animals is to see the distinctive herds and flocks in their own historic territory. So I've been on a long, personal mission through England, Wales, Scotland, the two Irelands and a scattering of smaller islands around the coast to meet the breeds. It would be impractical to include every breed here, but I've compiled my encounters, region by region, travelling anti-clockwise from my home in Gloucestershire and back again. Along the way I'll introduce you to a wide and wonderful range of native, traditional and truly rare British breeds, as well as a handful of extinct ones.

This, then, is a travelogue, it's a history book and it's a love story, but importantly it's as much about people as it is animals. It's about individuals who are committed, caring and yes, occasionally crazy. A few of them are well-known but most wouldn't be recognised beyond the small band of their fellow breeders and enthusiasts. Some of them are good friends while others I know only from our shared interest in saving Britain's rare breeds. And I decided to start close to home.

CHAPTER 1

The West Country

The old, wooden front door creaked open. Behind the familiar white beard was a kindly face, one I've known for as far back as I can remember. Friendly, twinkling eyes looked at me over the top of a pair of spectacles perched halfway down his nose. I had the distinct feeling that I'd disturbed the old man from his afternoon snooze. 'Hello Adam,' he said with a hearty chuckle in his voice, one large hand reaching out to shake mine before he ushered me inside.

When it comes to rare breeds, Eric Freeman is something of a living legend. In the last 50 years, he's probably given more to the local rare breeds movement than anyone alive today. We sit down at the large wooden table in front of the kitchen range. It's covered with newspapers, magazines and breed society journals, which Eric reads thoroughly from front to back –

nothing passes him by. On top of the pile of papers sits his pocket diary, full of invitations, events and reminders of important engagements.

At 86, Eric is still a member of his local Young Farmers' Club. What's even more impressive is that in 1944, at the age of just 12, he attended the club's first ever meeting. His life-long membership isn't simply a gesture either. He's still actively involved and is now a trustee of the Newent club. I've seen him at Young Farmers' conventions, surrounded by people 60 or 70 years his junior who are utterly rapt by his charm, enthusiasm and storytelling. In fact, first-hand tales are very much Eric's thing. He doesn't have a mobile phone, use social media, browse the internet or own a television – I suppose the nearest modern phrase to describe Eric would be 'off-grid'. Yet he's probably the most informed person I know. He's always on top of world events, knows exactly what's happening in the news and has an uncanny knack of always being the first to know the latest local gossip and goings-on. This is a man who doesn't need Facebook or Instagram because he has his own social networks. His warm, welcoming farmhouse kitchen is a magnet for visitors at all times of the day, his phone is almost always engaged and he's often heard popping up on his local radio station offering sage advice.

The more I thought about it, the more I realised that visiting Eric at home was an ideal starting point for any examination of Britain's livestock heritage.

Gloucestershire is the only county with breeds of the three main species: pig, sheep and cattle. Eric is one of the few people who has owned, bred and promoted all three big breeds of his beloved home county: the dotty, playful Gloucestershire Old Spots pig, the long-wool, lion-like Cotswold sheep and the majestic mahogany Gloucester cattle. More than that, he's been a driver for their survival and success in an official capacity as an honorary life member of the Gloucester Old Spots Pig Breeders' Club, past president of both the Cotswold Sheep Society and the Gloucester Cattle Society, as well as being Gloucestershire vice president of the Three Counties Agricultural Society in the year 2000 (the other two counties in the trio are Herefordshire and Worcestershire).

There's also the small matter of the Rare Breeds Survival Trust, the conservation charity with traditional livestock at its heart, which was the brainchild of my dad, Joe. When the project got off the ground in the early 1970s, one of the small band of enthusiastic founders standing alongside Dad was one Eric Freeman. His long list of titles is an impressive pedigree and Eric's collection of society ties must have outgrown his wardrobe years ago.

The Old Spots pig is the one rare breed from the county of Gloucestershire that is known by virtually everyone. The name helps of course, along with the fact that a spottier, piggier pig would be hard to find. So they're instantly recognisable, easy to remember, they look appealing and kids love them. It means the breed has become the poster-pig for British breeds – they appear on prints and postcards, mugs, dinner sets, egg cups, ornaments, tote bags, bookmarks, badges, jewellery, cushions, cuddly toys and yes, even piggy banks. Once you start looking, you see Old Spots 'stuff' everywhere, and a lot of that popularity is down to the cuteness factor.

Originally though, there was nothing cute about this very practical pig. They were once called the Orchard pig because they come from the low-lying, fruit-growing region between Gloucester and Bristol known as the Vale of Berkeley where they gorged themselves on the windfall apples that littered the ground beneath the trees. Folklore has it that the pork tasted of cider and that the spots on their backs were actually bruises caused by the falling apples. Another name, the Cottagers' pig, came from their popularity with smallholders in the country who would have a pig in the yard, which served as a living waste disposal unit for kitchen and garden scraps in spring and summer, then afterwards the carcass provided the family with meat throughout the autumn and winter.

Eric loves his Old Spots and bought his first one almost 50 years ago. His theory – he tells me with a grin – is that because their lop ears fall forward and cover their eyes it leaves them hard of hearing as well as blind, so Old Spots navigate by sense of smell. In recent years, as Eric has tried to downsize and make life a little easier for himself, he's held stock reduction auctions and a famous dispersal sale of all his livestock, which caused such interest that it was the subject of a programme on BBC Radio 4. Yet when the last of the buyers' trucks left the yard, there still remained one or two animals that Eric couldn't quite bring himself to sell. Among them was an Old Spots sow. Although, he's the first to acknowledge that his father would certainly not have approved: 'Their faces take too much washing' was Freeman Senior's graphic way of saying that he thought the whole business of keeping and feeding swine was troublesome and expensive.

As a modern Old Spots breeder, Eric is in good company. Another Gloucestershire resident, Princess Anne, has kept pigs on her Gatcombe Park estate near Stroud for years and is seen as a supportive, local ambassador for the breed. In 2009, the Princess Royal even accepted an invitation to become patron of the Gloucestershire Old Spots Pig Breeders Club and she takes her role as a figurehead for fellow Spots enthusiasts seriously. But there wouldn't be any pigs for her to champion if it wasn't for a maverick farmer who was prepared to ignore advice and shun fashionable ideas in the post-war years.

George Styles farmed near the town of Bewdley, on the banks of the Severn in Worcestershire, and so not traditional Gloucestershire Old Spots territory at all. And yet George was such a dedicated, passionate and prolific breeder of them that he's known as 'the grandfather' of the breed. Throughout the 1950s and 60s, when it seemed that every other pig farmer was following government guidelines and switching to fast maturing, so-called 'modern' breeds to make farming profitable, George stuck doggedly with his beloved spotty pigs. By the 1970s things were desperate, with only about 100 registered Old Spots sows left in the world, and 80 per cent of them belonging to George. It means that today, somewhere in the pedigree of every pure Gloucestershire Old Spots, is genetics that can be traced back to the Styles herd. What a legacy to have left us.

George knew the breed's survival wasn't just about numbers; no matter how large or small the worldwide population was, there also needed to be genetic diversity in the herds so that boars weren't inbreeding with closely related sows. The danger lay in any faulty gene which might be passed on by both the mother and father, something that could prove fatal for their unlucky offspring. So to make it as easy as possible for the owners, George pushed for a strict but simple identification scheme based on the lineage of breeding females, using colours and names. Sows were put into one of four colour groups (red, black, green and blue), all their male offspring were linked to their family line by one of four names (Sambo, Patrick, Gerald and Rufus). When they matured, the boars were then mated only with females from a different designated colour group. This was the Cyclic Breeding System, and

George Styles' vision not only worked a treat at avoiding genetic complications but also helped increase the Old Spots population.

The list of famous admirers of the breed is a long one and includes, randomly, the actress Liz Hurley, TV presenter Angela Rippon and even the last German Emperor. In the early twentieth century, Kaiser Wilhelm II took a fancy to owning a Gloucestershire Old Spots pig. He even selected and paid for a prime specimen to be shipped to Berlin. Sadly for Kaiser Bill, his timing was terrible, because just before his boar was due to leave, the First World War broke out. The pig never made it to Prussia. Could this mean that Britain is still in arrears to Germany to the tune of one spotty, floppy-eared pig? I'd hate to be the one to have to work out a century's worth of interest on that debt.

Eric Freeman is immensely proud of the fact that he tends to his Old Spots in a part of Gloucestershire west of the River Severn that his family have called home for generations. But another of his adored breeds originates from the other side of Gloucestershire entirely, on the high limestone hills where bemused visitors are often asked 'have you seen a Cotswold lion?'

The Cotswolds will always be home for me, as well as being my all-time favourite place. So I'm always keen to point out that there's a great deal more to it than just the heartbreakingly pretty villages and mandatory cream tea which features on every coach trip itinerary. Now, I love a scone and a gorgeous view as much as anyone, but importantly the region is also home to any number of intriguing stories about the people, history and landmarks, and the tale of the Cotswold lion is high up on that list.

The label was given to the Cotswold sheep breed because their long, lustrous fleece falls in ringlets round the face, forming what looks like a lion's mane (it's nothing whatsoever to do with the fun that can be had teasing tourists about big cats). Most day trippers never hear that many of the things they come to the Cotswolds to admire wouldn't be here at all without the sheep. The field patterns typical of the region are a remnant of the days when large flocks of Cotswolds grazed the hills, while many of the most photographed town houses, fancy manors and elaborate church towers were built by thankful, rich wool merchants with cash from the proceeds of the highly profitable Cotswold wool trade.

In the Middle Ages, English fleece was highly prized throughout Europe and the fleece of the Cotswold sheep was the most coveted of all. If you live around here and your local pub is called the Golden Fleece, there's a good chance the name refers to the great earnings made from Cotswold sheep. The secret of the breed's success is the sheer quality of the creamy white wool they produce. Apart from the lion's mane effect, it has a beautiful all-round crimp and a magic ingredient: lanolin. The Cotswold and a handful of other English Longwool breeds are famous for the large amounts of lanolin they produce, much more than other UK breeds. This results in a fleece that's waterproof, supple and soft to the touch.

The fleece of the Cotswold sheep was so celebrated that for 700 years the woolsack in the House of Lords, from where the Lord Speaker chairs proceedings, has been filled with Cotswold fleece as a symbol of the nation's mediaeval wealth and power. At least, that's what everyone thought. There are actually three wool-sacks in the Lords, which resemble large cushions. They are upholstered in red cloth to match the colour of the leather benches in the Upper Chamber. When I was making a film for the BBC in the Houses of Parliament, I was very honoured to be one of the few people allowed to sit on the woolsack, and I can tell you that it's wider, firmer and far more comfy than it looks.

I wasn't quite so delighted when I heard the real story of what's inside the woolsack, though. When my sister, Libby, was doing some research into Cotswold fleeces she discovered that in the 1930s the famous red seat urgently needed to be re-stuffed. When the furniture restorers opened it up, out fell heaps of old horse hair. Apparently, down the ages, the woolsack had been repaired and re-filled with the cheaper, coarser mate-rial instead of expensive Cotswold fibre. There was bitter disappointment in the Henson household when we found out, I can tell you. But at least the twentieth-century upholsterers came up with a modern take on the Golden Fleece of the Middle Ages. They replaced the horse hair and old fibre filling with a new filling, which was a blend of different types of wool from around Britain as well as fifteen other countries across the Empire.

Sheep people are proud of their animals and love a good story about their particular breed so I decided not to mention anything about horse hair as I headed off to Bourton-on-the-Water, one of Britain's best-known villages and a local tourist hotspot. That's where the Cotswold Sheep Society Summer Show was taking place, in a field in the grounds of a large country house. On the way in, I heard a rumour that the King of Jordan had been in the area a few days earlier and had taken an interest in the Cotswold sheep he'd seen grazing nearby. I made a mental note to give him a call next time I have a ram for sale.

A dozen people, mostly from the local area and all dressed appropriately in crisp white coats, had brought about 50 of the best examples of the breed to show off. Despite it being a small scale gathering, this is an event where there is serious silverware up for grabs, and those judged to have raised the best Cotswolds will win highly-polished, engraved trophies, and the prestige that goes with them. But this is nothing like the hard-fought, sometimes high-stakes sheep competitions that take place at county shows all over the UK. This relaxed, almost laid-back event was created in the 1970s as a way of encouraging new recruits to the society, away from the gaze of a formal agricultural show. One seasoned breeder confided in me: 'The pressure's off at this show, so you can make mistakes here.'

It's a sentiment that's shared by Lynne Parkes, the ever-smiling secretary of the Cotswold Sheep Society. She's delighted to see some fresh, younger faces at the show this time: 'As people drop out, new people take their place, the cycle is amazing,' she explains. Wherever Cotswolds are shown, you can guarantee that Lynne and her husband Steve won't be very far away. It's a partnership which started in 1974 when they met at the Tewkesbury Young Farmers' Stock Judging Dance, or what Lynne calls 'the countryside marriage bureau'. Today, they own about 20 breeding ewes and they travel thousands of miles every year taking the best of the flock to shows, sales and competitions all over England. Despite the long forms, long days and long hours on the road, Lynne is convinced it's worth all the expense and inconvenience: 'If you want a breed to survive, you've got to be in the public eye.' She's absolutely right, and there can't be many people who have done as much to promote Cotswold sheep as Mr and Mrs Parkes. So much so that their ewes have become minor media stars in their own right, with numerous appearances in the press, on radio and TV. I've featured the woolly wannabes on *Countryfile*, they've popped up on *Farming Today* and they've even met Prince Charles, bleating at him during a royal visit to a Cotswold craft fair. But nothing the flock has done in recent years has been grander or more regal than being granted an audience with national treasure and Dame of the British Empire Penelope Keith. The star of *The Good Life* and *To the Manor Born* interviewed Steve, and his ewes, for one of her TV documentaries about British villages, and Steve's friends love to remind him constantly of this particular moment of TV fame. Lynne just rolls her eyes.

Most of the people at the Cotswold Sheep Society Show see Eric Freeman as something of an elder statesman because he's been such a champion for the breed over the years, yet his devotion for traditional breeds began with an entirely different species. In 1971, he gave in to his curiosity and bought his first Gloucester cow at the weekly livestock market in the Cotswold town of Tetbury.

Historically, the cattle known as the Old Gloucester was always a jack-of-all-trades animal; it supplied milk, provided meat and the oxen were used as 'beasts of burden', pulling ploughs and farm wagons. But far from working to its advantage, being the local farmers' utility animal proved to be the downfall of the Gloucester because as a multi-purpose breed, it didn't excel at any one thing. So thrifty farmers with an eye on their incomes ditched the Gloucester as soon as they were offered higher-yielding dairy cows and meatier beef breeds. Meanwhile, in the early twentieth century, the few remaining working oxen, already outclassed by heavy horses, could only look on idly as the first afford-able tractors trundled into the fields, revolutionising farming and making the Gloucester utterly redundant.

I've always known that true Gloucesters should have a black head, black legs and a deep mahogany coat, complete with a distinctive white stripe all the way along the spine ending in the classic white tail. But it took a trip to see Gloucestershire breeds aficionado Charles Martell on his farm in the little village of Dymock to discover a characteristic I'd never known about. Introducing me to the herd he said, 'They've got to have a black top to their tongue too and a black roof to the mouth, if you care to look.' Cows' mouths hold no fear for me, so I looked, and he's absolutely right. Charles likes to point out Gloucester cattle's horns too, which should always be 'fine, wide and inclined to turn up'.

Looking at Charles' herd as they calmly graze in front of us, you'd never guess that this breed is a bit of a superhero in the animal world – it's thanks to a Gloucester cow that hundreds of millions of lives have been saved around the globe. The beast in question was a docile old milker called Blossom who lived in the dairy-rich Berkeley Vale. In May 1796, she played a central role in the discovery of vaccination and the eventual eradication of smallpox. Blossom had been infected with cowpox – a mild, contagious disease of the udders – and had passed it on to her milkmaid, Sarah Nelmes, who suffered ugly pustules on her hand. A local doctor called Edward Jenner wanted to prove an old wives' tale that dairymaids who had caught cowpox were immune to the deadly and disfiguring smallpox.

He used Sarah's infection to transfer cowpox to a small boy called James Phipps, and when he recovered, Jenner then exposed the brave little lad to a mild form of smallpox. The good doctor must have wept with relief when young master Phipps survived the ordeal without ever developing the fatal smallpox. Jenner was hailed as the pioneer of vaccination, Sarah went back to the milking parlour, James eventually married and had two children of his own and Blossom became the most famous Gloucester cow in history. When she died, Jenner displayed Blossom's hide in his coach house before it was eventually given to St George's Hospital in London where it's still on show today. I think the best reminder of dear old Blossom happens every time someone goes to the doctor for a jab, because the very word vaccination has its roots in the Latin *vaccinus* meaning 'from a cow'.

In Jenner's day, the milk of the Old Gloucester was used to make cheese but this practice pretty much stopped when the breed dwindled almost to the point of extinction during and after the Second World War. By the early 1970s, Charles Martell was intrigued and enchanted by Gloucester cattle and had already established a small herd when he took it upon himself to single-handedly revive the local cheese-making tradition. For him it was all about safeguarding our farming heritage: 'The Old Gloucester needed help and my way of helping was to bring back the cheese. If you keep a breed just because it's rare you'll keep it rare but if you give it a job of work to do, like producing milk to make cheese, there's a certain beauty in that and it also looks after the breed.' His approach makes sense today, but the whole idea was puzzling to many people in the so-called progressive 1970s.

There are two varieties of Gloucester cheese. In the past, the light, creamy white-coloured single Gloucester was the poor man's food. The cows often grazed on poor quality grass and the cheese was frowned upon by the well-to-do. Double Gloucester is orange, stronger tasting with a harder texture. Some folk even claim that it was called 'double' because cream from the morning milking was added to the evening milk. The problem for Charles in the early days was that despite wanting to restore traditional farmhouse double Gloucester, he didn't actually know how to make it. What was worse is that he'd already committed to having a go when a BBC TV crew arranged to visit him and film the momentous occasion. Luckily for Charles (and for the Gloucester cows), the method had been written down by a lady whose name has passed into legend.

Avis Colnett had the glorious title of 'dairy instructress for the county of Gloucestershire', and in the 1930s she had toured local farms recording, for the first time in history, the way that cheese was being made. She was a canny woman because these were basic, rustic dairies where recipes had been passed from mother to daughter by word of mouth and temperatures were measured by rolling up a sleeve and dipping an elbow in. Miss Colnett knew if Gloucester cheeses were to survive, she'd need to get to work with her thermometer. Years later, she recalled what she'd seen: 'The farmhouse double Gloucester had the personal touch, the person who was dedicated to cheese-making produced a more mellow, really fine type, typical double.'

For all her love of things Gloucestershire, Avis Colnett was actually from Essex. She'd trained at the East Anglian Institute of Agriculture in Chelmsford and at Reading University. Then in 1926 she founded the Dairy Students' Association to encourage farming families to make butter, cream and cheese from their surplus milk. More than 90 years on, the foresighted Miss Colnett has long left us, but her association is still going strong and continues to meet every month.

Although I love Double Gloucester, I'm not being unkind in saying that it isn't the best-known cheese in the world. In fact, looking around some of the local supermarkets, it might not even be the best-known cheese in Gloucester. When it comes to the international popularity stakes it's in a long queue well behind brie, cheddar, mozzarella and even Edam. But once a year, without fail, double Gloucester gets its moment of glory in the global spotlight.

Over the years, TV crews and press photographers from America, Japan and Australia, among others, have gathered at the bottom of an impossibly steep hill four miles outside Gloucester for what is either the most impressive amateur sporting event of the year, or the dumbest. This is the annual cheese-rolling event, when otherwise sane and well-adjusted people hurl themselves from the top of Cooper's Hill and crash down the 1:2 gradient in pursuit of a nine-pound wheel of double Gloucester. Enormous crowds turn up to cheer on the lunatics, which is just as well because the noise of the spectators helps to drown out the sickening thuds and crunches as flesh and bone hits cold, hard ground on the way down. It's obvious why the international media flock to this place, and it's not uncommon to spot the pained face of a TV personality among the battered, limping contestants at the finish. Ben Fogle, Paddy McGuinness and Rory McGrath have all taken part, and even a normally impeccably dressed and well-groomed TV newsreader Seb Choudhury has risked it all by bouncing headfirst after the fabled fromage. Thankfully he avoided becoming the only BBC news presenter with a broken face and a toothless grin.

When the media spotlight moves on and the cheese-rollers have all hobbled home, the work of the unsung, dedicated cheesemakers goes on. Following Charles Martell's creation of the first proper farmhouse double Gloucester in a generation, the 1990s saw him fight to get special protection for single Gloucester. His success means that cheese can only carry the name if it is made in the county from the milk of the Old Gloucester cow.

His hard work as a staunch defender of local tradition was rewarded in 2018 when, by royal appointment,

Charles became High Sheriff of Gloucestershire. The role dates back to Anglo-Saxon times and, while it's mostly ceremonial these days, High Sheriffs still help maintain law and order, supporting local magistrates and judges. Charles looked quite the part on the day he was sworn in at Gloucester Cathedral, arriving by horse-drawn carriage and swapping his cheesemaker's overalls for a black velvet doublet with lace ruffle and cuffs, complete with a silver sword of office.

Although he was surrounded by judges in wigs, mayors in red robes and councillors wearing heavy gold medals and chains, there were clues to his country roots throughout the cathedral, among the great Norman stone pillars. In the thousand years since the first High Sheriff was declared, I can't imagine there's been a more agricultural congregation for his swearing in. Apart from Eric Freeman, in his best tweed suit and silk scarf, there were old friends and familiar faces everywhere. Supporters had travelled down from the hills and high ground surrounding the city. There was Smiling Sally, who devoted every summer to showing Gloucester cattle; Big Albert, the maker of head-spinning cider; elegant Edna Powell, forever remembered for saving the Stroud Country Show from closure, and Robert Boodle, my father's former shepherd and a walking, talking encyclopaedia on Cotswold sheep.

What none of them would have been able to see as Charles was formally presented with the insignia of the

High Sheriff was the intricate detail on his badge of office. Sitting proudly between the Royal Crown and the crossed swords of mercy is the famous Golden Fleece – a depiction of a ram as a reminder of the importance of livestock to the lives of everyone locally, from the labourers to the lords and ladies.

It's been centuries since wool was king, but the old livestock breeds are earning a living once again. There are new markets for regional food which means fresh interest in Old Spots pork and Cotswold lamb. Gloucester beef that's raised on the Severn plain is making a return, and the public's love affair with British cheeses has been good news for double and single Gloucester. I think food tastes so much better when there's a story behind it. And what a story!

The 'Land of the Summer People' is in fact a phrase taken from Old English, though it sounds like it could be a good marketing slogan for the place we now call Somerset. This county is home to one of the UK's great seasonal spectacles. The grandly named Royal Bath and West Show is one of the 156 county and agricultural shows which crowd the nation's events calendar every summer. (There would be many more if you added all the annual game and country fairs to the list.) Just about everywhere in the UK has its own agricultural show, from Aberystwyth to Yeovil – I'd love to say that as a nation we can boast a genuine A to Z of summer shows, but sadly the Cornish village of Zennor and the Nottinghamshire hamlet of Zouch are too tiny to stage one. But everywhere else is treated annually to beefy livestock parades, sheep shearing, show jumping and dog agility, which alongside vintage tractors and the latest, hi-tech monster machinery draw the crowds and put the farming industry firmly centre stage.

I've been going to county shows since I was a small boy and I've seen them all – good ones, bad ones, big and small. But as a showcase for agriculture, the Bath and West is in the top flight. It's one of the oldest (first held in 1852), largest (240 acres), longest (four days) most impressive (around 4,500 livestock) and it was granted its royal status in the Queen's silver jubilee year (1977). The organisers are very proud of that regal association and they make certain that everyone knows it's the *only* royal four-day show in England.

But what's particularly interesting to Charles Martell and his cheesemaking colleagues of the south west and further afield, is that the show is also the permanent venue for the British Cheese Awards. It's hard to think of a better home for the competition, what with the Bath and West showground sitting just outside Shepton Mallet in the heart of Somerset dairy country and the village of Cheddar just up the road. The contest for medals is hard fought here and every year the Cheese Awards judges sniff and nibble their way through a thousand British cheeses. How many of us even knew there were a thousand cheeses made in Britain?

Today though, it's not the dairy products I want to see, it's the dairy cattle. Out of curiosity, I'm keen to gauge how well represented our rare, traditional and native cattle are among the more commercial breeds, such as the Limousins, Charolais and Simmentals. The Bath and West prides itself on the quality and the quantity of livestock on show to the public, and rightly. There are so many cattle here that, just as with many shows of a similar size and prestige, the dairy and beef breeds have to be housed in separate buildings – enormous structures which resemble big brick aircraft hangars.

I decide to start with the dairy breeds and pick my way along the cattle stalls as the owners brush and fuss over their animals. First there are the Holsteins. In fact, there are lots of large, angular Holsteins with their familiar broad faces and long, straight backs. Next in line come the Brown Swiss with their large, fluffy ears, and beside them, enjoying their bed of straw, is that universal black and white breed – the Friesian. All great dairy cows with a seriously impressive ability to produce large quantities of milk, but the names alone tell you these are breeds which didn't originate in the British Isles. Finally I see what I'm looking for: Jerseys, Guernseys, Ayrshires and Dexters.

Next door are the beef breeds. First the Belted Galloways, then British Whites, a row of ten beautiful Lincoln Reds, the giant South Devons, a chestnut-coloured Sussex, lots of lovely Longhorns and finally a few Beef Shorthorns. In a third building, small crowds wander around admiring Aberdeen Angus and

Hereford bulls. The number of cattle entered for the event is up on previous years, and it shows. I linger and look on, impressed at how attentive the owners are to their stock.

The unexpected doesn't happen until I leave the cattle lines and walk through the crowds towards the show's main ring. That's when I catch sight of a cow that hasn't been seen since it was declared extinct almost 90 years ago. To be clear, this fine exhibit that's so captured my attention is a detailed illustration covering an entire wall of one of the larger trade stands. It shows the image of a long-forgotten and long-dead variety of cattle called the Somerset Sheeted. This one's a short-horned cow with a long tail; she holds her head high, completely ignoring an old wooden pail and a ladle arranged neatly at her feet. The inscription underneath reads: 'Somerset Sheeted Cow circa 1840'. In the busy throng nobody else even gives it so much as a cursory glance, but I'm delighted and intrigued that this giant copy of a Victorian rare breed engraving is here.

The man responsible for making my day is Simon O'Brien, the marketing manager of Barber's, a family-run firm of cheddar cheese-makers. Their story starts in 1833 when Daniel Barber started making cheese to feed his family and the workers on Maryland Farm in the Mendip hills. Six generations later, the Barber family are still dairying on the same farm, although on a vastly bigger scale, and can claim to be the oldest surviving makers of cheddar cheese in the world.

They're as fascinated by British breeds as I am, and in a brilliant merchandising move they use old illustrations of dairy cattle on their packaging. The Somerset Sheeted adorns every pack of their vintage cheddar and it's an enormous version of that label that looms over Simon as he serves a long queue of customers. As breed names go, it sounds strange to modern ears but there was logic behind it. These brown-red cattle had a wide belt of white around their middle, and the West Country farmers thought it looked as if a sheet had been thrown over their backs. They originated sometime in the 1700s, when Dutch traders using the Bristol Channel brought their own belted cattle from the Netherlands which bred among the local red-coloured herds. However, by the 1840s numbers were dwindling and it's thought the last herd of Somerset Sheeted cattle died out in the 1930s, victims of tuberculosis. But reading about them in history books isn't enough for one single-minded county farmer I've heard a lot about. Andrew Tanner is on a mission to reinvent the Somerset Sheeted, a scheme which he blames on a dull football match.

In the summer of 2014, Andrew was so bored watching the World Cup semi-final between Argentina and the Netherlands on TV that he started idly playing with his son's iPad. Before long he was searching for native livestock breeds and found a reference to the extinct Somerset Sheeted. That was the light-bulb moment and, determined that like neighbouring Devon and Gloucestershire his home county should have its own local breed once more, he began investigating ways to recreate Somerset's belted cattle. Soon he was importing genetic material from the original Dutch belted dairy breed, the Lakenvelder, which was put to the local crossbred cows on his farm.

The first dairy calf was a heifer born in February 2018. It's a big step for Andrew, whose dream is to produce a beef variant of the Somerset Sheeted to rival the Aberdeen Angus for brand recognition and reputation. He wants quality meat from calves suckled by their mothers for six months then raised on grass for another 18 months to produce choice cuts bought by discerning customers from craft butchers.

It's a fascinating project but there's a long way to go. Not least because there are people who will need convincing that what Andrew is breeding is actually a Somerset Sheeted. For the doubters, a cow that's similar to the original simply isn't the same thing. But head of shows at the Royal Bath and West Show, Alan Lyons, is interested in Andrew's project and supportive. 'We're open-minded here, it's a platform for diversity, so the first place those cattle are brought out must be here at the Bath and West.'

Reputation is as vital in the business of showing as it is in the livestock world and two breeds which have impressed at the Bath and West over time are the region's red cattle – the Ruby Reds of North Devon and the Big Reds of South Devon. When the Pilgrim Fathers loaded up the Mayflower and sailed for the New

World from Plymouth in September 1620, they made sure there were 'the red cattle of Devon' on board to help give them a fighting chance when they landed in North America.

The North Devons really are ruby red in colour, and if you see a small herd grazing in the sunshine, the first thing you'll notice is the sheen of their coats. South Devons are lighter coloured with sandy or copper tones. Though both north and south Devon neighbours were traditionally kept both for meat and milk, today they're well established for their marbled, tasty beef. But there are still a few people who appreciate the creaminess of their milk and successfully rear them as dairy cows. One of them is an old mate of mine and a true Devonian, Rob Taverner. We played rugby together as young men and he's the biggest Exeter Chiefs fan I've ever met. Rob has created a niche market for South Devon milk and has capitalised on the cow's appearance with the name of his produce – Orange Elephant Ice Cream. It must have been quite a spectacle when Rob purchased his first South Devons and brought them home on foot, walking the herd across the hills and down the lanes to the family farm. There's a good display of Devon cattle at the Shepton Mallet showground and it's heartening to see as many as 26 Ruby Reds and a further 10 South Devons paraded around the competition ring.

With most of the judging over, I dash back to check the results of the British Cheese Awards. I'm very pleased to see that Charles Martell is among the medal winners. He picked up a bronze for his Hereford Hop, a variety which really is covered in toasted hops, and silver for Stinking Bishop – his most famous product and the cheese of choice for those plasticine pin-ups Wallace and Gromit in their debut feature film *The Curse of the Were-Rabbit*. For the record, there are silver medals for two double Gloucesters – though one is made in Shropshire and the other in Devon. I'm sure it's cracking cheese nonetheless.

Dartmoor is 200 square miles of high, harsh, wind-swept solid granite. It's been called England's last wilderness, a place that somehow manages to be bleak and beautiful at the same time. So you'd imagine it's not the sort of habitat in which to find ponies – at least if your idea of a pony is a delicate, flighty little creature. Dartmoor ponies couldn't be more different. They're small, certainly, but as hard as nails, strong and muscular with alert ears and a good nature, which helps them thrive in the wildest of weather. The typical Dartmoor will stand firm facing the driving rain as its long mane is whipped about by a howling wind.

Ponies have been on the moor for 3,500 years and they first appear in written records more than 1,000 years ago. Their tough character made them ideal working animals and they were used to haul stone in quarries and as pit ponies in the tin mines of the south west. They had another use too – as food. Pony meat was known locally as taffety, a Devon dialect word for 'delicate on the tongue', and until about 80 years ago it wouldn't have been unusual for Dartmoor families to sit down to roasted pony on a Sunday lunchtime. Taffety was low in fat, high in protein, with a slightly gamey taste and, if caught wild on the moor, certainly free-range.

There's an old story about one of the Victorian governors of Dartmoor Prison who wanted to own a wild pony, so went out with a party of men to round one up. They chose a fine-looking specimen, separated it from the herd and drove it on to some rocks, with a man on horseback following behind. They thought they'd cornered their target but the Dartmoor pony had other ideas and leapt clear over the horse and its rider to escape capture. Bear that gymnastic tale in mind the next time you see a Dartmoor in the Horse of the Year Show. In the 1940s, a Dartmoor cross had a short taste of fame, appearing in the cinema newsreels as Britain's answer to the Pony Express. Devon postman Henry Moore was nicknamed the 'mounted mailman' when he abandoned his GPO bicycle and instead chose four-legged transport to cover the tough, rocky terrain on his 18-mile delivery round across the moor. It was a typically jaunty, tongue-in-cheek film to please the public, but what it didn't reveal was the dramatic effect the Second World War had had on pony numbers.

During this time, the moor was used for army training. Six years of conflict when all energies were put into the war effort also meant that very few ponies were registered, and the trade in pony meat collapsed as Britons lost their appetite for horseflesh. Today the number of pure-bred Dartmoor breeding mares stands at around 500, putting them firmly in the endangered category. That figure is similar for the other great West Country equine on the opposite side of Devon – the original off-roader and the pony that was my introduction to the wondrous world of British breeds.

I've got three older sisters, and when we were small our dad came up with a clever way of getting us interested in livestock keeping, although I've got a sneaky feeling it was really about sharing his passion for rare and native breeds with us. He gave each of us a breed to call our own on the farm; we were responsible for looking after them and the incentive was that any money we made could go into our piggy banks. He was no fool! My breed was the Exmoor pony and I've adored them ever since.

Exmoors can be traced back to the first wild horses which roamed Britain after the Ice Age – that makes them the oldest of all British ponies and arguably the most ancient domestic breed in the world. The clue is in their primitive markings, and especially the eyes. Their colouring is much paler around the eye and on the nose, and there's a ring of raised flesh that circles the socket, called a toad eye, which protects their sight from the hardest rain and the coldest winds. The other link to their ancient heritage on the moor is their incredibly hard feet. When I was little, one of the first things I learnt about my Exmoor ponies was that primitive horses never need to be shod.

The first Exmoor ponies we had at home came straight from the moor and belonged to a wonderful, commanding countryman called Ronnie Wallace. That was in the 1970s, and 40-odd years later I repaid the favour when I helped Ronnie's son, David, to round up his herd of wild ponies on one of the wettest days I can remember. Every year teams of volunteers on foot, quad bikes and horseback corral about 30 ponies to bring them off the moor. They're brought back to the farm so the foals can be weaned from their mothers and a general stocktake of the young can be made. It took hours, but eventually seeing a string of dripping, dark brown Exmoors trotting through the mist was a magnificent thing to experience. Once I'd wiped the rain out of my eyes that is.

There is another moorland breed which never fails to make me smile whenever I think of it. The Whiteface Dartmoor is a hardy hill sheep with a thick, curly fleece and a history on the isolated heathland of southern Devon that goes back at least a couple of thousand years. You'll occasionally hear them called Widecombe Whiteface sheep after the village on the moor where a famous fair has been held since at least the 1850s, immortalised in one of Britain's best-known folk songs (' ... Old Uncle Tom Cobley and all').

I love the Whiteface and of all the sheep breeds they're probably my favourite. Their appearance is all there in the name; they have clean white faces, which combined with a black-tipped nose, gives them an inquisitive look. The harsh landscape they thrive in was described beautifully to me by an old Devon farmer and poet called Colin Pearce. He kept and cared for the breed for well over 60 years, and when he was approaching retirement, I bought 16 sheep from him to start a new breeding flock of my own. It was the first time in hundreds of years that any Whiteface sheep had left Dartmoor. As we gazed up through the drizzle at the misty, brooding moor above, Colin offered these weary words: 'When you can see Dartmoor it's going to rain and when you can't, it is.' With wisdom like that, he ought to be presenting the *Countryfile* weather forecast.

Colin stayed true to his beloved Whiteface Dartmoors despite decades when there was real concern that the breed faced being wiped out. Today the number of registered breeding ewes has grown to stand at more than 3,000, pushing them off the list of Britain's rarest and most vulnerable breeds. There are several reasons for the breakthrough. First there's the unglamorous and uncelebrated hard work of the breeders. Secondly there is a renewed interest in buying local, sustainable goods, and while the market for their meat is small, business in Dartmoor woollen products seems to be growing. Finally, there was a hugely successful heritage project in 2016 called 'One Hut Full' which told the story of Dartmoor sheep farming as part of a travelling exhibition. It was a really engaging way of promoting the breed to a whole new audience. So if a reversal in fortune can happen for Whiteface Dartmoor sheep, surely it can happen for the dozens of other breeds who face the threat of extinction?

In fact, Colin's home county is a wonderful example of what can be achieved. We know some areas of the British Isles have lost their distinctive local breeds, but there are others which give us heart that all is far from over, and Devon is one. Farmers there have looked after their county breeds, treasured them and kept them from going under. It means we can still see Exmoor ponies on the high moors, Exmoor Horn sheep grazing in the pastures and herds of Ruby Red North Devon cattle looking magnificent in the valleys. Does that add anything to a county or region in the fast-paced, highly-digitised commercial world of the twenty-first century? You bet it does!

The railway did wonders for Cornwall. Stunning pictures of summery cottages, charming harbours and wide, empty beaches shone out from thousands of classic Great Western Railway posters. The slogans promised 'Ideal Homes and Holidays' or 'Glorious Sands' and the duchy was labelled 'Land of Legend, History and Romance'. There are no posters like that anymore, instead food tourism is what grabs the attention, with pasties, clotted cream, Newlyn crab and saffron buns topping the lists of Cornish cuisine. But no one ever seems to mention bacon butties. That's a shame, because Cornwall is pig heaven for British breeds.

There are only eleven rare pigs on the UK list and two of them are Cornish. One's black, one's white and they're both great baconers. The Large Black certainly lives up to its name and was once even described as 'gigantic'. This is a pig that's all ears. They're so large and floppy that they fall right over their faces as far as the tip of their snouts. The breed was developed in Cornwall and Devon at the same time that a similar hefty black pig was emerging in Essex and Suffolk. By the 1890s the penny had dropped and Cornish farmers started using the East Anglian pigs to improve the breed and produce the Large Black we know today. The ups and downs of the Large Black over time is really the story of Britain's changing eating habits. But a hundred years ago no other pig could get near them for the sheer wow factor.

The Oscars of the livestock world at that time was undoubtedly the Smithfield Show in London, and in 1919 the leading lady was a Large Black sow. She was declared Supreme Champion and, not surprisingly, she was later put up for sale; probably still wearing her Smithfield rosette. The old girl changed hands for a remarkable 700 guineas, which today would be the equivalent of well over £35,000. Now that's an expensive chop.

However, by the 1960s things had changed. By then, farmers were being pushed towards keeping the leanest, fastest growing and most profitable pigs; herds were moved indoors and bred intensively. On the high

street, shoppers didn't want the sort of fatty cuts associated with the older, slower-growing breeds and people
were complaining to their butchers if they spotted
black bristles on the crackling. Before long, the Large
Black went from hero to almost zero. Now it's our only
surviving all-black pig and seriously endangered. But
I like to think I'm doing my bit to help. I bought my
first Large Blacks in 2017 and that spring we introduced them into our collection of rare breeds at the
Cotswold Farm Park in Gloucestershire; the two nine-
month-old pregnant sows were the first Large Blacks
on the farm since the attraction opened in 1971. I'm
very proud of that.

Cornwall's other pig – the white one – is a hog with
an identity crisis. It's been called the Cornish White,
the Cornish Lop, the Devon Lop and, most magnifi-
cently of all, the National Long White Lop-Eared pig
(only a committee could have come up with a name like
that). But it's better known simply as the British Lop
and like its county cousin, it's all about the large, floppy
ears. The Breed Standard is a strict checklist for all
breeds of livestock and acts as a sort of MOT for passing
inspections and for judging. The one for British Lops
doesn't waste any space describing their most promi-
nent feature: 'long, thin ears that blinker the eyes'. They
certainly do that. The Lop comes from the Cornwall–
Devon border country and was considered a local breed
on both banks of the River Tamar. It was popular on
modest farms and with smallholders, but unlike other

pigs, it never caught on nationally and stayed the south west's open secret.

The largest herd of Lops can still be found in Cornwall, just off the A30 near the harbourside town of Hayle. Trevaskis has always been a traditional mixed farm, rearing livestock and growing vegetables, like hundreds of others all over the west of England. But over the last 40 years, the 28-acre farm has become a talked-about tourist and shopping destination; first with its pick-your-own fruit, and now due to an impressive food market, including a deli, butcher's, fishmonger's, restaurant, an organic kitchen garden and a farm park.

But while peas, plums and pumpkins keep the farm staff busy, it's the local lop-eared pigs that are at the heart of the operation. Trevaskis is run by Giles Eustice whose family have been farming in the same parish for more than 400 years. He's proud of being the latest in a long line of enterprising pig men. 'My great, great grandfather was the first Eustice to keep pigs, that was back in the mid-1850s when the records refer to them as a Cornish white pig.'

The farm is home to 65 breeding sows, which I suppose could be called the flagship herd of the British Lop. As if he isn't busy enough managing the countless activities on the farm, Giles is the chairman of the British Lop Pig Society. 'I feel very responsible for the breed and I think of myself as the custodian of the bloodlines.' The Trevaskis pigs are on view to the public in the outdoor pens, and as part of a crusade to give rare breeds a viable role the meat is on sale a hundred yards away in the farm shop and the restaurant. On the menu are Lop bacon, ham, pork, gammon and sausages as well as hog's pudding, a Cornish speciality that's eaten at breakfast instead of black pudding. Giles believes his British Lop pork is sold on its quality and taste: 'It eats like butter'. But Cornish piggy pride alone isn't enough to get customers through the door, he explains: 'People don't tune in to the localness, but they are interested once they know.'

Do they know, and are they interested at Westminster, I ask myself? Is there a listening ear in Whitehall, mindful to the needs of livestock farmers and sympathetic to rare breeds? There should be, because Giles' brother is George Eustice, the local Conservative MP who became the Farming Minister in 2013. Before Westminster beckoned, the Honourable Member for Camborne and Redruth worked on the family farm, growing strawberries and taking his finest pigs to big county agricultural shows as far away as the Midlands – what the Cornish refer to as 'up country'.

Politics has taken over from soft fruit and practical pig farming for George now, but Giles is convinced the British Lops played their part in making his brother a more effective government minister – 'The farm background is a good influence and he knows what farming does for communities because he's seen the highs and lows.'

When it comes to his breed, Giles wants to win hearts, minds and stomachs. Like many rare breed enthusiasts, he's a strong advocate of 'eat them to save them'. He's the man behind the 'Love a Lop' campaign which aims to push up sales, increase demand and make British Lop a household name. Giles has the sort of entrepreneurship and a flair for publicity that makes you think he'll easily succeed.

According to another well-known Cornish breeder, the British Lop is 'a proper old outdoor pig' and Julian Collings should know – his father started breeding them at Liskeard in 1933 and he passed the business on to his son in the 1970s. Julian grew up with Lops and he freely admits that even love can't get in the way of a man's passion for his pigs: 'I got married in 1976 and during the honeymoon we went to the rare breeds sale at Stoneleigh.' These days Julian's summers are spent with his pedigree pigs going to a succession of agricultural shows – that means the Royal Cornwall, along with the Bath and West of course, the Royal Welsh, the Great Yorkshire and – though small by comparison – his local one-day event, the Oakhampton Show.

Life hasn't always been so kind to Julian though, and he gets visibly upset as he remembers the devastating effect that foot-and-mouth disease had in 2001. In a year marred by lockdowns, livestock culls and blazing pyres to prevent the disease spreading, Julian lost his entire British Lop herd, including five Supreme Champion pigs. 'People don't realise what farming families went through.' The deadly virus is appalling for all farm livestock, but for rare animals there's the potential to wipe out entire breeds. Extinction is a real fear if the population of a particular breed is concentrated in one small area, or if there are no stocks of genetic material in reserve; that's usually samples of frozen semen or occasionally embryos. So even greater efforts have been made in recent years by farmers and breed societies to disperse herds and flocks as widely around the country as possible.

Thankfully the British Lop breed survived the 2001 disaster and Julian picked up the pieces of the business and started again, but his herd has never been quite as big since. These days, all the Collings' porkers go to Trevaskis to be sold in the food market and restaurant there. It's obviously a good decision in terms of keeping food miles and carbon emissions low, but for Julian there are other reasons too: 'It's important to breed, sell and butcher locally, it's about pride.' When the conversation turns to Brexit, he sounds a hopeful note. 'If there's less red tape that could make it easier to rear Lops and other rare breeds. It's not a financial thing for me and I don't get any EU subsidy for my pigs, I just happen to think British is best. Yes definitely, British is best.' As he says it Julian begins to smile, thinking of his Cornish lop-eared pigs. I smile too, thinking what a great railway poster it would make.

Shoulder of Old Spot Pulled Pork Bap

Serves: 6

Ingredients
2.5 kg (5lb 8oz) boneless pork shoulder
olive oil, for rubbing
3 tbsp paprika
2 tsp mustard powder
2 garlic cloves
1 onion, halved
500 ml (18fl oz) hot water

To serve
barbecue sauce
6 soft baps
tangy slaw

1. Pre-heat the oven to 130°C/250°F/gas ½.
2. Rub the pork with the olive oil, paprika and mustard powder.
3. Heat a large, non-stick, ovenproof pan until hot and sear the pork on all sides until golden brown.
4. Add the garlic cloves and onion to the pan and pour in the hot water.
5. Take the pan off the hob, cover tightly with foil and place in the preheated oven. Cook for 5 hours or until the pork is almost falling part.
6. Remove from the oven, drain the juices from the meat and leave to cool slightly.
7. Shred the pork using two forks, discarding the fat. Mix the pork with barbecue sauce, according to taste. Serve in soft baps with a tangy slaw.

Andy Boreham
Head Chef, Cotswold Farm Park

CHAPTER 2

The South

This may come as a shock, but not all sheep are the same. There are even a few farmers who need convincing of that. When my dad first suggested opening up the farm and showing his collection of rare animals to the public, the idea was met with bemusement by the locals. Many simply didn't see the point and some of his neighbours objected to the council on the grounds that they didn't think the Cotswolds was the sort of place that should encourage such things. Dad loved to tell the story of an old farming friend who came to see him when word got out about his farm park proposal – 'It's not going to work, Joe. If you've seen one sheep, you've seen 'em all.'

I suppose if you squint at a distant field of grazing sheep you could be forgiven for thinking that those things that look like woolly clouds on legs are the same the world over. They're not and it's no surprise that I'm the first to point out that every breed is distinct: their size, shape, colour and the way they behave all differ; stories about their origins and how they have survived are never the same; their fleeces and meat vary enormously. Often those things have been dictated by the lie of the land and the local climate; whether the livestock was bred up hill or down dale.

There are five main groups of native British sheep. The first category is the Primitives which are the most ancient breeds and are our window on the Iron Age. Then there are the Longwools, such as the Cotswold, which are all remarkable fleece-makers. The next three types all describe habitats where the particular sheep thrive: Mountain, Hill and Downland. The south of England is where the highest concentration of Downland breeds are found – square, meaty sheep perfectly suited to the gentle southern hills. The broad sweep of counties from Dorset in the west across to the Kent border in the east is an area where shepherds have tended their flocks for thousands of years. Sandwiched between the English Channel and the Thames there are seven native sheep breeds – and they're so much more than just woolly clouds on legs.

Start with a map of the south coast and nestled snuggly beneath Devon and Somerset, like a child hiding under a blanket, you'll see the county of Thomas Hardy, Lulworth Cove and Blandford Pudding. Dorset is also home to England's first natural World Heritage

Site, the largest natural harbour in the northern hemi-
sphere and the biggest vintage steam show in the world
(the Jurassic coast, Poole harbour and the Great Dorset
Steam Fair respectively, in case you were wondering).
Dorset is chalk downs, lowland heaths and wooded hills.
It's also the historic habitat of three sheep breeds: the
Dorset Down, the Portland and the Dorset Horn.

The Dorset Down is an interesting combination of
English breeds, developed 200 years ago when
Berkshire, Hampshire and Wiltshire ewes were crossed
with pure Southdown rams (this is a trend you're about
to become very familiar with). The result was a stocky,
thickset animal with a dark brown face and short,
springy wool which was used in the making of socks
and provided the fine felts needed for pressing paper
and bank notes. In recent years the fleece has found a
new role, becoming really popular for filling Japanese
futons. Dorset Down rams are phenomenal mating
machines; they're virile, have high pheromone levels
and I've even heard a story about one male which served
20 ewes in a single day.

The second Dorset breed comes from what is effectively a county within a county. The Isle of Portland
pushes out from the mainland into the English Channel
at the end of Chesil Beach, the narrow finger of shingle
that's known all over the world. Thomas Hardy called
Portland 'the peninsula carved by time out of a single
stone' and it still has a lonely, isolated feel despite
thousands of homes, huge quarries, the old, grim

prison and reminders of the Royal Navy base that was here for a 150 years. There even used to be a torpedo factory nearby. This virtually tree-less island, four miles long, is the natural habitat of the Portland sheep.

Some say they date back to the Romans, others insist it was the Saxons, but the best-known story about Portlands is that they came to England by swimming ashore from the stricken, sinking ships of the Spanish Armada in 1588. Likely? Not really and nobody seriously believes it, but it's a great tale and who am I to ruin a popular legend? The story probably came about because the Portland shares some strong characteristics with the sheep of the Mediterranean. Rams and ewes both have horns but in the Portland males they're long, outward curling and really impressive, just like the Spanish Merino.

While most of our native breeds come into season in the autumn and give birth in the spring, the Portland is one of the few that can lamb at any time of the year. When the lambs are born they're a lovely foxy-red colour and it never completely disappears, the fleece always has a hint of tan to it. A magazine journalist recently described the wool as latte-coloured, but maybe that was just the caffeine talking.

A millennium ago, the Domesday Book recorded 900 sheep on Portland (which admittedly demolishes the Spanish Armada theory), and at the peak of their popularity in the 1840s four thousand were roaming the island. Sadly, by the 1920s they had all gone. But thanks to a determined rare breeds enthusiast called Su Illsley, the Portlands have returned, and if she has her way, they're back for good. She runs Fancy's Family Farm, a community project housed on the site of the island's old radar station. Here, Su and her volunteers look after a flock of more than 40 Portland sheep. It's been a decade since she restored the breed to their traditional home and she's adamant that Portland sheep belong on Portland – 'If we lost them it would be like Shetland without ponies or the Isle of Man without the Manx cat.'

In 2010, I filmed Su and her flock for *Countryfile* on a freezing cold day. Since then, things have moved on considerably. 'We've gone from a rickety old barn with some sheep and a few goats to having an education centre, oodles of animals and we're now open to the public every day,' she updates me. Her flock is twice the size it was when I first visited and they now graze on the highest point of the island, even closer to Portland Bill Lighthouse than before. She's expanded her rare breed collection to include Eriskay ponies, Bagot goats and a Clydesdale horse, with the dream of becoming an officially recognised conservation farm park sometime in the future. Crucially though, Su has made a personal commitment to sharing the story of rare breeds with the next generation; she arranges school visits for around 600 pupils every year, and the farm hosts daily classes for a handful of children with social and emotional needs who can't attend a mainstream school. 'We sometimes have our work cut out explaining that a Portland sheep isn't any old sheep you just happen to see on Portland and a few kids get confused when they see a girl sheep with horns.'

It's thanks to the Portland that the county of Dorset has a third sheep breed to call its own. Sometime in the nineteenth century (nobody knows exactly when), they were crossed with the ever-present Southdowns to produce the stocky, white-faced Dorset Horn. Sure enough, the males have those classic Portland horns and the females share with Portlands the ability to breed all year round. That's the reason Dorset Horns became very popular in south and south-west England, as they could produce lamb ready to put on the table at Easter. The fleece is amazing and when you grab a handful of wool on the back of a Dorset Horn it fills your palm. It's dense, fine wool which protects the sheep from the hard winter weather. As top breeder Francis Fooks once said, 'a good jacket is absolutely vital'. Francis is devoted to the breed and is a man who was born to look after Dorset Horns – his great grandfather, Frederick, was a Victorian shepherd on the hills above Bridport and established the flock at about the time that Thomas Hardy was writing his Wessex novels. So when a national newspaper published the Fooks family story it was just too tempting not to use the ingenious headline: 'Baaa from the Madding Crowd'.

To add a bit more variety, and to confuse things a little bit, there's also a Dorset Horn which doesn't have horns. It's called the Poll Dorset – poll and polled are old terms for hornless livestock – and it was developed in Australia back in 1937, possibly by accident. It's believed that some Dorset Horn ewes escaped and mated with a Corriedale ram, a breed that's naturally hornless and popular in New South Wales for its bulky fleece and tasty meat. The lambs they produced were born with no horns and, realising they could be on to something, the owners kept breeding the offspring back with pure Dorset Horns to supply a polled sheep with all the other characteristics of its English ancestors.

The man responsible for bringing them to the UK was an inquisitive farmer called Bunny Lenthall from the little west Dorset village of Burton Bradstock. In the mid-1950s, he travelled to Australia, working his passage on the long sea voyage Down Under and taking a consignment of sheep with him. But his main motivation was to check out what the Aussie breeders were up to, and he spent two years visiting cattle and sheep stations all over the country on the trail of hornless Dorset Horns. Bunny eventually found what he was looking for in Tasmania and returned to the UK in 1956 with a stud ram and a young ram lamb – the first Poll Dorsets to ever set foot here.

Over the border, in neighbouring Wiltshire, there's another horned breed that's raised for its meat and this one's the original easy-care sheep. What makes the

Wiltshire Horn stand out from the crowd is the fact that it's a hair sheep. The skin of a Wiltshire is similar to a horse or a goat and they have a very short fleece which sheds naturally. So farmers love rearing them because they don't have to pay to have them sheared and vets' bills are lower because flocks don't suffer from fleece infections or infestations.

Two hundred years ago, the chalk hills and pastures of the Marlborough and west Wiltshire downs were a mass of free roaming Wiltshire Horn sheep, or Westerns as they were known by some flock-masters. They were everywhere. At one time, the total number in the county was thought to be around 700,000, easily making them the number one breed in Wiltshire. They were a tough sheep in a soft landscape, described as being 'perfectly white in their faces and legs, with Roman noses'. Those official breed society descriptions are full of lovely phrases, and surely the aim of every serious breeder of the Wiltshire Horn is to produce a sheep that is 'proud and stately on short legs with certain grandeur of carriage'. It might sound like a line from a furniture catalogue but it gives a perfect picture of how they should carry themselves.

In the 1700s, Wiltshire Horns were bought and sold in large numbers at the Westbury Hill Fair, an annual open air sheep auction held close to the massive Bratton White Horse chalk carving. According to the records, Wiltshire Horns were traded along with other flocks brought up from Dorset and Hampshire, as well as ponies from the New Forest. There are accounts of stalls, sideshows and peddlers selling everything from bootlaces and gingerbread to sticky handfuls of cold plum duff. It seems to have been a lively atmosphere to say the least – sermons were even preached in Bratton warning local youths about the moral danger they might face if they went to the Hill Fair. It all sounds like chaos.

Sheep were also traded at the weekly market, with shepherds droving their flocks through the streets to the town centre auctions. Big, strong Wiltshires didn't mind being herded like that, and on some of the long, sprawling farms the men would drive their flocks to the top of the downs every morning and bring them back to the low land every evening. Naturally, thousands of sheep on manoeuvres meant a lot of droppings, but this provided a free and simple way of fertilising the poor quality grass. One very distinguished and well-spoken gentleman farmer used to raise a laugh when he referred to Wiltshire Horns as 'mobile muck carts'.

As they couldn't be sheared and the fleece collected in the conventional way, the breed fell out of favour with many Victorian shepherds, who depended on selling wool to make a living, but there were enough enthusiasts to save them from disappearing completely. A breed society was started in 1923, and in the 1930s and 40s they became popular in the Midlands where rams were used as terminal sires, or in other words, for breeding to produce good quality butchers' lambs. In the twenty-first century, that important role in the meat industry is still one of the main uses of Wiltshire's old county breed.

The heavyweight of the southern flocks is the Oxford Down, easily the largest and heftiest of all the Downland sheep. Once again, it's a breed that started out with Southdown ewes, crossed this time with Longwool Cotswold rams, to produce a black-faced sheep with black ears that point straight outwards and a woolly topknot which make it look like its wearing a toupee. The first sheep I could truthfully call my own, when I was about 16, were Oxford Downs, partly because our farm is just a few miles from the Oxfordshire border, so it was very much thought of as a local breed in that part of the Cotswolds. I was given some excellent advice on how to rear them for market and I tried to sell them commercially but without much success. Let's just say that I think of it as a learning experience.

The breed first appeared in the 1830s and it really took off with stockmen in western Oxfordshire, along the route of the lazy River Windrush and especially in the fields around the blanket-making town of Witney. In need of a name that would catch on they were called Cotswold Downs for a while until, sensibly, the Downland sheep of Oxfordshire became known as the Oxford Down.

The most impressive gathering of Oxford Downs in the whole of England was always the Oxford Ram Fair, held close to the River Thames on the outskirts of the city every August for generations. This was an occasion that definitely saw itself as superior to rough and ready events like the one at Westbury; Oxford was a serious, dedicated sheep sale. I've seen black and white film footage of the fair in 1930 showing row after row of old wooden hurdles arranged to form hundreds of large holding pens, which stretched out across the flat, open land beside Binsey Lane. Thousands of calm, obedient sheep filled the pens and circling around them were crowds of smartly dressed men, some in trilbies and others in caps, but every single one wearing a hat of some sort. Among the farmers, livestock managers and spectators you can spot the occasional pipe-smoker and a glimpse of a watch chain hanging from a waistcoat, but the thing that most dates the scene to anyone watching it today is the total absence of any women. In the thirties, buying and selling Oxford Downs, or even just watching the auction from a distance, was obviously deemed to be 'men's business'.

The Ram Fair started to peter out in the late 1950s and it had ceased completely by 1964. The fortunes of the event really mirror the rise and fall in popularity of the breed. Its size is impressive, but this proved to be its downfall because when butchers and their customers wanted a small, fat, early maturing lamb, the large and lean Oxford Down no longer fitted the bill. It fell out of favour and became a rare breed.

At about the same time that the Oxford Down was being developed, the Hampshire Down was making its first appearance. The person responsible was a vocal and assertive man called John Twynam who farmed near the upper reaches of the River Test at Whitchurch, a town summed up in the nineteenth century as being 'as big as a good-sized pocket handkerchief. It has three shops and nineteen public houses.'

Who knows if Twynam came up with his best ideas in the pub, but he did spend a lot of time campaigning, cajoling and petitioning on behalf of farmers as well as sharing the wisdom of his opinions with the readers of the *Hampshire Chronicle*, writing letters and columns in the paper for a remarkable total of 70 years. He crossed old Hampshire ewes with Cotswold rams to produce the first Hampshire Down type, which was then improved further with some of the breeds from the neighbouring counties: Southdowns, Wiltshire Horns and the now extinct black-faced, long-tailed Berkshire Nott. Once called 'the glory of the county', you can spot a Hampshire Down straight away because it looks as if it's wearing a woolly balaclava with a pair of brown ears and a dark nose poking out from the fleece on its head. They give birth to lively lambs that breeders like to describe as 'vigorous'; in the words of the Hampshire shepherd's rhyme, the newborns are 'looking for the teat before they're on their feet'.

The man to thank for the success of the Downland breeds across the southern counties and beyond is John Ellman, a tenant farmer and stockman from Glynde near Lewes in Sussex, who was one of the founders of

London's great agricultural gala, the Smithfield Show. In the late 1700s, Ellman took the local breed of lean, short wool sheep that grazed on the Sussex hills and threw all his efforts into developing them into a smaller, fast-growing, high quality butcher's animal with a light, fine fleece. This was the Southdown, the signature sheep of top-notch meat. The aristocracy took an interest in Ellman's work and he advised the Earl of Egremont and the Duke of Richmond on how to start their own Southdown flocks on their Sussex estates, at Petworth and Goodwood. He flirted with royalty too, meeting King George III and selling a pair of Southdowns to Emperor Paul I of Russia. More work was done by other agriculturalists later, as it almost always is, and the breed only declined when farmers discovered that dairying was more profitable and many bought milking herds to replace their sheep flocks. But it's Ellman's Southdown which weaves its way through the story of the south and links the sheep breeds of the downlands.

Everyone who keeps Southdowns knows Gail Sprake. In fact, most people who keep any sort of traditional breed know Gail. Somehow she manages to juggle running the Southdown Sheep Society and the chairmanship of the Rare Breeds Survival Trust with looking after her own collection of about a hundred animals on her Suffolk farm. There are cattle, turkeys, hens and sheep of course, but it's the Southdowns which have a special place in her affections. Gail's Southdown flock is now up to 50 breeding females. She bought her first ewes in the 1980s, because in her eyes they were aesthetically pleasing – 'If you're going to keep livestock you need to like what you look at.' She's got a point. There's a boxy, no nonsense quality about a Southdown. Soft, dense wool that looks from a distance like fur covers their small ears as well as their mouse brown face, giving them a teddy bear appeal.

Gail explains, 'I wanted to do my bit for a breed on the danger list.' She's also taken the decision to sell the lamb directly to her local, independent butcher who specialises in rare breed meat. It's all about localness, transparency and traceability: Gail knows exactly what has happened to her lamb, the butcher knows the provenance of the meat and in turn, the consumer can be confident and informed about what they're buying. She talks about it all with cheerfulness and positivity that's combined with an old-fashioned shepherd's loyalty to their flock.

I'm sure Gail's glass-half-full approach was a big factor in her becoming the longest serving chairman in the history of the Rare Breeds Survival Trust as well as a popular figure at events around the country. Despite having two busy national roles, she never misses a chance to help her local rare breeds support group and she'll sometimes travel for hours to spend her weekend working as a steward, livestock judge or main ring commentator at county shows and country fairs. 'The success of the four-legged animals depends on the two-legged animals who run the breed societies. I never forget the importance of the people behind the breeds.'

As mottos go, 'We wunt be druv' is about as unlikely and defiant as you can get. It's an old country dialect saying that translates as 'We will not be driven' – meaning pushed around or forced to do anything against our will – and, believe it or not, it's the county motto of Sussex. For me, the delight in this old phrase comes from its supposed farming roots. It's said that Sussex pig men respected the free-spirited, independently-minded swine they bred and the phrase came about as a way of describing the stubbornness of their herds. What we don't know is if the pig connection refers to a breed specific to Sussex or just any pigs that happened to be reared in the county?

You won't find any pigs of the long-extinct Sussex breed refusing to be druv these days, but we do know what the county hog of years ago looked like thanks to the author and agriculturalist Richard Parkinson. In 1810, he described the Sussex pig as a 'very good kind, distinguished by being black and white but not spotted; frequently black at both ends and white in the middle'. He talks about their superior rind (the skin for eating), their pointed ears and long, thin snouts, describing the county breed as 'small' and 'handsome' (though he doesn't mention if they minded being druv).

If the belted Sussex pig that Parkinson portrayed had survived into the twenty-first century, it sounds like it would have been a colourful addition to the list of

British pigs, pushing the number of pedigree breeds up to a round dozen and its distinctive markings might even have given the Gloucestershire Old Spots a rival in the porcine popularity stakes. I'd love to have seen a black and white Sussex pig living up to the county motto at the South of England Show.

I'm glad to say that another old breed associated with Sussex is very much still with us. Sussex cattle are medium-sized, muscly beasts with long, straight backs, sturdy legs, strong feet and big oval ears. Despite their bulkiness, they're a really easy-going, docile animal which can happily graze even on poor grass. I can clearly remember a Sussex breeder once telling me, half-jokingly: 'We call them idiot's cows, anyone can look after them.' They have rich, red coats with a white tail switch and the big claim is that they're 'the Great British beef breed'. But that reputation for good eating is relatively new. They're such powerful animals that it's no surprise that they were being used as working cattle long before anyone thought to use them primarily for beef. As horses and then steam ploughs replaced oxen, pockets of Sussex remained trapped in the past, with teams of eight cattle continuing to pull old-fashioned wooden ploughs on local farms, even as the Victorian era came to a close. Remarkably, one or two individual Sussex draught cattle were still working in fields near the village of Ditchling as recently as 1940.

Today's Sussex herds can be traced back to the red cattle which lived in the forests that stretched across the southern counties of England more than a thousand years ago, before the Norman invasion. The area is still called the Weald, which is the old English word for forest.

A millennium on from the Battle of Hastings, and the current Queen is helping to save the breed from extinction. The Queen's farm manager, Mark Osman, introduced me to the royal herd of Sussex cows as they grazed close by the famous Round Tower of Windsor Castle. The animals spend most of the year out in the Great Park with their calves and are only housed in winter when the ground is too wet and the pasture is too thin. Mark told me that Her Majesty may be the monarch and the resident of the castle, but she also sees herself as the farmer of the Windsor estate. He explained that the Queen takes a leading interest in how the farm is run and the future policy of the enterprise, with Mark working directly for the ranger of the park – better known to us as the Duke of Edinburgh.

The first Sussex cattle came to Windsor in the mid-1990s when 30 animals were bought for the farm, a decision prompted by the Queen and Duke who wanted to rear a traditional local breed. Her Majesty was equally concerned that more should be done to help a British beef variety at risk, and at the time there were fewer than 6,000 breeding Sussex cows. Today, the royal herd is more than 2,000 strong, making it the largest collection of Sussex cattle in the world and a sign of the Queen's serious commitment to our native livestock. But I can't help wondering if the royal officials missed a trick when the Duke and Duchess of Sussex were married. After Harry and Meghan's wedding ceremony at St George's Chapel in 2018, instead of taking a horse-drawn carriage pulled by a pair of Windsor Greys through the town, the royal mews really should have harnessed a couple of Sussex bulls. To borrow the words of the old county motto, they definitely would be druv.

We've got a lot to thank *Downton Abbey* for. First it was a Sunday night TV sensation. Then it became a ratings winner in America. Now there's due to be a movie version. But somewhere along the way, the aristocratic Crawley family in their fabulous stately home gave a much needed boost for one of the breeds of southern England.

The Oxford Sandy and Black pig had almost disappeared from view and most people had never heard of it. That is until the fictional Lady Mary brought a herd to Downton and they won first prize at the Malton Fatstock Fair. It was publicity money just can't buy. Suddenly everyone was talking about the lovely ginger pigs with the big black blotches and demand for sows suddenly went up as people fancied owning a pig or two of their own. Visitors to farm parks and spectators at county shows also started recognising the breed and calling it by name. Which all goes to prove the power of Downton.

The Oxford Sandy and Black pig, or OSB if you're in a hurry, has been rootling around in the woodland of its home county for 300 years. They were used in the Wychwood Forest to clear fallen nuts and prevent cattle being poisoned by acorns, so they were known locally as the Oxford Forest pig, and occasionally their distinctive markings earned them the nickname of the Plum Pudding pig.

But for decades their numbers were so low that most people thought they'd died out. As long ago as the 1940s, only one new pure-bred boar was being licensed each year, and without a dedicated breed society to safeguard its wellbeing, the Oxford Sandy and Black slipped out of public view. Thankfully the OSB had a saviour in the shape of the late, great Andrew Sheppy.

Known to everyone as Shep, he was a true man of the Somerset soil, a member of the famous Sheppy's cider family and the sort of person who felt most at home when he was on the farm dressed in a mud-splattered old boiler suit. At heart he was a poultry man, the best in the country, but he loved his cattle and pigs too.

Rare breeds of farm animals were being raised and cherished on the Sheppy family farm back in the 1950s, long before it seemed anyone else knew or cared. When the first real census of British breeds was carried out in the 1970s it showed OSBs were scarce, and as their origins couldn't be confirmed and there were no written records, it was decided that the breed was extinct. Andrew was having none of that. He discovered small herds of them and fought for years to have them recognised, eventually compiling enough historical information for them to be finally adopted as a living, breathing British rare breed.

Much more recently, DNA tests were carried out to establish once and for all if there was any genetic variation between various types of rare breed meat on sale. For decades people had argued that there was no difference between the meat in, for example, an Old Spots sausage and one labelled as Tamworth. As it turned out, when the results came back from the lab they showed that the Oxford Sandy and Black was genetically distinct and could be clearly distinguished from other pork. Shep had been vindicated.

My first encounter with OSBs came about thanks to another man with a passion for British breeds – a Witney farmer and stockman called Bob Brickell. Although it's fair to say his real love was Shire horses rather than pigs. In 1946, he had set up a stud which became one of the oldest and largest of its type in Great Britain, producing horses for customers as far away as Russia, South Africa and the United States.

Despite the widely-held view that Oxfordshire's own breed of pig was extinct we had heard that OSBs were, in fact, alive and squealing down on Bob's farm. Forty years ago this was intriguing news so I went with my dad and sister to check out the Brickell herd and do a spot of business with him, as Bob wanted to swap some of his pigs for a few of our working horses. When we arrived on his farm there were OSBs everywhere; sows and piglets in his red brick sties, a yard full of recently weaned young, four or five boars and some older females who were about to be used for breeding. There must have been 250 pigs there.

It was my 'unicorn' moment. It's difficult to explain just how remarkable it is to see a creature running around in front of you that you've always been told doesn't exist. We were ushered into Bob's magnificent, chrome-trimmed caravan, full of horse brasses and beautiful china figurines. We had tea, there was banter, but mostly it was a day of bargaining, bartering and haggling. He was a tough negotiator – the EU's Michel Barnier is a pussy cat compared with Bob. In the end though the deal was done and we got our elusive Plum Pudding pigs.

Oxfordshire is now the stronghold of the OSB with the biggest concentration of herds in that county, but there are also breeders dotted all over the UK from Selkirkshire to Somerset. The Sully family have been fans of the breed since 2004, attracted by the pigs' colouring and their easy, docile nature. Chris and Katie started breeding small, hairy Kune pigs before they 'went big with OSBs' for judging on the agricultural show circuit. Their daughter Hollie first took part in livestock competitions when she was just four. Now aged 16 she's spreading the word among her peer group: 'My best friend moved nearby when she was 13 and had never seen a pig. I showed her how to deal with them and within a few weeks she was in the young handlers' class at the Royal Bath and West Show.' Hollie is at college with thoughts of becoming a midwife, and she's very aware that being among farrowing sows and raising piglets since she was a toddler may have influenced her career choice: 'But whatever I do, I'll always have pigs.' Meanwhile, Mum Katie is confident that the OSB's future is secure: 'People like the meat, it's delicious, the fact it's a rare breed is appealing, and of course since Downton Abbey they've become a household name.'

I decide not to mention the Henson family connection to Downton. But the role of 'cheerful' Charlie Grigg, the old song and dance partner of Mr Carson in the series, was played by my uncle Nicky. He was pretty good too, even if I say so myself. But then again he didn't have to appear alongside any of those scene-stealing Plum Pudding pigs.

Every Jersey islander carries a picture of their famous local breed with them wherever they go. Even if most don't even realise it. But ask any resident of the sunny Crown Dependency in the English Channel to empty their wallet and there it is. When they hold a Jersey banknote up to the light, the watermark image of a Jersey cow comes into view. A good choice to symbolise the island, in my opinion, although the authorities could have chosen a potato, some knitwear or Jim Bergerac I suppose. Yet the native cattle breed, with its aristocratic air, does the job splendidly.

The Jersey cow is the standard bearer for the Channel Island breeds, and for milk that's rich and creamy. Jersey milk is pretty special and hailed as a healthy option because it's high in protein, calcium, butterfat and minerals, with a lot made of the claim that a small glass contains as much potassium as a banana. The cows it comes from are small and toffee coloured with a friendly nature, big eyes and long lashes which gives them an irresistible deer-like quality. You can see straight away why people love them. These dainty animals are likely to be related to ancient 'Celtic' cattle (they share characteristics with the small, ancient Kerry dairy cattle from Ireland) mixed with traits of tropical, Indian or yellow-skinned Caspian types which found their way to France. The Russian Tsar Alexander II was certainly sold on the breed and kept a herd as pets. Winston Churchill also had a Jersey, presented to him as a gesture of thanks from the people of the island at the end of the Second World War. But despite those famous owners, it's rare for Jersey cattle to make the news, so quite a fuss was caused when one calf on the island hit the international headlines in 2015. Named Fairy, she was born on a farm at Maufant in St Saviour, and shortly afterwards her owner, Andrew Le Gallais, noticed a white marking in the exact shape of the island of Jersey on her back. The outline was perfect, leading to a flutter of activity on Facebook and suggestions that Fairy should become the island's new mascot.

I can't claim to have ever seen maps on cattle hides but I have to confess to a liking for Jerseys. I'm keen on them because the breed has a unique place in the Henson family history. It's the breed that helped convince my dad as a small boy that he wanted to be a farmer. At that time, he didn't live in the country; home for him and my grandmother was a small house on one of the main roads through Northwood in Middlesex. This was the 1930s and the marketing men at the Metropolitan Railway had invented a glossy name for London's ever-spreading suburbs and commuter estates: Metroland. Northwood was right at the heart of this new development and in fact the Metropolitan Line Underground station wasn't very far from Dad's front door. But further away, down the Rickmansworth Road, was a place that would capture his young imagination and lead him on the path to a life on the land. Park Farm was about as old-fashioned as you could get and the sort of place where the cows were hand-milked, horses did most of the heavy work and chickens ran around in the rickyard. It was a picture-book farm and Dad fell in love with it from the age of four, going there with his mum whenever he could, to see the animals and help collect the eggs.

The farm was run by the Nichols family who had taken it on in the 1880s. Pigs and sheep were reared a mile or so away at 'Top Farm', while the four-bedroom farmhouse, offices and the entire dairy operation were based at 'Bottom Farm'. I've been lucky enough to discover two ladies who lived near Park Farm in the 1930s and 40s and can remember it clearly. Joscelyn Reeve and her sister, Marguerite Treglown, might be in their late eighties and early nineties respectively, but you'd never know it. They're both remarkably youthful with pin-sharp memories of old Northwood. They were friends with the farmer's daughter, a girl called Joy, and together they played on the farm as children. With no one turning a hair, the sisters remember riding in the hay carts, playing hide and seek in the yard and even walking the cows across the road from their pasture to the milking parlour. Marguerite can recall the appearance of the farm as my dad would have known it: 'There was nothing terribly posh about the place, but it hadn't moved with the times and really was a Victorian farm, even in the 1930s.'

Joscelyn and Marguerite lived in Gate Cottage which stood opposite the farm and beside a sturdy timber-framed, redbrick pub called, not surprisingly, The Gate. The pub building has been a local landmark for the best part of 400 years and it became one of the first Victorian 'beer houses' in the district when Northwood wasn't much more than a hamlet. Gate Cottage and the public house marked the site of the old turnpike, or toll road, which crossed the boundary between Middlesex and Hertfordshire. Travellers, tradespeople, herdsmen, their livestock, carriages and carts all had to pay to use the road until 1840, when tolls were abolished for pedestrians using the turnpike. This, apparently, inspired a burly local blacksmith called Alfred Hodgekinson to come up with an early form of tax dodge. Every time he passed the toll house he carried his horse on his shoulders to avoid being charged. They were obviously made of sterner stuff back then. The quiet, rural feel of the area may have gone, but you can still pop into the pub for a pint, and despite refurbishments, extensions and big chain ownership, it's kept the old Gate name, even if it's more of a food destination pub these days.

Joscelyn and Marguerite told me that the Park Farm dairy herd was made up of about 40 cows, just enough to provide the neighbourhood with a daily supply of milk. Householders would come out on to the street to fill their ceramic jugs from a metal churn carried on the back of the Nichols's horse-drawn cart. More than half the herd were Ayrshires, a classic and popular milker, but the rest were beautiful, genteel Jerseys. They were the cows that stood out and caught Dad's eye all those decades ago. Thanks to Joscelyn and Marguerite, I've been able to pinpoint the Jersey as the breed that sparked his fascination with British livestock, and Joscelyn was even able to draw me a map of how the farmyard looked when my dad knew it. Marked in pencil on a half-sheet of paper she outlined the very heart of this lovely family farm, with two milking sheds, one for the Jerseys and the other for the Ayrshires.

The sisters have vivid memories of the cowman too, a tall wiry man called Mr Carter, and how he would sit on an old three-legged wooden stool. He always wore his flat cap while he worked on the farm and he would have to turn the peak round to the back so he could lean into the cows as he milked them. When the entire herd had been milked, he carried the pails to the dairy, two at a time, hanging from a yoke across his shoulders. The sisters also remember seeing the hay cart being hauled by two working horses; a Shire called Boxer and a Suffolk who couldn't avoid being christened Punch. It sounds idyllic, and when Dad eventually left school he was delighted that the farm he'd adored as a child gave him a job, which means that I can say with confidence that the first cow he ever milked was a Northwood Jersey.

Dad's arrival on the staff at Park Farm is still remembered by Marguerite. 'When I saw him that first time I immediately noticed his head of curly hair,' she recalled, as if it happened yesterday. 'Of course I wanted to know who the new boy was and what he was doing on the farm. I'd often watch him going out across the fields to bring the cows in.'

Dad always called his childhood home 'leafy Middlesex', and that's still the case, more or less, but an awful lot of other things have changed. The farm he would have known is gone and a fitness club with an enormous car park has been built on the site.

After Northwood he went to work with Jerseys again, this time on a dairy farm near Taunton in Somerset. Not long after he arrived the head cowman was injured in a motorbike accident and, as there was no one else to take on the cattle, Dad found himself in charge. His dilemma was that the cattle all looked identical to him and he was meant to be recording their individual yields. The solution was sheer genius, as Dad recalled more than 60 years later: 'They stuck auctioneers' numbers on the cows' rumps for me and I had to learn their names before the writing wore off which I did, and when I got to know them, every cow was different and I knew them all.'

The learning curve was steep because it's also where he discovered just how difficult it is to milk an entire herd of Jerseys by hand. If you're a novice in a full-scale milking parlour it really takes it out of you, and after just a few minutes all the muscles in your hand will ache and your thumb will pound. So to milk 20 Jersey cows with full udders three times a day must have been agony for Dad. He once admitted to me that at the end of his first shift he was crying with the pain.

Before he left Taunton, the Ministry of Agriculture began an ambitious programme to eradicate tuberculosis (TB) in cattle, which was endemic at the time. They tested every animal in the UK, beginning in Cornwall and moving slowly and painstakingly up the country. Those animals which reacted to the test were slaughtered, just as they are today. One of Dad's favourite cows failed the test and had to go, but her young female calf was clear and was given to him as a leaving gift. She was the first pedigree animal registered in his name. He called her Panola, joined the Jersey Cattle

Society and founded the Jersey Cattle Club at Cirencester Agricultural College.

It might seem odd that despite Dad's affection for Jerseys and the part they played in his life, we only ever had one Jersey cow on the farm at home when I was young. Just like Highland cattle, the Jersey isn't a rare breed in the sense of being endangered, but the public love to see them and of course Dad was a great one for giving his customers what they wanted. Our Jersey was a lovely gentle old house cow called Pookie. It must have been at least 40 years ago now, but every so often I still meet visitors who remember seeing Pookie at the Farm Park in the days when we milked her in front of the public.

Until recently, the cows on Jersey were a closed population, so although they've been taken off the island for many years and exported all over the world, on their home turf the herds remained pure island stock. Sensibly, semen from some of those indigenous bulls was stored, but commercial necessities and the need to increase production meant that in the early 2010s improved Jersey genetics from overseas had to be reintroduced. I know there are some people who disagree with that decision, but the reality is that farms have to be viable and without action there was the real prospect of the famous Jersey breed disappearing from their island home. That would have been a sad and painful outcome, but as one breeding expert explained 'the blood is now flowing in both directions'.

Jerseys were also responsible for one of my most memorable filming assignments on *Countryfile* and one which earned us acres of great publicity in the national newspapers. To mark the programme's thirtieth anniversary in 2018, we were given permission to go behind the scenes on the royal estates at Windsor, Sandringham and Balmoral for a three-part series under the title *Queen and Country*.

The royal dairy herd of 165 beautiful Jersey cows graze in Home Park. One bloodline on the farm dates back to 1871 when the first Jersey, Pretty Polly, arrived at Windsor, given to Queen Victoria as a present. Her genetics survive in the cows which graze the Windsor estate today, making her descendants the oldest herd of Jerseys in the country. Their milk is made into Windsor Castle ice cream, which is sold in the estate's own farm shop and at Buckingham Palace every summer.

Victoria's husband Prince Albert personally oversaw the building of one of the gems of the Windsor estate: the royal dairy is home to an ornate and finely-tiled creamery in the Italian Renaissance style with its arches, columns and beautiful stained glass. What an honour it was to be the first person to film inside the creamery and capture the high painted ceiling and the rows of wide marble tables. The building has been preserved exactly as it was when it was constructed in 1848. At the time it was the height of dairy technology, though of course it's pretty basic compared with the set up today.

The twenty-first century royal herd is milked in a robotic parlour with the aid of laser-guided milking cups. In the cattle shed there's an automatic cow brush while another 'bot sweeps the floor and the slurry is collected for recycling as fertiliser. But the biggest surprise was seeing where the Queen's Jerseys sleep. As I turned to walk between two rows of cattle stalls, I noticed the floor of each berth was moving slightly. That's because the cows rest on their own water beds – huge liquid-filled pillows designed to soothe the animals and take the pressure off their shoulders and hips while they sleep. I never thought I'd meet a cow which spends the night floating.

If fog hasn't grounded flights at Jersey Airport, the journey to the second largest of the Channel Islands only takes 20 minutes. Sitting 60 miles from the UK and within sight of the French coast, the Guernsey climate makes any visit feel like a holiday. The winters are markedly milder than at home, the summers are long and warm with gin-clear skies, and there are areas of this beautiful island that remain remarkably unspoilt. Despite its compact size, just nine miles by six, the scenery is spectacular. In the north, there are award-winning sandy beaches while the south coast is one of high, rugged cliffs that drop dramatically to the waters below. But it's inland where the terrain gets really interesting and the agricultural landscape is like nowhere else. The land here is divided into small fields, each about one-and-a-half acres in size, separated by a system of ancient earth banks and hedges creating an intricate pattern of interwoven plots on the ground.

It's essentially a medieval field system and old maps reveal that not much has changed in hundreds of years. The reason that the hedgerows and bank boundaries have remained is that almost every field is owned by a different person. The curious field structure doesn't lend itself to large scale arable farming but it's perfect for the island's own bovine superstar: the Guernsey cow. The doe-eyed, short-horned golden beauties have a calm and contented temperament – although sticklers will insist that Guernsey cattle are various shades of fawn rather than gold. Larger and sturdier than the Jersey, they also produce bigger yields of milk than their island neighbours.

The Guernsey cattle's heritage is firmly French, although no one seems to agree on the exact details. The most popular theory is that they came from herds of Froment du Leon cattle, possibly brought from Brittany by tenth-century monks, which were crossed with the larger Isigny breed from Normandy, transported from Cherbourg in the 1060s. What's not in doubt is how vital the dairy industry has been to the economy of the island. Guernsey milk is deliciously smooth and creamy. In fact, traditionally, the milk on sale to islanders had to come from the local Guernsey herds; it was a custom that was great news for milk drinkers, dairy farmers and the cows alike.

The milk is so famous that it overshadows the other, lesser known Guernsey cattle product: fantastically tasty beef. If raised on milk and allowed to grow good muscle, these cows provide excellent meat that's marbled with distinctive yellow fat, a result of the high percentage of carotene they retain from the grass they eat. That's something that startles anyone who's only used to seeing white fat on their plate, but it's especially popular with islanders who eat local and stay loyal to Guernsey. The local cattle ruled the roost for generations here thanks to a law in 1789 which banned imports of other breeds to the island. The knock-on effect was a unique genetic purity and, importantly, meant the Guernseys on Guernsey avoided many of the animal diseases which, over time, affected herds on the mainland.

Cartons of their milk and cream seem to be sold everywhere on Guernsey, as you might imagine. But a taste of the Channel Islands is the last thing you'd expect to find among the luxury skyscrapers, sumptuous shopping malls and glittering nightlife of Dubai. With the Persian Gulf on one side of the city and the scorching, dusty Arabian desert on the other, there's not a lot to remind you of lush green island pasture. But in the crowded investment hub of the United Arab Emirates, the latest trend among the rich, fashionable elite is for cream teas, and the clotted cream they're going crazy for is made from the milk of Jerseys and Guernseys. The rest of the world seems smitten too, with export markets in Japan, China and Australia.

The company behind this British success story overseas is Rodda's. This Cornish organisation is fiercely
loyal to its roots, and is responsible for making a remarkable 250 million spoonfuls of clotted cream every year
from a mix of Jersey and Guernsey cream – although
the trademark soft golden crust on the top of every
potful is solely down to the Guernseys' contribution.

Rodda's is a family firm that's been making rich,
sticky clotted cream from local herds around the village
of Scorrier in north Cornwall since 1890. They're almost
as proud to have had six generations of the family in the
business as they are of having their cream served as
part of the meal on the final flight of Concorde. In my
job, admitting to having favourite breeds is a dangerous thing to do (of course they're *all* my favourites, I
cry), but there's one Channel Island variety that has a
special place in my heart. I'm not the only one either.
The Golden Guernsey goat is cheeky, charming, occasionally naughty and completely unique. Peter Girard
says of his experience with the goats: 'I hear people say
they're bad tempered but I disagree, I've always found
them placid, good natured and a really great goat to
look at'. His family have been on Guernsey since the
1600s, and while Peter earns a living with his hands as
a cabinet-maker and joiner, he devotes his spare time to
caring for his herd and carrying out his duties as president of the Guernsey Goat Society.

While goats are reared all over the world for meat
(it's claimed to be the most consumed red meat in the

world) the Golden Guernsey is bred, like its bovine counterpart, for its outstanding milk. It's rich, creamy and tasty, but that high quality isn't enough to put it on the supermarket shelves; it can't compete in the commercial world because Guernsey yields are too low. But as a small, nimble animal they make great household goats and if you fancy keeping a few animals and like the idea of having a ready supply of goats' milk for your own consumption or for making cheese, then I'd recommend the Golden Guernsey every time.

There's no such thing as a 'typical' Guernsey goat, and although we call them golden, their coats come in a variety of shades from a pale blond to a fox red. They can be horned or polled, have short or long hair and come with or without white markings. Apart from their colouring it's the Guernsey's ears that people love: they're large, forward pointing and have a slight tilt at the ends as if they're straining to hear what you're saying.

The story of the saviour of the Guernsey goats would make a terrific movie. If not a thriller then it could easily compete with *'Allo 'Allo!* for the most improbable way to thwart the enemy. Back in June 1940, Nazi troops bombed and then invaded the Channel Islands, imposing a curfew, outlawing alcohol, banning radios and requisitioning cars. The occupying forces controlled all the crops grown and every fish caught by the islanders, while farm livestock were often slaughtered to feed German soldiers. In 1944, when supplies from Germany were cut, the situation on the island became desperate and starvation loomed for islanders and occupiers alike.

Every Guernsey goat was destined to be used for food and the breed would have certainly become extinct if it wasn't for the heroine of the hour, Miriam Milbourne. She had started rearing Golden Guernseys in the 1930s and was determined that German oppression on the island wouldn't be a death sentence for her beloved breed. So she bravely hid her goats from the occupying soldiers to literally save their skins, and although she probably didn't think of herself as a Resistance fighter that's exactly what she was. Tricking the Nazis would have been a nerve-wracking experience for her, and it must have taken all her guile and ingenuity to keep a herd of goats quiet and undetected on such a small island. If she'd been discovered by the Nazis we can only imagine what the consequences would have been.

One popular myth that definitely isn't true though, is that Miss Milbourne hid her animals in local caves. The only caves on Guernsey are tidal and fill with water daily, so the goats wouldn't have lasted very long there. It's unlikely that they ended up in a cellar or basement either. Islanders who knew Miss Milbourne agree that she would have concealed the animals in the rooms of her house, which makes the story all the more remarkable.

As for today's great defender of the Golden Guernsey, it was the outbreak of foot-and-mouth disease in 2001 that prompted him to take action. The threat to live-stock populations throughout England made Peter Girard wonder about the numbers of Golden Guernseys. So he bought a pure-bred female kid and from there his herd grew; he now has 30 pedigree goats. Peter's not alone in taking the Golden Guernsey to his heart. 'The total population is up to about 1,200 now, and I'd say in the last eight years the number of goats actually on the island has increased too, so there's definitely much more interest,' he says. He puts it down to the power of the media; his goats have been on network television at least three times, and the exposure means publicity and that equals awareness. Perhaps now would be a good time to suggest that a statue of Miriam Milbourne wouldn't be a bad idea.

It seems so much of Guernsey is golden – not just the sunshine and the beaches but also the cattle, the goats and, most intriguing of all, the much talked about but never seen Golden Guernsey donkey. Over the years I've heard it mentioned on many occasions, and once or twice I've seen its name in print, but the only thing that's ever said is that it's a long extinct breed. There are no other clues and it's impossible to find references or descriptions in the old farming journals and agricul-tural text books. That's saying something, because even breeds which died out 200 years ago or more are usually mentioned somewhere deep in the archives. In 2016, a donkey (though not a golden coloured one) fea-tured in a series of special Guernsey postage stamps celebrating the island's animal life, and the blurb accompanying the set even explained that it was included 'to pay homage to the original Guernsey golden donkey which is now extinct'. But there was nothing substantial to help pin a tale on this elusive donkey.

There's no shortage of regular donkey connections on the island however. A donkey called Joey was the famous mascot of the Royal Guernsey Light Infantry in the First World War; there's a statue of a donkey and foal in the centre of St Peter Port, and there are toys made by a cottage industry called the Little Guernsey Donkey Factory. But none of them can claim to be a donkey of the Golden Guernsey variety.

Have we confused folklore with fact? Like most places there's good old local rivalry between communities, and in the Channel Islands a tradition still exists of giving jokey animal nicknames to the neighbours. So Jersey Islanders are called 'toads', on Alderney they're 'rabbits' and the people of Sark are called 'crows'. Guernsey residents are known by the others as 'donkeys', and there are at least three reasons why the name came about. First, because the steep streets of St Peter Port meant donkeys were needed to transport supplies. They did all the jobs that horses normally do, not just carrying goods on their backs but also pulling carts, wagons and ploughs, so in time the image stuck. Secondly, if a Guernseyman hadn't married or been to London by the time he reached 25 his mates would call him a donkey. And finally, there's the obvious image of a mule being stubborn and wilful with a powerful kick. Although on Guernsey they prefer to say strong and determined! Perhaps there's been a misunderstanding about Guernsey donkeys, and at some point long ago a gentle quip has been taken literally?

I think an expert opinion is called for. The Priaulx Library occupies a handsome three-storey Georgian town house in St Peter Port, overlooking the harbour with views across to the islands of Herm and Sark, and it's been keeping the heritage of the Bailiwick safe since 1889. Sue Laker is the chief librarian and there's not much about the island that she doesn't know. There's not an ounce of doubt in Sue's mind: 'There isn't and never has been a Golden Guernsey donkey. It simply doesn't exist.' She tells me that she's searched for evidence in numerous books, agricultural files and newspaper cuttings in the archive but has drawn a blank. There are no photographs, copperplate etchings or lithographs of a distinct local donkey breed either. 'Donkeys yes, lots of them,' says Sue, 'but no Guernsey breed and certainly none that are golden.' Undaunted, goat breeder Peter Girard is a little more romantic about the whole donkey legend: 'I have no reason to disbelieve it, despite the fact there's no evidence we can put our hands on. Call me a man of faith if you like.'

Heading north east, the last and least well known of the Channel Island cattle breeds is the Alderney. Although its obscurity is hardly surprising since its story has echoes of the Golden Guernsey goat with one final, tragic difference. The cattle of the fortified little island of Alderney didn't have a saintly rescuer like Miriam Milbourne, and so the breed has been extinct since the Second World War, when the last surviving animals on the island were slaughtered and eaten by the occupying German troops. In 1940, just before the Nazi invasion, most Alderneys were taken off the island and transported to nearby Guernsey, where they ended up cross breeding with the herds there. A few pure Alderneys remained on home turf, but in 1944 the last of them were butchered to feed Hitler's men. It was a shocking end for what had been a beautiful and widely admired dairy breed. So impressive in fact that in 1912 it was described as 'the best butter cow in the world'.

These placid-natured cattle were smaller, more slender and even more deer-like than their neighbours, the Jersey and the Guernsey. Again they were related to the cattle of northern France and had a nickname – the crumpled horn. Sure enough, old photographs show milking cows with short, wayward horns pointing in different directions.

There was a theory that the Alderney wasn't a separate breed at all and was just the collective name for all Channel Island cattle. It came about because, as the most northerly of the islands, Alderney was the last port of call for vessels carrying cattle to England. Workers on the dockside would be waiting to unload livestock from the 'Alderney boat' and that's how the confusion came about.

Although the living, breathing animals were wiped out, the memory of Alderney cattle lives on in the world of literature. It's known that Jane Austen's mother owned a pair of Alderneys and it seems to have inspired the author to include the breed among the dairy herd owned by the Martins of Abbey Hill Farm in her classic novel *Emma*. An Alderney also pops up in Elizabeth Gaskell's *Cranford*, kept by Betty Barker and treated like a daughter by her.

But on the printed page the Alderney is best known as the cow that features in A. A. Milne's timeless children's poem *The King's Breakfast* about a fussy monarch who had 'no butter for the royal slice of bread' and the hard-pressed dairymaid who tries to help. The poem was published in 1924 and it's still popular with young children today, but I wonder just how many teachers and parents explain what an Alderney is, or if they even know themselves?

Cotswold Lamb Koftas

Serves: 6

Ingredients
500g (1lb 2oz) lamb mince
2 tsp ground cumin
1 bunch fresh coriander, leaves picked and roughly chopped
2 garlic cloves, crushed
1 tbsp fresh mint leaves, roughly chopped
olive oil, for brushing
salt and pepper

To serve
6 pitta breads, warmed
crisp lettuce leaves
raita dip

1. Pre-heat the oven to 180°C/350°F/gas 4.
2. Add all the ingredients to a bowl, mix well and season with a pinch of salt and some pepper.
3. Divide the mixture into 6 equal portions, then roll into 6 sausage-like shapes.
4. Thread the each kofta onto a metal skewer and brush with oil.
5. Place on a baking tray and cook in the preheated oven for about 12 minutes, or until cooked through.
6. Serve the lamb koftas in warmed pitta bread with crisp lettuce leaves and a raita dip.

Andy Boreham
Head Chef, Cotswold Farm Park

CHAPTER 3

London and the Home Counties

G azing up at the concrete pillars of the Chiswick
flyover, dodging the non-stop traffic on the
Uxbridge Road or watching airliners on their final
approach to Heathrow airport, it's impossible to
imagine the fields, farms and livestock which were once
dotted all over what is now London's urban sprawl. But
the capital, and the 'capital county' of Middlesex, have
their own place in British agriculture and the story of
our native farm breeds.

Well into the Victorian era, the high roads and back
streets of this area were full of traders who earned their
living from livestock, in dairies, slaughterhouses and
butchers, as tripe sellers, game and poultry dealers,
cheesemongers, wool merchants, skinners, saddlers,
tanners and leather sellers as well as some in some
trades we barely recognise today, like horners (crafts-

men who fashioned items from horn) and tallow chandlers (who made candles from animal fat).

But there was, and still is, one place where big money changed hands. Close to the heart of London, Smithfield is the UK's biggest meat market and it surely must be the world's best known. Beef, pork and poultry have been bought and sold there for more than 800 years. From at least the 1100s there was a livestock market on the site, described at the time as being 'a celebrated rendezvous of fine horses to be sold' with 'vendibles of the peasant, swine with their deep flanks, and cows and oxen of immense bulk'. The sale of live animals lasted at Smithfield down the centuries until the 1850s, when stock auctions were moved to a new site in Islington because of concerns about hygiene and welfare at the ancient market, along with fears that livestock might escape into the surrounding streets.

Smithfield meat market was rebuilt and reopened in 1868 to truly embrace the railway age. For the first time, fresh meat from all over the country could be brought by wagon straight into underground railway sidings, where it was moved by hydraulic lifts up to the traders on the market floor.

Smithfield also has a special place in the family history of the Hensons. My Victorian forebear Joseph Lincoln Henson was among the city's principal sellers of tripe and offal – admittedly not a glamorous career, but at that time a remarkably lucrative one. He set up business at Smithfield in 1895 and went on to supply brine-soaked meat to the many salt beef bars that were popular throughout the East and West Ends a century ago. Henson Foods Limited is still going strong and, while it bowed to the inevitable when it stopped tripe production in the 1970s, the firm has forged a reputation as a high quality catering butcher and it's known in delis and restaurants all over London for its modern grass-fed brisket salt beef; a contemporary makeover which has helped keep the company thriving.

Just like the rural counties of the UK, the capital used to have its own local farm breed – the intriguing and mysterious Middlesex pig. I wouldn't expect anyone in Brentford or Uxbridge today to have even heard of the breed, but these places were a stronghold during its heyday in the 1840s. Unfortunately the passage of time hasn't been kind to the Middlesex pig and detailed records don't seem to have survived the last century and a half.

An account we do have shows that, at the Smithfield Christmas Show in 1843, an obviously well-nourished Middlesex was commended by the livestock judges. The *Farmers' Magazine* reported that Jacob Crawther from Isleworth fed his 31-week-old pig on 'boiled potatoes, fine middlings and skimmed milk'. Middlings is a wonderful Dickensian sort of word for animal feed made from the by-products of milling wheat. I don't suppose this concoction looked very appetising, but modern day nutritionists will be pleased to hear that this particular porker was getting a good mix of carbohydrates, protein and calcium.

Old portraits of the breed are hard to find, but in the Wellcome Collection, London's excellent free museum and library on the Euston Road, there's an etching of three improved Middlesex pigs beside a thatched out-house. The artwork is in the classic exaggerated English naïve style. In it, the pigs look like three enormous black barrage balloons each with a face at the front. The eyes, snouts and mouths look unnervingly human and beneath their shiny, obese bodies they have spindly little legs which, honestly, would struggle to hold up a flimsy coffee table.

Distorted perspective was the trademark of the naïve artists because in many cases they were being paid by the farmer to promote their skill as breeders of prize-winning fatstock. You could call it the earliest example of spin. The inscription below the image of the Middlesex pigs in the Wellcome Collection gives it all away: 'Bred and fed by Mr William Mills Barber of Uxbridge for which the first prize of £10 was awarded and the Silver Medal at the Smithfield Cattle Show, December 1848.'

There is another pig with such a strong association with the capital that it became known as the London Porker. This cockney's favourite was the Middle White. Although, it's not a native of the south east at all, but actually comes from the West Riding of Yorkshire, where in 1852 a weaver and pig breeder called Joseph

Tuley caused a stir with his swine at the Keighley Agricultural Show. The judges were stumped because Joseph's sows were too small to be classed as Large Whites and too big to be eligible as Small Whites. But they all thought that 'the merits of these pigs were so extraordinary' that they couldn't simply be disqualified. Unable to agree what to do, the competition organisers eventually created a third category and called it the 'Middle Breed'.

The first thing you notice about a Middle White is its face. You'd never call it pretty with its short, squat, upturned snout, small heavy-lidded eyes and large, open, pointed ears. More than once they've been called bat-faced. But what they lack in the looks department is compensated for in their meat. As a specialist pork breed it came into its own about a hundred years ago and helped satisfy the enormous demand for meat in and around London. Small joints were popular around this time, and butchers in the capital discovered that the Middle White was easy to cut and just the thing to keep their customers happy.

In the 1920s, the London Porker even caught the attention of the future wartime prime minister, Sir Winston Churchill, who kept a small herd of them at Chartwell, his country home and retreat in Kent. He was a real animal lover with a menagerie which also included cats, dogs, ducks, swans, horses and a herd of dairy cows. There's no question that Sir Winston was a man of many talents, but unfortunately he could never be described as an accomplished pig farmer. His herd won prizes but they never made money, partly because he believed you could never send an animal to slaughter after you had wished it good morning.

In 1926, when finances were tight, he had to make economies and many of his farm animals were sold, but he was too attached to his Middle White pigs to get rid of them. In fact, Churchill is credited with one of the most famous pig quotes of all time: 'Dogs look up to you, cats look down on you. Give me a pig! He just looks you in the eye and treats you as an equal.' If you've ever kept pigs you'll know how right the great man was.

Of course, London is full of unusual and unexpected delights, but I was still genuinely surprised by events at the Natural History Museum. The ornate Victorian landmark in South Kensington is famous for its dinosaur bones, whale skeletons and millions of very old, very dead exhibits. Still, I don't think many of the five million people who visit the museum every year go there expecting to come face to face with living, breathing exhibits, particularly ones that bleat. As well as a three-ton meteorite, Dodo fossils and a stuffed polar bear, the museum also owns a flock of Greyface Dartmoor sheep which graze in the wildlife garden within the grounds of this great palatial institution.

The Longwool breed from Devon is descended from the ancient hill sheep that lived on the wild moors and is a quiet, slow growing and very cute-looking animal. I always think of it as the Eeyore of the sheep world, and at county shows even the best Greyface Dartmoor will pootle slowly past the judges with its downturned head and ears, making it just about the least showy sheep you'll ever see. But they hold special memories for me because when my sisters and I had our own adopted breeds on the farm when we were youngsters, Mum decided she didn't want to be left out and fell in love with the Greyface Dartmoor. At that time, very few farmers were keeping them outside Devon and I can well remember that the breed society was never entirely convinced that the sheep Mum raised in the Cotswolds were anywhere near as good as the ones from Dartmoor. We even had an orphaned Greyface lamb that was suckled and reared by a doting nanny goat that had lost its kid. It was a beautiful thing to see and the lamb grew to be a thumping great adult ram, but even he couldn't sway the exacting guardians of the Greyface Dartmoor breed.

The Natural History Museum calls the sheep its 'cutest members of staff' and 'fuzzy lawnmowers' which is precisely what they are; their speckled faces are the only part of the sheep that's not covered in thick wool. These shaggy-coated garden trimmers munch their way through long grass and weeds, helping to keep plants healthy and improving biodiversity. The small flock spends most of its time at the London Wetlands Centre on the Surrey bank of the Thames, but every year since 1999, after the wildflowers have bloomed and they start to set seed, the trampling sheep help to press the fallen seed into the ground outside one of London's top visitor attractions.

Nine miles east of Exhibition Road SW7, there's another surprise and a truly exceptional example of the urban and the rural coming together. In the middle of the Isle of Dogs, on a derelict plot that was once earmarked for an estate of tower blocks, sits Mudchute Farm. You'll know the place if you watch *EastEnders* – in the opening titles it's where the River Thames loops round to form a 'U' shape. The land was originally spoil from the construction of the nearby Millwall dock and got its name because the mud was channelled through chutes. So its back story couldn't be more industrial, but since the mid-1970s this patch has been a public park and a conservation farm – a much needed green 'lung' surrounded on three sides by the world's most famous waterway.

In the shadow of the enormous tower of Canary Wharf, the staff care for at least 15 British breeds. There are Tamworth, Large Black and Middle White pigs, Oxford Down, Whitefaced Woodland and Manx Loaghtan sheep, Golden Guernsey goats and a small but growing herd of Dexter cattle. Seeing those little black cows grazing within mooing distance of city skyscrapers really is something to behold. Beyond the metal and glass superstructures, there are ten million people living and working in the London area, but somehow Mudchute maintains a peaceful, country atmosphere and the 32 acres of farm, parkland and meadows act as an antidote to all the noise and commotion of the metropolis.

But you'd be wrong if you thought Mudchute was simply a curiosity for city dwellers, it's so much more than that because behind the fun there's proper education and serious conservation work going on here. It's won a Green Flag Community Award for the standard and biodiversity of the open space the team have created for local people. In 2018, Mudchute also joined the ranks of officially recognised farm parks with approval from the Rare Breeds Survival Trust for its work. The RBST sets the bar high before it gives its backing to any business or organisation, which means you have to be doing something pretty special to earn a place on the approved list.

A few weeks after the award was announced, a smart white plaque to celebrate the farm's achievement was unveiled by Cyrus Todiwala. He's the top chef and restaurateur who made a big impact when his TV series *The Incredible Spicemen* hit our screens in 2013, and we've been fellow judges at the BBC Food and Farming Awards. Cyrus is a gift for the rare breeds movement and not just because he's a high-profile supporter. He really embraces the idea of giving the animals a purpose so that there's a practical reason for rearing them, and what could be better than delicious, traceable and truly British lamb, pork and beef. He's particularly keen on creating dishes with Middle White pork, Manx Loaghtan lamb and North Ronaldsay mutton because, he says, 'They're as interesting to look at as they are to cook.'

Cyrus also just happens to be a dab hand at making a tasty meal from woodland-reared Old Spots pork. I discovered this when we were filming together, and he not only created a delicious, spicy grilled pork sausage but he also roped me into making the bangers with him. As I struggled with meat, chopped onions, crushed garlic and sausage skins, I found that we share the same views on eating for conservation.

'It sounds rather strange but the more of the rare breeds you demand as a meat, the more the chances of the breed surviving,' Cyrus told me. I couldn't have agreed with him more when he told me that, as a chef, he feels he has to do justice to the work of the farmers who have provided him with beautiful meat, reared with 'passion and love and affection'. Cyrus makes a point of buying directly from farmers for his London restaurants and he'll often take, and find a use for, the whole carcass (what's often called nose-to-tail cooking).

It's plain that rare breeds aren't just ingredients for Cyrus to show off his culinary skills, for him its food that tells a story about British farming. I've always said that if more butchers, high street shops and super-markets sold rare breed meat, numbers of many of the most threatened varieties of sheep, pig and cattle might be lifted out of danger and I wondered if Cyrus agreed. 'Yes, but I think we need to start with the public because the public dictate where food trends go,' he explained.

If there's one thing they really love at the Royal County of Berkshire Show, it's the Berkshire pig. The annual event started before the First World War as a horse show on a farm to the west of Newbury. Now it has grown into a two-day jamboree of all things rural on a 150-acre showground next to the M4/A34 junction and just a welly chuck away from the Chieveley motorway services. It's certainly an unconventional location for an agricultural show but it works; it's simple to find and easy to park, there's barely any traffic noise and if you want a trucker's breakfast, it's right on the doorstep. The lack of pigs at that first Newbury Show in 1909 is more than made up for now; you'll find more Berkshires here than at any other agricultural show in the country. I counted almost 50 in the pig tent, and although the livestock marquees were lined up in a row at the furthest edge of the showground, there was still quite a crowd wandering by and peering into the metal pens to admire the county breed.

Berkshires aren't the biggest of pigs but their black coats, six white points (snout, feet and tail) and their large pointy ears make them unforgettable. They're the same colour as a decent pint of Guinness and when you see a Berkshire, you're looking at English history on legs. They've existed for centuries and were originally a variety of colours from tawny red to black, sometimes with spots and white patches, but it wasn't until Oliver Cromwell's troops noticed them that the first written records were made. That was more than 350 years ago at the height of the Civil War when the Parliamentarian forces were in winter quarters near Reading. Cromwell's Roundheads were impressed by the size of the local hogs they encountered in the area and praised the quality of its ham and bacon (remember, these were cold, hungry soldiers).

By the end of the 1700s, the breed was well established, particularly around the market towns of Faringdon and Wantage. Later, Queen Victoria became a fan. She kept a large herd at Windsor Castle, including a famous one called Ace of Spades which went on to become the first registered Berkshire boar in America when serious breeding began there in the 1870s. News that they were Victoria's favourite breed, and their reputation for being sweet natured, friendly and easy to manage, soon saw them being called the ladies' pig. The phrase was a shorthand way of describing their size and temperament, but it caught on because the breed was popular with aristocratic wives of the age (who didn't so much tend their herds as simply own them).

There's a chance a Berkshire pig is on your bookshelf. The Empress of Blandings in the P. G. Wodehouse novels is a Berkshire sow; Pig-wig in *The Tale of Pigling Bland* was based on Beatrix Potter's own pet Berkshire and George Orwell made the tyrannical Napoleon in *Animal Farm* a fierce, threatening Berkshire boar.

At the Newbury showground there were no overbearing boars – in fact, the pig tent was the most peaceful part of the Berkshire Show. It was full of sleeping, snoozing and snuffling pigs, mostly sows and gilts (young, unmated females) with their snouts buried deep in straw bedding, only getting to their feet with an oomph when fresh water arrived. The highlight of the whole weekend was the Berkshire pig Champion of Champions, when 23 rosette-winners from this and 17 other summer shows competed for the top honour.

Among the hopefuls were an eight-year-old sow called Pips and her two-year-old granddaughter, Flora. They're owned by Chris Hudson who's particularly proud of Pips, the 'old lady' of his herd. 'She can be awkward at times but she'll run to me when I call her name.' Pips has a great track record for winning prizes, and she's been a supreme champion twice before, as well as farrowing 140 piglets in her life. No wonder she was fast asleep in her pen. The good mothering instinct of the Berkshire sow was one of the deciders for Chris when he was choosing which pigs to rear. 'I researched all the breeds and made my mind up that I liked the Berkshire most, a lovely temperament and you won't get crackling like a Berkshire from any other breed.'

The crackling is the clue because, despite the rosettes and the adulation, it's not Pips who pays the bills, it's her numerous litters. Chris runs a hog roast company, serving spit-carved Berkshire pork with all the trimmings at birthday parties, business lunches and especially weddings. 'I've been breeding pigs for showing and the hog roast pays for my hobby.' He promotes the meat as home bred, outdoor reared, rare breed pork, and he seems to be winning his customers over to the idea of eating something that's traditional and slow-grown. 'Different breeds have different flavours through the fat and with the Berkshire, people say they like the slightly gamey taste.'

It's that flavour and succulence that's made the breed a hit in the Far East. Chris has exported half a dozen gilts and boars to Japan where the Berkshire is treated as a speciality black pig and the pork is known as *kurobuta*. It's such an important market that a delegation of Japanese breeders visited the Berkshire Show and was treated to a special one-off parade of the very best Berkshires in the judging ring. One hundred and fifty years after those early exports to America, and then Australia and New Zealand, it's good to see that foreign interest in the breed continues. Although I can't help thinking how ironic it is that while Berkshire pork is treated as a delicacy 6,000 miles away in Tokyo, there would have been some people from Berkshire visiting the county show who will never have even heard of their own local pig. That's the enigma of rare breeds, I guess.

It's not for want of trying though and I've got to hand it to the Berkshire Show organisers who do a tremendous amount to put their county breed forward. When the whole event was rebranded in 2014 they chose a rather handsome looking, prick eared Berkshire pig as the new logo, and in the weeks running up to the show you see that image in all the region's newspapers and on billboards everywhere. Then there's Rasher the

Pig. She's a life size cut-out of a Berkshire sow (or in the words of the show society, a 'nearly real animal') which tours local schools, and helps teach kids about different cuts of meat as well as promoting British Sausage Week every November. The show team are doing all the right things, and wouldn't it be a huge leap forward if their hard work led to the Berkshire pig becoming the official symbol of the royal county?

I could have stayed in the livestock section all day, but there's something else I was curious to see and it was only a short walk away. In another large, long marquee people gathered around a table watching some food experiments, an old farming film was flickering away on a screen in the corner and one visitor was even wearing a virtual reality headset. It was all part of the display put on here every year by a team of friendly, outgoing staff from the University of Reading.

The university has been at the forefront of serious agricultural research since 1893, but there's another side to their work. The team at Reading knows that for the general public to understand the impact and importance of farming and country issues, the information needs to be presented in an attractive and entertaining way. My dad would always say that people must have fun in order to learn, and of course he was right. I was never very academic at school but I do remember that I absorbed more from the teachers who could share a joke and made their lessons enjoyable. They understand that at Reading, so for the last seven decades the university has run its own visitor attraction, the Museum of English Rural Life, or MERL for short.

It's like *Countryfile*, *Springwatch* and the *Antiques Roadshow* all rolled into one. It opened in 1951 as a touring exhibition at county shows, before it was moved to a permanent home in Reading, Berkshire's county town. The launch of MERL happened at a significant time for farming: meat, sugar and butter were still on the ration; *The Archers*, billed as the everyday story of country folk, started on the BBC Light Programme (the Radio 2 of its day), and it was the first year that tractors outnumbered horses working the land on British farms.

The MERL collection is vast, totalling more than 25,000 objects. There are Victorian portraits of massive Hereford cattle, prize pigs and Southdown sheep; a horse-drawn milk cart; an old wood turner's workshop; a farmer's vintage Land Rover and a six gallon teapot. In the archive there are tape recordings, farmers' diaries from the 1700s and more than a million photographs. But the highlight for me is a fascinating collection of beautifully restored wooden farm wagons. These four-wheeled icons of our rural past represent the same regional diversity that British farm breeds do. Just as livestock varied around the UK, so it was that every county had its own style of wagon, designed specifically to suit the landscape, the soil or the type of produce that was grown locally. For example, the Devon wagon-makers crafted small, thick wheels to give stability on the West Country hills, while in East Anglia they built big-bodied wagons to accommodate the heavy crops grown in the flat lowlands.

There's certainly nothing stale or dusty about this museum. For a start, the building is alive with sound – birdsong, neighing horses, a rainstorm, the blacksmith's forge and a delightfully plummy voice on an old film about Cheshire cheesemaking. There is also what the museum calls digital interactives. These are smart touch-screens which immerse you in rural life. The most popular one puts you in the shoes (or should that be wellies) of a sheep farmer at lambing time. Guy Baxter, the museum's associate director, is eager to point out that innovation like this is as much a part of his role as preserving the past, and he's already started experiments in archiving tweets and digital-only information.

It's Guy's responsibility to manage and promote the archive here. He explains how the museum relies on the support of people who are passionate about the history and traditions of English rural life: 'We can't preserve and collect everything and it would be impractical for us to be in charge of, say, all vintage tractors or Shire horses. Instead the enthusiasts do the work and we support them, safely archiving their important documents and artefacts.'

That's precisely what's happened with the heritage of the nation's feathered farm stock – chickens, ducks, geese and turkeys. MERL is now looking after the treasured possessions of the Poultry Club of Great

Britain, and some of its antique books and pamphlets were on display at the Berkshire Show. One of Guy's jobs in the university marquee was to keep a fatherly eye on what must have been the oldest thing exhibited on the showground that weekend – an intact and obviously cherished copy of the *Poultry World Annual* from 1914, still in its original dust jacket (printed by the Poultry Press and priced at one shilling). South-east England was the starting point for several chicken breeds and the Poultry Club's irreplaceable papers and publications chart their origins and popularity. There's the Sussex which was reared in Victorian Heathfield as a bird for the table; the Orpington, which developed in Kent as a fowl 'of handsome appearance', and the Dorking from Surrey, whose ancestors were noted by the Romans for having five toes instead of the usual four. All the Poultry Club's records are now securely housed at the museum, but Guy Baxter knows just how easily our heritage can be lost. 'We don't want herd books, newsletters and posters being left under someone's bed or dumped in a skip.'

MERL might not attract the sort of attention the big, famous museums do, but I think it deserves to be much better known. You definitely don't need to be a farmer to enjoy it – I'd recommend it to anyone. And if you are a rare breeds buff like me, turning up some of the items in the museum's archives is like finding buried treasure, because they contain items which can never be

Porcine perfection and unmistakable markings – the Gloucestershire Old Spot pig.

Old Gloucester cattle showing off their beautiful mahogany coats.

Cotswold shepherd Robert Boodle is a walking, talking encyclopaedia when it comes to sheep.

The Golden Fleece in all its glory.

Exmoor Ponies are the four-legged friends I've loved all my life.

The Large Black pig is one breed which really does live up to its name.

Portland sheep are being bred on the Isle of Portland in Dorset once again.

One of my favourite photos of Dad, at home with our Golden Guernsey billy goat.

The Aylesbury duck –
Buckinghamshire's most
famous export and the
inspiration for Beatrix Potter's
Jemima Puddle-Duck.

Dad passionately believed
that there was still a role for
working horses.

Horse breeder Nigel Oakley putting a pair of Suffolk Punch horses through their paces.

A stunning White Park cow – the White Park is the face of the rare breeds movement.

Back from the brink – the Norfolk Horn sheep was saved from extinction.

The Bemborough herd of Bagot goats was established in 1976 from a small group which came from the breed's ancestral home at Blithfield.

Every Herdwick lamb is a black sheep in the family until the fleece grows grey as they get older.

recreated. Search the files for England's lost varieties of pig for instance and you'll find photos of the Cumberland, Dorset Gold Tip, the Lincolnshire Curly Coat and the Yorkshire Blue and White. Seeing them captured in their prime before they died out is fascinating and sobering at the same time.

There is something in the displays to raise a smile though, in the shape of a very unlikely board game. 'Grade Up to Elite Cow' was billed as a 'game of skill and chance for dairy farmers'. It's essentially a dairy-farming version of Monopoly, which, instead of top hats and old boots going round a board buying expensive property on London landmarks, is all about cattle breeding, bank loans and artificial insemination. I don't know if it was meant to be taken seriously or not but I like the suggestion of the person who tweeted that the game should have been called Moo-nopoly.

Perhaps one day Pips' collection of prize rosettes will be stored away for posterity at MERL. It's exactly the sort of thing they like to have at the museum and it's a timely moment to think about it, as Chris Hudson has decided that Pips' days in the competition ring are over and this year's Berkshire Show is her swansong. She's certainly going out with a bang, not a whimper, after being judged Champion Veteran sow and making it to the final round of the Berkshire Champion of Champions. Chris is delighted. 'I think she's earned her show retirement,' before adding quickly, 'although she'll hopefully produce a few more litters for me.'

'The world, according to the best geographers, is divided into Europe, Asia, Africa, America and Romney Marsh.' These words of the humorist Thomas Ingoldsby give you some idea of the special nature and isolation of this corner of the Kent countryside. If he was around today I bet old Ingoldsby would be thrilled to know that Romney Marsh has its own website called the Fifth Continent. In the southeast corner of the most south-easterly county of England, the marsh is a hundred square miles of flat, featureless wetland. It's technically four neighbouring marshes that are dotted with villages; a place of enormous skies, narrow, twisting lanes and fields dissected by ditches and streams. For at least 800 years, a hardy and resilient breed of sheep has been a feature here.

Romney Marsh sheep have sometimes been called Kent or even Kentish sheep and are a breed with a big frame, open faces and a heavy fleece as 'white as a piece of writing paper'. I really like them, we've had them on the farm at home for years and, along with a Welsh breed, the Lleyn, they're the basis of my commercial flock. The wet conditions on the marsh mean Romney Sheep have developed good, hard feet which protect them from foot rot, a common problem among other breeds. They're also more resistant to parasitic worms, a trait that's thought to have developed because they grazed separately on the marsh so were less likely to pick up infections from each other. Looking at them grazing away, you'd never believe that the Romney's story includes a tale of crime and violence.

Wool was the first commodity to have an export tax imposed on it back in the thirteenth century, and once the revenue men became involved, a black-market economy soon followed and fleece smuggling became rife. In the seventeenth and eighteenth centuries, the wool of the Romney was hugely valuable to smugglers, and with the French coast easily in sight on a clear day, armed criminals would often be out on the wild, remote marsh. The Romney sheep wool was their prize and they were prepared to kill anyone who got in their way.

The Fifth Continent website calls the Romney 'the best-known sheep in the world', which is a bold claim, but I think they could be right. Although they're not as numerous here as they used to be, around the world they're bred in their millions – from the United States and Canada to Patagonia and the Falkland Islands. The breed society keeps a track of all exports and they'll tell you that 'the sun never sets on Romney sheep'. It's a nice image. They were first shipped to Australia in 1839, then 14 years later the original consignment of 20 sheep left Kent on the migrant ship *The Cornwall* bound for New Zealand. The Kiwis liked them so much that now well over half the country's 27 million sheep are Romneys.

However, the New Zealand Romney nowadays is very different to the ones you'll find grazing in Kent, because on the other side of the world they've become a super sheep. Down Under they breed their livestock to be much tougher than ours, so they can survive in the vast, harsh landscape with as little human contact as possible. Over here if an animal gets into trouble the farmer will intervene; if it develops foot rot we'll treat it. This means we've bred an animal that needs attention. The sheer size of the average grazing land in New Zealand means that shepherds there have no time for sick and lame animals, or ewes that have problems lambing and they'll dispose of them immediately. That's imposed selection pressures which have resulted in a sheep that's incredibly good at looking after itself.

I discovered the difference on a trip Down Under in 2016. I helped muster a flock of 5,000 Romneys in New Zealand's South Island, moving the sheep from one hillside to fresh pasture on another. It was a massive flock compared to my 700 sheep at home but my guide, a charming bloke called Bill Brownlee, explained that some Kiwi farmers think nothing of having to herd 10,000 or even 15,000 sheep at a time. Bill's family have reared Romneys for more than a century and as we walked across a steep mountainside track with the enormous flock moving slowly ahead of us, Bill pulled no punches: 'They're not mollycoddled like they are in the UK.' That hit home! But it made me think about building more resilience into my own sheep, and when I was back home I decided to buy a pair of New Zealand-bred rams to introduce a bit of the survival instinct to the flock. The tups weren't cheap, about £1,000 apiece, but I was taken with the idea of breeding animals with narrower shoulders for easy lambing and an ability to grow well on grass alone. In fact, there's now quite a trend for introducing the genetics of New Zealand's tougher strain back into our domestic flocks. The Romney has been around the world, and like all good travellers it's being welcomed home again at long last.

Drop the word Buckinghamshire into a conversation and hardly anyone will think of ducks. But mention Aylesbury and you'll get nods and knowing looks. It's been the county town since the days of King Henry VIII, boasts an excellent Roald Dahl museum and is home to statues of Ronnie Barker and David Bowie. Yet for most people the name of the old market town on the clay-rich plain between the Chilterns and the Great Ouse will only ever mean one thing: Aylesbury duck.

Humans have wanted to get our hands on ducks for thousands of years, first hunting them before we domesticated them for exactly the same reasons we started farming sheep – to provide us with food from their carcass and warmth from their covering. A primitive, prehistoric market was created for duck eggs, duck meat and for their soft downy feathers, and in that way our demands haven't changed very much since our first farming ancestors raided the wild duck nests they stumbled on.

The sight of paddling, dabbling ducks is guaranteed to put a smile on my face at any time – I've always loved waterfowl expert Tom Bartlett's description of them as 'beautiful, comical things'. I didn't know when

I first heard this that he was quoting the words of the Great War poet and fellow Gloucestershireman, Will Harvey.

Tom was a big character, heavily bearded with jet black hair, even in middle age, and he absolutely bubbled with enthusiasm about his birds. He'd started keeping them as a boy in the 1930s and, until he retired about twenty years ago, he ran Britain's biggest waterfowl conservation centre just a few miles away from our farm in the Cotswolds. Every year around 40,000 people used to visit Folly Farm, just a mile or two off the route of the old Roman Fosse Way, where Tom kept well over a hundred different breeds of ducks and geese. He gave names to his birds, spoke to them as if they were his children and made a particular point of introducing visitors to Josephine, a large grey Cape Barren goose who liked to be fed by hand. In essence, what my dad was doing to save rare farm livestock, Tom was doing for rare ducks and geese just a short waddle away at a place he called Duck Pond Valley.

My main duck flock at home are Indian Runners, renowned for being flightless and walking upright like penguins, but I've also got a British county breed which was one of Tom's favourites: the Silver Appleyard. It's named after the Suffolk man who developed them in the 1930s, Reginald Appleyard. On his waterfowl farm near Bury St Edmunds he wanted to create the ideal duck, a bird that was good for producing eggs, providing meat and beautiful enough to exhibit.

Unfortunately, after the war things took a downward turn and the breed became close to extinction as people lost interest in keeping chickens and ducks. Then in the 1970s and 80s it was revived, in the nick of time, by Tom who tracked down Mr Appleyard's daughter and discovered that she had a painting of the original duck in her attic. Tom used the picture and some of Reginald's writings to confirm the true colouring and bred them back to the original standard. He eventually re-established the Silver Appleyard in the UK and is recognised internationally for his work developing the miniature Appleyard. It's what enthusiasts call a heavy breed, and today the Appleyard is mostly known as a meat bird. They're not ready for the table until they're at least six months old but the wait is worth it because the flesh is dark, well textured and it has a strong meaty flavour which fills your mouth in a way that faster-maturing, commercially bred duck meat doesn't.

Reginald Appleyard is almost a folk hero in the poultry world and he clearly knew what he was doing because he was responsible for a further breed of white bird. The Ixworth chicken, another meat and egg breed, made its first appearance in 1932 and was named after the village where Reginald lived and worked.

In books or TV features about British breeds, poultry and waterfowl can sometimes get overlooked in favour of the big agricultural breeds. It's true that the heritage of some poultry, ducks and geese can be more complicated than that of our native four-legged beasts, but there are some stand-out varieties with proud county connections. As we've heard, Buckinghamshire is a great example and is the birthplace of the loudest and whitest duck in the land, the Aylesbury. In the same way that Gloucestershire Old Spots became known as the cottagers' pig in the West Country, so the Aylesbury was considered the cottagers' duck. Rather than being kept in yards and orchards though, the ducks were reared in the homes and sometimes even the bedrooms of families living in the 'duck end' of Aylesbury.

Two hundred years ago this was the poorest part of the old town, notorious for its slum dwellings and the lack of proper drains, sewers or even refuse disposal. Originally bred for their meat and to satisfy the demand for feathers to fill quilts and bedding, by the 1800s the duck eggs were being bought from the town farms to be hatched, and the ducks fattened for market by labourers and householders keen to earn a bit more money. Raising ducklings was seasonal work between Christmas and the summer which could be done in cramped conditions with the women of the house often employed to feed and eventually pluck the birds.

Aylesbury ducks grew out of the Old White English breed, but by the 1800s the name of the Buckinghamshire town where they thrived had become a byword for these large, pure white birds with their pink bills and orange feet. Aylesbury ducks were popular in London too, where they could fetch the highest prices. Before the arrival of the railways made transporting the ducks straightforward, some flock owners (or duckers) walked their birds to the capital. To survive the 40-mile journey, the ducks' feet were often covered in tar and coated in sawdust to toughen them up.

The best known breeder of Aylesburys in the 1940s and 50s was a character called William 'Ducky' Weston (what else?), who by then had become known as the last duck man in the town. Ducky came from a long line of breeders who were already rearing Aylesburys by the early 1800s. The legend is that William and his father (also nicknamed Ducky) could kill and pluck six birds in ten minutes. Sixty years ago, William gave several interviews to the press and on radio in which he told a story about the early days of breeding when cottagers used to mark their birds with a dab of paint to identify them before they were marched through the streets to the local stream. He explained that at nightfall the birds would return to their owners, making their way back like homing pigeons.

But by the mid-1960s the cost of farming the birds was beginning to bite and the business eventually closed, bringing 200 years of duck breeding by six generations of the family to an end. In the 1970s, the site of the Westons' duckery was bought by a developer for new homes. But the industry in Buckinghamshire is far from over. Today the home of true Aylesbury table ducklings is 15 miles away in Chesham. That's where Richard Waller prides himself on selling birds for eating that are directly descended from the stock his own ancestors bred in the county back in the 1700s.

The only way is Essex. To be frank, there's no other choice after you've emerged from the Holmesdale Tunnel and crawled slowly with the rest of the clockwise traffic on the M25. Once the unlovely motorway carries you over the River Lea you've arrived in England's most mocked county. A small boundary sign reads 'Welcome to Essex', but dwarfed by roadside warehouses and massive depots it looks more like an apology than a greeting. That's a shame because industrial units and rush hours that last all day don't reflect the true Essex. Neither do the reality TV stars of *TOWIE* or those corny jokes about fake tans, white stilettos and loose morals. Away from London's orbital motorway, the urban towns which follow the Thames to the sea and the holiday resorts such as Southend and Clacton, Essex is a charming, picturesque and surprisingly rural county. In fact, a few years ago the area around Saffron Walden in north-west Essex was ranked the most desirable place to live in rural Britain. Who would have guessed that?

There's also a distinct Essex dialect. But it's not the one you think it is. It isn't the 'mock cockney' accent known as Estuary English that we hear on *EastEnders* and which everyone now assumes is native to the county. The few remaining speakers of true Essex have a soft, lilting East Anglian accent and use long vowels, similar to traditional Suffolk and Norfolk. Their dialect words include *hoss* for horse, *ship* for sheep and *shote* for a young hog. This lovely rural way of speaking is the almost vanished English of the old Essex farm worker. It's now so rarely heard that in 2009 the County Records Office felt compelled to release a CD of Essex dialect speech and song from its archives in an effort to alert locals to the threat posed by the 'invading' London-speak. It would certainly have been the language of the swineherds who raised the local breed, the small, fat Essex pig.

There were several strains of Essex pig over time, as a result of mixing and controlled breeding. Like all British breeds, the first Essex emerged from the local wild boar population. In the 1800s it's thought they were bred with Chinese or Asian pigs which had arrived here aboard ships from the East – meaty animals that were intended to be eaten by the crew. The result of that breeding was the Black Essex. But that's not the whole story, because following on there were various crosses and strains including the New Black Essex, the Lord Western Essex (named after the gentleman farmer who developed it), the Essex Half Black and the Improved Essex. I hope you're keeping up with all this.

By far the most popular Old Essex pigs were the sheeted variety (black with a white middle), the marking we now call saddleback. That became standard for the Essex, along with its trademark white feet and white tail tip. A really good pork breed and an excellent bacon pig, especially when crossed with a Large White, it did well during the Second World War, and even as recently as 1954 the Essex made up 10 per cent of all registered sows in the UK. But it couldn't last. The end of the Essex started with the rise of the Danish bacon industry. The fatal blow came in 1955 when fears that British pig breeders weren't competitive enough led to the publication of the Howitt Report.

The end of rationing and a return to free markets after the war had focused minds in Whitehall on the competitiveness of British agriculture. Sir Harold Howitt was an accountant who had a distinguished military career in the First World War and in peacetime took up a series of important public roles in Westminster. He was charged with investigating the pig industry and his report called for a major reorganisation. It declared that the diversity of pigs in the UK was holding farmers back and recommended to the government that the future lay in just three breeds: the Welsh, the Large White and the Landrace. The Howitt reforms changed pig farming forever – it meant a more scientific approach to breeding, the testing of pig genetics and artificial insemination. But it also led to many old breeds going into decline and for some even extinction.

Twelve years after the Howitt Report was published, the Essex was amalgamated with a similar breed that had grown up in the New Forest and Wiltshire and which shared the same black and white colouring, the Wessex pig. Cross breeding had been going on for years between the two but they had very different reputations – the Essex was thought of as the toffs' pig (because the leading breeder in Georgian times was Lord Western) while the Wessex was definitely considered to be the farmers' breed. The merging of the bloodlines formed the British Saddleback that we see today. It's large, black and lop-eared with that old Essex/Wessex band of white around the shoulders and down the front legs. Looking at a Saddleback side on it's got a distinctive piggy profile – round at the rump and pointed at the snout.

Dylan, an eight-month-old Saddleback boar, fits the picture perfectly. Just like pedigree dogs at Crufts, the best pigs also have proper 'posh' names. These pedigree names are made up of three parts – the herd name (often the farm), the line name (after the piglet's mother or father) and the pedigree numeral (which shows how many pigs have been bred from each line). Dylan's pedigree name is Watchingwell Dominator 130, and he's spent the summer appearing at 11 different county shows, on what his owner calls 'Dylan's UK tour'.

His owner, Sharon Groves, started out with several native breeds including Old Spots, Middle Whites, Tamworths and Berkshires before being swayed by the Saddleback's easy-going temperament and friendliness. In fact, Dylan got his name because he reminds Sharon of the cool, laid-back rabbit on *The Magic Roundabout*. His bloodline, Dominator, is one of the rarest with only eight registered boars in the country, although in 2015 it was down to just a single male. It's what motivates Sharon to put her pigs in the spotlight: 'We must educate the public not to buy what I call plastic meat and seeing them at shows is vital to that process.' I think it's reassuring to hear that people take an interest in Sharon's herd and it's lovely that she spends time answering all their questions, although she's taken by surprise occasionally: 'One lady looking at my black and white Saddlebacks told me she'd thought all pigs were just big and pink, and said she didn't know there were different shapes and colours.' Sharon's quest to educate the public is obviously a work in progress.

There's a serious point that she wants to share though, because while she was 'on tour' with Dylan, unsettling news broke about animal welfare. Confirmed cases of African swine fever were reported on mainland Europe. The virus is highly infectious and potentially fatal to pigs, so prevention is very much on Sharon's mind. She says, 'The English Channel is a good protector from disease but we must have strict laws about what livestock are brought into the UK.' Interestingly, livestock movement didn't feature much in the 2016 referendum campaign and it's only now that post-EU disease prevention has become a real talking point.

For Sharon though it's about vigilance at home as well as at the borders: 'People must keep good biosecurity both on farms and at shows. That's vital if we want to ensure the health of these animals.' In practical terms, biosecurity is anything that prevents an infectious disease from spreading, and includes disinfectant foot dips, hand sanitisers and security fences. As Sharon shares her thoughts Dylan gives a contented grunt, which sounds to me like he agrees.

There's an intriguing footnote to the story of the Saddleback's predecessor, the Old Essex pig, and it involves the farmer and TV presenter Jimmy Doherty. He's known by millions of viewers for *Jimmy's Farm* and his telly escapades with his old mate Jamie Oliver, but away from the cameras Jimmy is serious about British breeds and the Essex pig in particular. He's been the public face of moves to re-establish the breed in its own right after claims emerged that a herd of pedigree Essex pigs had survived.

In the 1990s, a breeder came forward to say he had kept his herd pure when amalgamation with the Wessex happened in 1967, and although he'd registered them as Saddlebacks he had actually preserved the Essex bloodlines in the decades after. Exactly 30 years after the breed officially ceased to exist, the Essex Pig Society was restarted and a new website launched by a small group of enthusiasts who 'have within their hearts a love of the Essex pig'. Jimmy gave the cause a big publicity boost by talking about the breed in the media and promoting Essex sausages produced from his own herd.

So is the Essex pig really alive and well, and has it survived against all the odds for 50 years in plain sight? Well it's a topic of great debate in the pig breeding world and for every person who backs the claim, there's another who'll be quick to rubbish it. Certainly for the time being the Essex remains officially extinct while questions are asked about genetic purity. But who knows what the future will bring, and for now, the rise and fall (and possible rise again) of the Old Essex adds a bit of curiosity and wonder to the whole rare breeds story.

Before leaving Essex there's a place I'm keen to see. Rochford is a small, handsome town which lies close to the little rivers, creeks and marshy inlets which are typical of the east Essex coast. Also typical of the area are the traditional weatherboard cottages, and Rochford has done a good job of saving them from being modernised, pebble-dashed or bulldozed. People here are very proud of the royal connections. In the sixteenth century, Rochford Hall was owned by the Boleyn family and local legend has it that it's where Henry VIII first set eyes on Sir Thomas Boleyn's daughter Anne. True or not, it guarantees good business for the Anne Boleyn pub, which is rumoured to be haunted by the ghost of Henry's poor beheaded Queen. Remarkable when you discover that the pub wasn't built until 1901.

The whole area is dominated by a large commercial airport on the outskirts and dwarfed by its brazen, boisterous neighbour, Southend-on-Sea. But I'm here because Tuesday is market day in Rochford. In fact, Tuesday has been market day in Rochford, on and off, since the year 1247. The market place isn't big by anybody's reckoning, and for the rest of the week it's a free car park. There must be a dozen stalls here, almost all of them with green and white striped canopies. The trestle tables underneath are crammed with crates and boxes full of bargains. There's dog food, moccasins, wrist watches, toothpaste, baseball caps and Jaffa Cakes plus a hundred and one other items you didn't know you needed. Steve's Bags has put on an impressive display of suitcases, holdalls and backpacks but it's the shop behind his stall that really catches my eye. Many small towns like this have lost their local, independent butcher's shops but in Rochford it's a different story and Gleadell Meats is doing brisk trade today.

For once though, it's not the steaks and Sunday joints I want to inspect. I'm interested in what's on the walls. All around the shop are big, framed photographs from the days when it wasn't Christmas cards and candles that were sold on market day, it was cattle. The once-thriving livestock market here also traded in sheep, pigs and poultry at various times, and the black and white pictures seem to capture the atmosphere of those far off days. They show the makeshift animal pens in the middle of the square, cattle lined up along the pavement and farmers' carts at rest. In one photo, prospective buyers are inspecting a pair of horse-drawn ploughs and another one shows the local saddler watching the commotion in the market place from the front of his shop.

The last time animals were auctioned here was in 1959 and the memories of those days are fading with the passage of time. But some remnants of the old livestock market have returned to the square and they've been placed on permanent display just a few yards away from Gleadell's shop window. A replica of the tall, ornate town pump which served the market place from 1820 onwards has pride of place once again. Next to it is the original 1902 stone cattle trough which was commissioned to mark King Edward VII's coronation and provided the livestock with refreshment on sale days for decades. Local homeowners could take water too, as long as they paid 'a farthing a pailful'. The trough was retrieved from a local wood where it had been left unloved for years and smartened up by the local council.

Of course, this is just one small town, tucked away in a quiet corner of the bustling south east. But what's impressive about Rochford is that it's in touch with its farming past and it has gone out of its way to show the close relationship which existed between town and country. When small herds and flocks for sale were penned just yards from town centre bus stops and post office, it was a visible expression of the importance of agriculture and a way for non-farmers to see livestock at close quarters. The market place reminders on show in Rochford represent an almost untold story that was true for hundreds of small communities all over the country. These town auctions weren't big operations and served farmers living only in a five- or six-mile radius. They were very different from the major livestock centres like Banbury in Oxfordshire, once the largest in Europe, or Gloucester, which I knew so well as a boy when it had one of Britain's leading calf sales. Rochford's auction was less formal, closer to the people and almost everyone in town on market day would have known each other. We can only imagine what local breeds might have been bought and sold here in the 700 years between the granting of the first market charter and the final livestock sale. How many Essex pigs or Golden Essex hens changed hands here? What about neighbouring breeds such as Suffolk Dun cows, black Suffolk swine, Middlesex pigs or Buff Medway chickens? Like the weekly livestock market, they're all gone forever. If only those old butcher's shop photographs could talk.

Orange Roast Chicken

Serves: 6

25g (1oz) butter
1 small onion, finely chopped
2 large garlic cloves, finely chopped
55g (2oz) celery, finely chopped
140g (5oz) fresh breadcrumbs
1/2 tsp dried rosemary
2 tbsp chopped fresh parsley 2 oranges
1.6kg (3lb 8oz) whole chicken
2 tbsp olive oil
50 ml (2fl oz) white wine
salt and pepper
watercress sprigs and orange twists, to garnish
300ml (1/2 pint) hot chicken stock

1. Preheat the oven to 190°C/375°F/gas 5.
2. Melt the butter in a pan and sauté the onions, garlic and celery until soft. Add the breadcrumbs, half the rosemary and the parsley. Take the pan off the heat.
3. Grate the rind of 1 orange and add it to the stuffing mixture. Peel both oranges, chop the flesh and add it to the mixture.
4. Put the chicken into a large roasting pan. Spoon the stuffing into the chicken, brush it all over with the oil and sprinkle over the remaining rosemary. Pour the wine into the roasting pan.
5. Roast in the preheated heated oven for 1½–2 hours, basting occasionally with the pan juices and wine.
6. Transfer the chicken to a serving dish, cover loosely with foil and keep warm while you make the gravy.
7. To make the gravy, skim the fat from the juices in the roasting tin, pour in the hot chicken stock and heat through on the hob.
8. Garnish the chicken with watercress sprigs and orange twists and serve with the gravy, roast potatoes and parsnips and lightly steamed carrots.

Bronwen Watts, Swansea
The Rare Breeds Survival Trust

CHAPTER 4

The East

C ambridge is a city famous around the world for its university and architecture. So you'd think there must be dozens of things that have been named in honour of Cambridge. Well there's a Duke and Duchess, an Austin motor car popular in the 1960s and lots and lots of pubs and hotels. But how many people hear the word Cambridge and immediately think of sheep? Yeah, I thought as much.

The Cambridge sheep is not a rare, traditional or heritage breed. It wasn't brought here by the Romans, the Vikings or the Normans and you won't find one in the Cotswold Farm Park or on the rare breeds danger list. In fact, it doesn't come close to qualifying for inclusion in any book about historic or endangered farm livestock, except for the fact that it's a perfect lesson in how to 'make' a breed and a great modern-day version of what the ingenious animal improvers were doing two or three hundred years ago.

The Cambridge is a real mishmash of genetics from several historic Welsh and English breeds mixed with some serious Scandinavian blood. The story starts in 1964, a few months after Harold Wilson promised an educational and scientific revolution in his 'white heat of technology' speech. The mood was for creating a 'modern' post-war Britain, and the dream in the live-stock world was to develop a commercial sheep that could produce more lambs and therefore make more profit.

A pair of university researchers, Professor John Owen and Dr Alun Davies, looked across the North Sea for inspiration and were impressed by the Finnish Landrace, or Finn, one of the family of North European short-tailed sheep that includes some Scottish breeds such as the Shetland, Soay and Hebridean. Owen and Davies were aware that the fine-boned, pink-skinned Finn were prolific 'baby-making' sheep. The rams could mate from the age of four or five months and the ewes were excel-lent mothers, able to give birth to several lambs at a time producing plenty of milk for their offspring. So the duo imported Finn rams and put them to 50 ewes from a variety of native breeds: Clun Forests from Shropshire, Llanwenogs, Lleyns and Kerry Hills from Wales as well as Suffolks crossed with Welsh halfbreeds. The resulting males were then used in a crossbreeding programme and what emerged was a new hornless breed with short, tight white wool and the sort of dark face that would keep traditional East Anglian shepherds happy. With so much blood from Wales it's no surprise that the Cambridge also became a popular breed in the Welsh borderlands.

The aim of the project was always to increase fertility but in the early days the Cambridge proved to be a bit too successful. Four, five and even six lambs became the norm for the new breed, instead of the usual one or two. Numbers like that are fine for smallholders with just a few sheep, but serious breeders with flocks in the hundreds, or more, would face the prospect of having huge 'litters' of lambs to care for and sell on. Today that prolificacy has been harnessed, and while you probably won't see them on display at a summer county show, the Cambridge will be quietly getting on with being one of the world's top commercial sheep for cross-breeding. We know how British breeds get their names: Portlands are from Portland, Greyface Dartmoors have grey faces and Hill Radnors live on hills, so just hearing their names conjures up a picture of the sheep or the place where it grew up. The Cambridge is unique in being named after the university where it was developed. There's nothing romantic or resonant about that, but the Cambridge is important as a modern link to the Agricultural Revolution of the eighteenth century and Britain's long custom of selective breeding.

Football and farming might be two worlds that rarely collide, but Suffolk's keen football fans, and anyone who watches *Match of the Day*, will be familiar with one of the rarest of all our livestock breeds. Although unless they're really hot on club trivia, most Ipswich Town supporters will be totally unaware that the animal that's so well known to them is a specific, named breed, and one with a very special place in the story of agriculture.

The official club badge is dominated by the strong, sturdy outline of a Suffolk Punch, the majestic-looking heavy horse that was developed for pulling, ploughing and carrying loads on the farms of the eastern counties. The Suffolk's muscle, versatility and sheer clout mean that owners will almost always describe them as 'good do-ers' and in its heyday this gentle, docile animal was literally the work horse of East Anglia. In the archives of the Suffolk Horse Society, founded in 1877, is an early description:

> *The Suffolk Horse, smart between the shafts in harvest, quick at the ends of the plough, a fast walker on the harrows after the drill, and a staunch slave at the collar, be it flour, timber or chalk behind him, is unsurpassed by any breed of horses in England or Scotland either.*

A job reference like that takes some beating. Whether Ipswich Town fans could name the breed on their club's badge or not, it's there for reasons I'm sure they'd all support. The Blues' previous crest was an old-fashioned affair, featuring a three-masted ship and a golden lion in the centre of the elaborate Ancient Borough of Ipswich coat of arms. So in 1972 a competition was held to find a new, more meaningful image for the club. The Suffolk Punch design was the work of John Gammage, well known as a leading light in the supporters' club, and his handiwork was chosen as a symbol of strength, nobility and local pride. You can almost hear the Town fans in the Bobby Robson Stand cheering at that.

The Suffolk horse logo was obviously a good omen because six years after it was adopted Ipswich won the FA Cup and in a brilliant piece of theatre the winning team paraded the famous trophy at a packed Portman Road stadium with the players lined up behind one of the finest, strongest Suffolk stallions that could be found. Rowhedge Count II was a huge beast, and on that famous day in 1978 he was decked out in his full show finery with tail ribbons, rosettes and a beautifully braided mane decorated with flights. In fact he looked exactly like the Suffolk on the club badge and he delighted the crowd. It was all a long time ago but Rowhedge Count II's name is still spoken with reverence among Suffolk horse enthusiasts. The great stallion showed strength to the very end and miraculously survived being struck by a bolt of lightning, although the physical effects of his ordeal eventually led to him being put down. A sad end for a remarkable horse.

The breed is the oldest variety of heavy horse to survive in its present form and the remarkable thing is that every Suffolk alive today can trace its ancestry back to just one stallion which was foaled way back in 1768. It was owned by Thomas Crisp from Ufford near

Woodbridge and was known, not very imaginatively, as Crisp's Horse. True Suffolk horses are always one of seven different shades of chesnut ranging from a dark liver tone through to a light mealy colour – and that's not a typing error by the way, chesnut really is spelt without a 't' in the middle when referring to the Suffolk Punch. Their other distinguishing feature is the lack of feathering, or long hair, on the lower legs and fetlocks. On Shires it almost covers the hooves, but because the Eastern counties have notoriously heavy clay soil, the feathers were bred out of the Suffolk Punch to make work in the fields cleaner and easier. After all, a day ploughing the old-fashioned way is hard enough without having to get loads of sticky mud off your horse when you get back to the yard.

The biggest gathering of Suffolks anywhere in the world happens every year in the breeds' native territory, East Anglia. The twenty-eighth annual Suffolk Horse Spectacular and Country Fair took place on a hot and beautifully still Sunday in September at the Marks Hall Estate, a secluded park, garden and arboretum which covers more than two thousand acres. In many ways it's the perfect venue because Suffolk Punches are still put to work in the woodland at Marks Hall to remove timber. It's a job they're able to do without causing damage to the soil or to precious plants, something which often happens with heavy machinery. The Suffolk Horse Spectacular isn't a working day though, with thirty mares, geldings and foals on show to the public, it's an event with the emphasis very much on pleasure, pride and publicity. The gathering is organised by the Suffolk Horse Society, a charity which isn't shy about putting the horse front and centre as a promotional exercise. 'Save Our Suffolks' is printed across all the banners and leaflets, the phrase 'critically endangered' crops up everywhere and there's lots of publicity on how to donate to the charity by text message. I'm impressed. This is effective marketing with a consistent message, although there's a nagging worry that the organisers might be preaching to Suffolk Punch converts. I ask one of the competition judges about this, who allays my concerns: 'How many people here know about heavy horses? I'd say about 25 per cent, probably less.'

The reason Suffolks need saving in the first place is the drastically low numbers of pure-bred young in a working world where heavy horses have been replaced by machines. And the figures are shocking. In 2017, only 25 pedigree foals were registered in the entire UK with a prediction that, without action, the breed will be extinct within a decade.

If the Suffolk horse is in need of promotion then one of the best adverts for them is Nigel Oakley. He's a charismatic, flat-cap wearing countryman with a soft Suffolk accent and a red blush to his cheeks which is a sure sign of a person who's spent a lifetime outdoors. I've been to his farm near Bury St Edmunds where he keeps nine Suffolks, as well as a pair of Shire horses, and I know how deeply he cares about them. On the day of the Suffolk Spectacular he seems to be involved in every aspect of the show, from organising the arena programme to putting up the fencing. He finds time to talk, though, and we retreat to a quiet corner of the judges' hospitality tent, next to a table of cakes that would put the *Great British Bake Off* to shame.

'The Suffolks are part of our national heritage and just as important as famous landmarks like the Tower of London and Westminster Abbey,' he says. I like Nigel. And it seems that I'm not the only one. Every few minutes we're interrupted by people who want to say hello to him, share a joke or give him cash to put into the charity's funds. Between visitors, he talks about the Suffolk's temperament, how he breaks them in and the bond of trust between a horse and its owner. 'We're in dire straits unless we tackle the bloodline issue though,' he says, referring to the large number of interrelated Suffolks available for breeding, with a glance towards the animals in the main ring.

Before long, Nigel dashes off to commentate on the parade of horse-drawn vehicles. His place in the shady marquee is taken by the society's chairman, George Paul, looking every bit the country show steward in his striped blazer, official tie and Panama hat. 'I don't know what we'd do without Nigel, he's a stalwart of the society and this event would be nothing without him,' he says. Only later do I discover that before he retired George ran a large national company and was the chairman of Norwich Union, one of Britain's biggest insurance businesses, overseeing its transformation into what is now Aviva. Yet despite his career in the City, his roots are firmly in the country: 'When I was a boy I was taught how to follow the plough and I will never forget the hiss of the yielding soil and the smell of the newly turned earth.'

The Punch is one of three breeds from the county which make up the 'Suffolk trinity', a trio of farm livestock which inspires pride among farmers and animal-lovers. The other two are Suffolk sheep and Red Poll cattle. Two hundred years ago, Red Polls weren't always red, and their name wasn't fixed either, with farmers calling them Norfolk and Suffolks or Polled Suffolks until the first herd book sorted things out in 1874. The classic dual-purpose breed came about from combining the milky Suffolk Dun and the meaty Norfolk Red to produce beautiful dark red-brown cattle, once described as having the same colour as a conker shining in the sun. They're not picky eaters and they'll happily graze away on poor grass, weeds and hedgerows. But from that low quality forage they're able to rear good calves which produce high quality beef, something that still sells well in East Anglia. Their creamy milk was popular too until the mighty-milking Friesian overtook it in the 1960s.

Red Poll milk was the perfect ingredient for farmhouse cheesemakers and in 2013 one particular herd caused a stir in dairy circles again. Cattle farmers Alan and Jane Hewson revived an old traditional English cheese called Colwick, driven by a desire to produce something different, distinctive and befitting one of England's native breeds. It had been invented in the seventeenth century in the village of Colwick on the banks of the River Trent in Nottinghamshire and celebrated as a perfect summer cheese. Soft and curdy with a texture like cream cheese, the Hewson's Belvoir Ridge Colwick caught the eye (and the taste buds) of Jamie Oliver and gave Alan and Jane's cows, the country's largest milking herd of Red Polls, more than just five minutes of fame.

Heavy horses and obliging cattle aside, the buildings and landscape of Suffolk tells you this was always sheep territory and a cluster of towns in the south had a particular reputation for wool. Haverhill, Clare, Lavenham, Sudbury, Hadleigh, Long Melford and others grew wealthy off the back of the 'golden fleece' in the Middle Ages and even now they're known as the Suffolk Wool Towns.

The little fifteenth-century village of Kersey is a perfect example. It was built on a hill, which is a rare thing in East Anglia, and gave its name to a fine type of warm woollen cloth called Kerseymere. Famous for its twill weave, it was used to make gentlemen's breeches, pantaloons, waistcoats and tunics in the early 1800s. If you were a Georgian dandy, Kersey was the place.

Walking around the cluster of mellowed Wool Towns today is like stepping back to medieval England, with streets lined with olde worlde inns, thatched cottages and timber-framed buildings. The wool and weaving heritage here is similar to the Cotswolds with trade in the Middle Ages bringing employment, wealth and a lasting legacy in wood, stone, brick and mortar. Just as it is in Gloucestershire, the prosperity of the past can still be seen in the fine houses and elegant churches.

The last breed in the trilogy of Suffolk livestock gives me a chance to share my theory about *Shaun the Sheep*. Everyone's seen Aardman studios' *Wallace and Gromit* spin-off, most under-fives love his TV adventures down on Mossy Bottom Farm, and I'm prepared to bet that the star of that show is the best-known Suffolk sheep ever. Shaun's got all the classic Suffolk characteristics: the dark black face, the big black floppy ears and a tight clean fleece. He does have a woolly topknot, which Suffolks don't, but I'm happy to put that down to a bit of Shropshire influence along the way.

The Suffolk sheep is not only the classic sheep of the English vales and one of the most important breeds in the country, for many farmers it's also the most popular and profitable native terminal sire of them all (that's the ram which is put with commercial ewes to produce the very best lambs for the butcher). Even if most people couldn't pin a name to this breed on sight, they are what everybody thinks of when they imagine a sheep. Suffolks grow quickly and are fast to mature so a ram will be ready to run with the ewes and mate by the time he's seven months old. Being the Lothario of the sheep world is a big boast but living up to that reputation depends on several things, and one of them might surprise you: having decent legs. Large, strong legs and clumpy feet are essential for Suffolks to carry their heavy weight, and when the most important job for these real-life Shauns is to mount as many ewes as they can, it's the back legs that need to be the sturdiest. Spare a thought for the average male Suffolk which will be required to serve more than a hundred females over the course of two or three weeks, and you can appreciate they need to be well anchored to the ground.

The Suffolk came about when farmers in the north of the county crossed thrifty Norfolk Horn ewes, which were excellent mothers, with the improved Southdown to create a magical combination of a box of meat on legs that had the fleece to generate a lot of wealth. The first ones were bred near Bury St Edmunds well over 200 years ago when they were known officially as Norfolk Southdowns but simply called Black Faces by the local farmers. The earliest record of them dates from 1797 when an agriculturalist called Arthur Young wrote that their mutton was 'superior texture, flavour, quantity and colour of gravy'. Praise indeed. But it took almost 80 years before a group of 26 flock masters gathered in the Fox Hotel in Stowmarket on a cold, windy January afternoon in 1886 and decided to get a breed society off the ground. Their flocks, like now, were long in the body, carried good flesh and were one of the fastest-growing breeds in the country. The

Suffolk looks good in the field too with a strong Roman nose, a wide head, and it's what some older shepherds call 'clean of horn' (meaning no horns at all). It's a sheep with its own internal thermostat as well, so it can happily live in hot or cold climates, which makes it a brilliant British export (one of our greatest gifts to the world in fact), and there are now big flocks in North and South America, Australia, New Zealand, South Africa and every country in Europe.

In Norwich the flags are out. All over the city there's bunting, banners and posters in the county colours of black and gold. It's the last week in July and the reason for all the hullabaloo is that celebrations are underway to mark the first ever Norfolk Day. It's even caught the attention of Prince William who gave his backing to the initiative months ago. Then again, he does have a home in the county, a couple of miles from Sandringham, so he's obviously been keeping up with the local news.

The aim of Norfolk Day is for residents and businesses to show their pride in the place they live and work. I'm not sure exactly why 27 July has been chosen as Norfolk Day and nobody I speak to seems to know either. Unlike other county celebrations in England it doesn't coincide with a Saint's day (such as St Piran's in Cornwall), commemorate a famous person (like the preacher John Bunyan in Bedfordshire) or mark an historic event (Lincolnshire remembers the Catholic revolt of 1536). If Norfolk picked a date at random then they did well by going for a summer's day at the start of the tourist season. Although I couldn't help noticing that this new county celebration was announced just a few weeks after one of Norfolk's best-known companies, Colman's, revealed it was closing the Norwich factory where it had been making mustard for 160 years. You don't need to know the city well to realise just what a blow that news was and how it affected working families in the area. If Norfolk Day restores a bit of local pride and injects a bit of 'feelgood' then who cares what date it's on? An impressive 300 events are planned, with street parties, concerts and a new Norfolk business summit. The town criers are in full voice and church bells toll away merrily. A new Norfolk pie is being launched and I spot special roast Norfolk Turkey lunches. But this year at least, I can't find anything that celebrates or even just mentions the remarkable tale of the Norfolk Horn sheep.

It's a meaty, leggy, black-faced sheep which is Norfolk through and through, and whose story should sound a klaxon for anyone who cares about conservation. Descended from the Saxon sheep of the eastern counties, the Norfolk Horn came from Breckland, the dry sandy heathland that sits on the border of Norfolk and Suffolk, long before anyone thought of creating Thetford Forest. Brecks was the name given to fields that were broken from the heath and used briefly for growing until the soil was depleted. If you've never heard of Breckland you're not alone, it's firmly in the shadow of better known and more popular visitor areas such as the Norfolk Broads and the East Anglian beaches.

In the Medieval wool boom, Norfolk Horn fleece was used to make warm, strong worsted cloth. In the 1400s, worsted, named after the village of Worstead, was considered to be the glory of Norfolk. The sheep were rangy animals, meaning that they would literally range the landscape, roaming the gorse-covered countryside covering miles every day to find enough grass good enough to survive. But the decline of the breed was long and slow. Two hundred years ago it was said to be facing extinction; numbers were down to one flock shortly after the First World War and by 1950 there were just a dozen. If there was one rare breed which rang the alarm bells, this was it. Though sometimes there were false alarms, like the newspaper headline in November 1930 which declared 'The Last of its Breed!' accompanied by a photograph of a slightly startled looking Norfolk ewe. The sheep was exhibited at the Norfolk Fat Stock Show and the article revealed that, 'This is the last one and is to be given to Norfolk Museum where there is already a stuffed ram.'

Incredibly, those two examples of the taxidermists' art mentioned in this article still exist, and even more remarkably they remain on public display, although not in Norwich. For years they've been on show at the Gressenhall Museum near Dereham, an excellent attraction and a working rare breeds farm which has been depicting all aspects of life in Norfolk since it opened to the public in 1976. I found the celebrated ewe, looking in surprisingly good shape after 90 motionless years, in one of the main galleries where she stands alongside an old shepherd's hut and essentials of the flock-keeper's art, such as a decorated Victorian crook, a whistle and a pair of woollen mittens. The stuffed ram really should be displayed next to her, but isn't. Instead he's on the floor above where he's surrounded by a far more varied collection of items from a bygone era: cow bells, a glass butter churn, a hand-cranked corn grinder and jars of Tomlinson's scaly leg ointment. If you didn't know better you'd think the old taxidermied tup was keeping guard on all these precious heirlooms.

As we've seen, farming can be a fickle business and the decline of the poor old Norfork Horn was largely down to the incredible success and popularity of the Suffolk sheep. At the end of the 1960s there were three rams left and five infertile ewes, which is pretty much as close to extinction as you can get while still having sheep to look at. Something needed to be done quickly and all eyes turned to Bemborough, where Dad put one of the last remaining rams, named Enoch, to a group of Suffolk ewes. Their daughters were then put to one of the other survivors and so on in a cycle – this is known as a 'breeding back' programme.

By the time the last pure-bred ram had died of old age we'd created a new Norfolk Horn which was more than 80 per cent pure and went on to be accepted as a modern continuation of the breed. It was a great personal success for Dad and it helped put the Rare Breeds Survival Trust on the map. So there's a lot of Henson heritage in a Norfolk Horn and understandably there's never been a time when they haven't been a major attraction on the farm at home. They say that if the ravens ever leave the Tower of London then the building and the Crown will fall, and I can't help feeling the same way about the Norfolk Horn and the Farm Park.

So a century after the Norfolk Horn was down to a single flock, and almost 50 years since it was 'reinvented', how's the breed faring now? Well it's still very much a rare breed with fewer than 3,000 registered ewes in the UK, and the latest figures even show a slight dip in numbers. But I can take some heart from the fact that on the annual danger list it's in the minority breed category (or the 'least worst', if you prefer). The truth is that the Norfolk Horn has been so closely associated with my home and such a figurehead for rare breed conservation generally, that I'll do everything in my power to ensure it's around for a very long time to come.

Yellowbelly is the name for anyone who is Lincolnshire born and bred. It sounds as if it should be an insult but it's a label that's embraced and even celebrated by the locals, and as soon as you cross the county border you'll start seeing car stickers with the slogan 'Proud to be a Yellowbelly'. If you fancy starting an argument in Lincolnshire just ask a few people where the nickname comes from and the disagreements will begin straight away. There are lots of theories. Some say it's from the officers of the Royal North Lincolnshire Militia who wore yellow waistcoats in battle, others that the Lincoln to York mail coach had a yellow undercarriage and another claim is that newts (or possibly frogs) in the Fens had a distinctive yellow underside. But the story I like best is the one about the local sheep which grazed in the mustard fields, and as their long wool dragged across the flowers it was stained yellow by the pollen. It sounds ridiculous, but so what?

I met quite a few Yellowbellies when I launched a new item on *Countryfile* called 'Adam's County Breeds'. The idea was to tap into my fascination with the way that different farm animals, and the methods of agriculture, varied from place to place depending on the local land-scape. We made several films covering the breeds of Suffolk, Yorkshire, Oxfordshire and Devon as well as Lincolnshire, and they were shown on an occasional basis over several months. I would love to do more, and with 92 counties to cover in the UK, many with several local breeds to call their own, it could keep me busy for quite a while. Perhaps it'll make a TV series in its own right one day.

Lincolnshire was our first destination because over time the county has been able to boast a full set of breeds – sheep, cattle, pig, horse and poultry. My first stop was the tiny hamlet of Risby on the Viking Way in the Lincolnshire Wolds. With a view of the towers of Lincoln Cathedral away on the horizon, the landscape here is beautiful and so are the sheep. Ian and Louise

Fairburn have been breeding Lincolnshire Longwools at Risby Grange since they moved here in 2004 and realised that 50 acres of land would take some looking after. From their initial six ewes and a ram their flock has grown to 70 sheep, which is almost 10 per cent of the entire UK Lincoln Longwool population.

The breed has a reputation as a big sheep and their heavy, flowing fleece makes them appear even larger. The wool hangs down in long, broad locks – that's the staple which is crucial in deciding the quality of the wool, and for Lincolns the wider it is, the better. On the finest sheep it skirts the ground like a curtain and if that's hard to picture, just think of Dougal from *The Magic Roundabout*. The size also means they're great mutton sheep.

I called on the Fairburns a few days before they were due to take their exhibition ewes to the Lincolnshire Show, so the flock was in top form. From a distance, Lincolns look a lot like my own Cotswold sheep, another Longwool breed with a similar history. But when we walked amongst the sheep and Louise showed me the wool close up, I could see the difference in the quality of the staple as soon as she started to separate the thick fleece. It's almost as if the ewes are covered in soft, creamy-coloured dreadlocks.

Louise admits to being 'absolutely crazy' about Lincolns and her wedding photos prove it. When the Fairburns were married in 2009, Louise's wedding dress was made from the wool of one of her flock, an agreeable ewe named Olivia. Fashion designer Caroline Chamberlain used the fleece and Louise's outline sketches to produce a stunning dress. The bodice was crocheted from hand-spun Lincoln wool decorated with crystals and the back was corseted with Longwool felt, trimmed with handmade felt roses, while the skirt was created from lengths of natural wool staples stitched on to woven cloth. The national newspapers couldn't resist printing beautiful pictures of Louise in the sunshine wearing her fleecy frock, holding a shepherd's crook with a pair of ewes at her side. Once the photos were posted on social media, the gown went global. People all over the world loved it and reaction, likes and retweets are still happening all these years later. It's a fair bet that being a viral sensation has given Lincoln Longwools the best publicity the breed has ever known.

Ian and Louise are also doing their best to keep the heritage of another local breed alive. The original Lincolnshire Buff chicken was large, heavy, easy to rear and quick to fatten making it a popular choice in the meat markets of London. The bird also had a fifth toe on each foot which is a rare trait they shared with the Dorking chicken. The breed was named after the orange-brown colour of their feathers and they were raised on Lincolnshire farms in their tens of thousands from the 1850s through until the 1920s, when they died out after being outdone in the popularity stakes by the newer Buff Orpington. But careful breeding with blood from historic fowl has reproduced their characteristics for a new era. It was work started in the early 1980s by the Lincolnshire College of Agriculture and Horticulture, and when that fizzled out the task was taken on by Brian Sands (a poultry-keeper since he was a boy and a self-proclaimed Yellowbelly). He took the college flock and carefully bred them back to the original standard so that by 1994 he was confident enough to enter them into the National Championship Poultry Show. The next year Brian set up the Lincolnshire Buff Poultry Society, and then in 1997 his hard work to re-establish the breed was given the approval of the Poultry Club of Great Britain.

If Lincoln sheep are the most famous breed in the county, then the next best-known must be Lincoln Red cattle. Their story goes back to the Vikings who brought large, rugged horned cattle with them when they invaded Britain and established the ancestral herds which would later become the Reds. The descendants of those Scandinavian animals would have been a common sight all over East Anglia and they were eventually used as working cattle on the fields and farmland of Lincolnshire. Three hundred years ago, the breed we know as the Lincoln Red emerged from this old type of draught cow when it was crossed with Shorthorn bulls from the north of England to produce cattle that in the early years could be either red and white coated or occasionally dun in colour. A century ago they were considered a classic utility cow, good for meat as well as milk. Their clout in the dairy caught the attention of spectators at the Royal Show in 1913, who commented on 'the size and scope of the matrons and their magnificent bags' – which even then was an odd way of describing a full udder. It's a breed that's been transformed since the 1950s. Until recently, these big, deep cherry-red coloured animals were still being called by their old name, Lincolnshire Red Shorthorns. The horns have largely gone, selectively bred out so that most are now naturally polled, and where they used to be dual purpose cattle now they're a specialist beef breed.

I set off to see some local Lincoln Reds for myself at the delightfully named Sunnyside Up Farm near Market Rasen where Julian and Hazel Hammond introduced me to their 40-strong herd. Dozens of lovely-looking cows and a hefty bull trotted over to greet us as the previous year's calves followed tentatively behind. The Hammonds told me they'd been keeping their local breed since the early 1990s, but Julian admitted the current demand for Lincolnshire Reds looked unlikely at one stage: 'They haven't always been popular, there was a stage when they went out of fashion and smaller animals came along like the Angus and the Hereford.' Imports of continental breeds in the 1980s and 90s had a damaging effect and then when beef sales slumped in the wake of the BSE crisis, it was a double whammy. Now, with the help of clever promotion and interest from beef farmers nationwide, the Red has bounced back and consumers have got a taste for Lincolnshire beef again.

Julian and Hazel found the best way to market the meat from their herd was to open their own farm shop. Their butcher is Nick Bradeley who cuts, prepares and sells all the meat. 'I think people more and more want locally sourced food,' he explained as I looked along the chill cabinets at trays of Sunnyside Up Lincoln Red beef alongside Lincoln Longwool mutton, rare breed pork from Old Spots and Berkshire pigs as well as wild venison from Welton Woods.

That link between place and produce, what we've started calling provenance, is particularly welcomed by Alan Stennett. At his home on the southern edge of the Lincolnshire Wolds, Alan gets up early every Sunday morning. Very early. He's at his work when many farmers are still asleep, most Sunday newspapers are still undelivered and certainly before the majority of vicars have practised reading their sermons out loud. Apart from his reputation as an early riser, Alan is a well-known Lincolnshire history buff, a writer with eight books to his name and a railway enthusiast. In fact, he's so keen on the days of steam that he even lives in a former Victorian railway station near Woodhall Spa. But none of those passions are the reason he's up and about before the dawn chorus on a Sunday. In the gloomy chill of an early morning, Alan is in his study, once the station master's parlour and now converted into a little radio studio, where he's preparing for his weekly show on BBC Radio Lincolnshire. It's the perfect job for him because I doubt there's another person alive who knows as much about the county, its agriculture and its rural heritage. His programme is called *Lincolnshire Farming* (of course) and if the BBC ever decides to issue long-service awards, Alan should be first in the queue because he's been presenting the show every week since the station launched in 1980. He's on air at 7 a.m. and at that time on a Sunday the only other person he sees while he's broadcasting is the paperboy, waving at him through the office window.

When the breeds of Lincolnshire are in the news, Alan can speak with an authority that comes from years of experience. He and his wife Sue are successful native breed farmers, and in 2005 one of their Lincoln Reds, Kirkstead Andromeda II, broke the record for a maiden heifer (a female that hasn't been put to a bull). 'People are definitely more aware of the county breeds than they used to be,' Alan tells me, with a hint of pride in his voice. 'But that's not an accident. It's down to a combination of independent butchers, niche marketing, the work of the Rare Breeds Survival Trust and the dedication of the local support groups.' Changing attitudes have also been noticed by Sue, a farmer's daughter who first milked a cow when she was a child: 'We're looking at the meat quality of native cattle now rather than just breed shape, it's a positive thing that's been good for the Red.'

As the Stennetts know well, there are three Lincolnshire breeds that we'll never see again, sadly.

The first to disappear was the Lincolnshire Black, a huge, strong horse that was sometimes called the Old English Black. Their roots go back to the time of the Norman invasion of Britain in 1066 when the French introduced us to the idea of using horses as working animals in place of cattle. Lincolnshire, Leicestershire, Huntingdon and Nottinghamshire became the counties of the cart horse, and these animals were used for ploughing, pulling and the heavy work needed for the draining of the Fens, while smaller, more agile Old Blacks became cavalry horses.

It's been 150 years since anyone saw a Lincolnshire Black in the flesh, but there are reminders everywhere. All over the country there are old pubs and former coaching inns called The Black Horse and many of them were named after Lincolnshire's own sturdy steed. But there's a living, breathing legacy too in the nation's most famous horse, the Shire.

In the late 1700s, the man they called the 'Father of Animal Husbandry', Robert Bakewell, used Old Blacks as the foundation stock for his improved breed, crossing the stallions with continental mares from the Netherlands and in-breeding the offspring to create the great horse of the English Shires that we know and love today. A painting of Bakewell in the National Portrait Gallery shows him on horseback (sadly not a Shire), looking well-fed and wearing a wide-brimmed hat as he sits bolt upright in the saddle. While Bakewell powered on with his new breed, many Fenland horse owners tried to stay true to the old, unimproved Black, before progress and a lack of bloodlines killed it off for good. Nevertheless, there's still a lot of Lincolnshire in the Shire.

'They're powerful but gentle,' says Victoria Clayton, the secretary and chief executive of the Shire Horse Society. 'It's a kind animal, it wants to work and to please you.' Victoria is not only the first woman to hold the top post in the society since its creation in 1878, she's also the first person under 40 to do the job.

Despite being a British icon, or perhaps because of it, Shire horses are popular with buyers from Europe, especially Germany, the Netherlands, Sweden and Spain. They'll often visit the UK in the autumn and buy foals to export back home, with the best animals selling for around £5,000 a time. It's important revenue for breeders here, vital even, and means Victoria and her colleagues have been seriously contemplating Brexit, tariffs and the strength of the pound against the euro. The worry is a common one, that any future financial barrier will stop continental buyers coming here and instead they'll use their existing Shires throughout the EU as breeding stock. So with that background, what are the prospects for the breed? 'There's potentially a bright future in new uses,' Victoria predicts. 'Riding Shires has taken off in the last 15 years, helped enormously by a Heavy Horse riding class at the Horse of the Year Show, which is drawing in more enthusiasts and hobbyists.'

It was a Shire called Sun Ray who briefly became the most famous horse in Britain and brought a lot of glory to the Farm Park. Sun Ray was a beautiful and faithful mare who was owned by a lovely lady called Joanna Neave; her husband John was Dad's old friend and business partner, so together the Neaves were like second parents to me and my sisters. In 1978 the Royal Mail marked the centenary of the Shire Horse Society by issuing a set of commemorative postage stamps featuring horse breeds, and the renowned Gloucestershire wildlife artist Patrick Oxenham was commissioned for the job. He was a great animal lover and decided Sun Ray would be the perfect model for his Shire horse portrait. We had to wait until July to see the finished work, but on the first day of issue there was Sun Ray, taking prime position on the nine pence stamp. She looked pristine and ready for action, wearing a leather and brass horse collar, bridle, blinkers and chains with an old fashioned single-wheeled plough in the background.

The other stamps featured Patrick's equally splendid paintings of a Shetland pony, a Welsh pony and a Thoroughbred. It led to Sun Ray having another starring role later that summer in a BBC Two programme called *All the Queen's Horses*, which followed Patrick at work as he made his original sketches and created the superb artwork for the stamps. It was an enormous honour for one of our animals to be chosen, but the most remarkable thing of all is the thought that there was once a time when you could actually post a letter for nine pence!

There was another equine breed from Lincolnshire, but it's less well known than the Old Black/Shire and there are precious few surviving documents about it. The Lincolnshire Fen pony was thought to be distantly related to the Dales pony from the Pennines and the Fell pony of north-west England. Apparently it was small with a large head, a straight back and big feet which helped it cope with the soft wetland soil. They had all the characteristics of a good pit pony and there are reports that they were sold to work in the lead mines of Derbyshire and the coal mines of Nottinghamshire.

The Wildmore Tit sounds as if it should have been a bird but it was actually the name of a strain of pony found on the Wildmore Fen north of Boston and highly regarded by all accounts. Thousands of these local ponies would have changed hands in Horncastle at the Great August Horse Fair during its heyday in the 1800s, when it claimed to be 'the largest held in the British Dominions and therefore in the world'.

The final breed of Lincolnshire is the strangest, the most fascinating and the most tragic of the lot. The Lincolnshire Curly Coat pig was a curious beast, a lop-eared monster of a breed renowned for being big, fat, hardy and hairy. The largest had powerful shoulders that were 'higher than a man's waist' and would easily tip the scales at 40 stones or more. It had all the qualities of a pig but looked just like a sheep with a covering of thick, curly hair resembling wool. This was the original sheep-pig long before *Babe*.

We know how unusual the Curly Coat looked because Lincolnshire County Council owns a number of black and white photographs showing sows and gilts in sties, at yard sales and one or two prize-winning champion pigs posing for the camera with their proud owners. But moving pictures of Curly Coats are much harder to find. It's a tragedy that no footage has survived of the 30-stone sow which appeared live on the legendary *Tonight* programme with Cliff Michelmore back in 1960. Mark Crowder remembers it though because he was at the studio on the night in question. His father, John, loved the breed and owned 40 pigs, which was the country's biggest herd of Curly Coats at the time. Even so, some farmers were already predicting the breed's extinction and the plight of this fast-disappearing old curio had caught the attention of the TV producers. So Mark, then just 12 years old, joined his dad and their chosen pig on the long journey from Lincolnshire to the BBC's regional studio in central Birmingham for the live link to London. All was going well until it came to getting the enormous animal up two flights of stairs and along a highly polished corridor in time for the broadcast. 'Father struggled a bit to be honest,' recalls Mark, who must be a master of the understatement. Not only did the sow disgrace herself along the entire length of the corridor, when John finally managed to get her into the little studio, she knocked over three or four expensive TV cameras. But even when the interview had finished, Mark remembers that the fun wasn't over: 'Getting her down the stairs was worse than going up.'

Now that sounds like TV gold to me. The only existing footage of Curly Coats I know about is in the safe keeping of a wonderful magpie-like enthusiast from Gloucestershire called Jim Wilkie. He loves old agricultural films and for the last few decades he's spent his free time searching industrial dustbins, skips and junk piles to rescue any obsolete, unloved and discarded 16mm reels that catch his eye. A few years ago, he really struck oil when he came across what's thought to be the last surviving footage of the Lincolnshire Curly Coat. Jim stumbled on a metal canister containing film of the 1947 Royal Agricultural Show, which was held that year in Lincoln, and among the usual scenes of parading cattle and excitable crowds was a fleeting shot of a Curly Coat being primped and prepared for judging. Blink and you'd miss it, but Jim knows history when he sees it.

The end of the story of Lincolnshire's utterly unique pig breed is a sad one: the last Curly Coats went to the abattoir in 1972, just as the conservation movement was starting and only a year before the Rare Breeds Survival Trust was created to bring a halt to just such extinctions. Timing, as they say, is everything.

British Mutton

Serves: 6

1 leg or shoulder of mutton, approx. 1kg (2lb 4oz)
2 sprigs mint
2 sprigs rosemary
1 large onion, roughly chopped
1 large carrot, sliced
850ml (1½ pints) lamb gravy (stock cubes are fine)
2 garlic cloves (optional)
salt and pepper

To serve
steamed baby potatoes or mashed potatoes
seasonal vegetables

1. Preheat the slower cooker or crock pot if necessary; see the manufacturer's instructions.
2. Trim away any excess fat from the joint, then put into the slow cooker or crock pot.
3. Add the mint, rosemary, onion and carrot to the slow cooker or crock pot.
4. Season the gravy and add the garlic, if using. Pour the gravy over the joint, cover and cook, on low, for at least 6 hours (it won't spoil), checking the liquid level occasionally.
5. Serve with potatoes and seasonal veg.

Pam Hall
The British Galway Sheep Society

CHAPTER 5

The North Country

'B ritain in miniature'. That's how Yorkshire is sold
to visitors from around the world and it's a pretty
shrewd observation. Stretching from the North Sea
coast to the far side of the Pennine Hills the landscape
is ever changing, encompassing moorland, mountain,
vale, dale, chalk cliff, river valley, wide tidal estuary,
hay meadow and even peat bog. The essence of the
White Rose County was captured in the 1840s by the
Reverend James Barclay in his *Complete and Universal
Dictionary*: 'It is very fertile, and produces in great
plenty corn of all kinds; there are excellent pastures,
where cattle, sheep, horses etc are reared in abundance.'
Almost two centuries on that description still works,
and if the good Reverend ever had Yorkshire's native
breeds in mind, he could have added pig and poultry to
that list.

Wherever they're from, people here will defend their own particular corner of the county but 'the Yorkshire Dales is the centre of the earth'. The big, bearded actor Brian Blessed made that declaration when he was president of the Council for National Parks, so it could be said he was playing to the gallery, but who's going to argue with him? I hardly need say that Yorkshire is fiercely independent. I've always admired the anonymous number-cruncher during the London Olympic Games who worked out that thanks to the likes of Jessica Ennis, Nicola Adams and the Brownlee brothers, Yorkshire would have come twelfth in the medals table if it was a separate country. There are plenty who think it already is! Not long ago I saw a farmer on TV explaining how he defines home. Starting with England then on to Yorkshire, the Dales and specifically Wharfedale until finally, 'You say you're from Upper Wharfedale – you can't go any higher than that, you're on the peak of human achievement.'

Sheep farming is the old calling of the Yorkshire Dales and it's reckoned that the area is home to 600,000 sheep – that's a ratio of one person for every 30 sheep. For hundreds of years, the coming and going of the seasons has been marked here by tupping, lambing, shearing and selling. It's that culture that led to a local breed, the Swaledale, being adopted as the official symbol of the Yorkshire Dales National Park, and I bet Brian Blessed approves of that.

The Swaledale is as tough as old boots and exactly how you'd expect a no-nonsense sheep to appear. Bold, confident and not afraid to look you in the eye. To cope with the hardest winters, its fleece is thick and rugged, or what Dalesmen call 'good, hard hair'. The tail is long and woolly, both sexes grow low, spiral horns and if you told me they bleated in a Yorkshire accent, I'd believe you. The old hill shepherds used to count their Swaledale ewes in a curious sounding dialect that was rooted in the language of the ancient Celts. So instead of 'One, two three ...' they counted 'Yan, tan, tethera ...' at a pace and rhythm that probably hadn't changed since the end of the Iron Age. There's something comforting in knowing that northern textile workers used the same method for counting stitches too.

At more than 1,700 feet above sea level, Tan Hill is known for having Britain's highest inn, but it's also the location of the big event in the Swaledale breeders' year – the Tan Hill Sheep Show. On the last Thursday in May, a long stream of cars, trailers and muddy Land Rovers make the steady climb to the isolated, windy hill top and if the weather's good (or even just good-ish) the crowds guarantee the inn's busiest day of the year. The first show was held in 1951 and there are 30 classes, from Best Ewe and Aged Ram all the way to the most prestigious of the lot, Overall Champion. When a documentary crew filmed the goings on at Tan Hill in the 1980s, one ruddy-faced character captured the spirit of the day perfectly: 'It's a queer job this showing, you get prizes and surprises.' Winning here is considered more important than getting a rosette at one of the big county agricultural shows. I can't imagine there are many farmers still attending the show who were here at the beginning, but I have heard that the Lofthouse and Middlesmoor Silver Band has performed at every event.

Next to Swaledale is the broadest and possibly best-known of all Yorkshire's ancient river valleys, Wensleydale. It's an evocative, utterly English word that rolls round the mouth as you say it. Here the waters of the Ure flow east, linking the northern Pennines with the great, flat Vale of York. The area used to be called Yoredale after its river, like all the other dales in the North Riding. If you eavesdrop on some of the older and more stubborn local farmers you can hear them still using the traditional name. Sometimes old habits never die at all.

It's in this open countryside with its network of dry stone walls and field barns that the famous Wensleydale cheese has been made for the last thousand years. In the 1100s, French Cistercian monks moved here and established a monastery, and when they started to make cheese they followed the old custom of using sheep's milk. They found ewes in the area which would give a pint each at every milking.

It was 700 years later that the Wensleydale name became associated with a specific breed – a great big, swishy, Longwool sheep with a fleece that drops down to its feet and a blue face that emerges from its soft, white fringe like a circus performer peering through the drapes before curtain-up. If you hear a Dales shepherd mention the 'topping', it's that fleecy forelock on the Wensleydale he's talking about. The hit-and-miss way that many improved breeds came about means that pin-pointing an individual founding male (or female) is almost unheard of, but with the Wensleydale we can. Bluecap was a big, prolific long-woolled Leicester ram that was born in the village of East Appleton near Richmond in 1839. His owner, Richard Outhwaite, modestly called him the best ram in the north of England and hired him out to local farmers for crossing with their ewe flocks of Teeswaters, an old type from County Durham. Suddenly a breed was created.

'I ended up with Wensleydale sheep by accident,' admits John McHardy, a former mechanic who was more used to repairing old buses than rearing young ewes when he first encountered the breed. That was during the foot-and-mouth epidemic in 2001, when strict biosecurity measures stopped a neighbour from tending a small flock which grazed a field next to John's house – 'He asked me to feed and look after them and I got the bug.' Now he cares for a dozen of his own Wensleydales which he breeds mostly for their wool. The long, lustrous fleece is silky to the touch and much sought after by hand-knitters and upholsterers as well as overseas, especially in America and Italy, where it's used in cloth-making for fashion lines. It means buyers are prepared to pay the best prices to get their hands on

Wensleydale wool. 'I'm very proud to produce some-thing that's so in demand,' John says as he flashes a wide smile, 'the value certainly was an added bonus when I found out.'

Jim Thompson is someone else who never planned on owning sheep, which is saying something when you con-sider that he's been both the president and the chairman of the Wensleydale Longwool Sheep Breeders' Association. Many years ago, he was owed some money for an order of straw he'd supplied but the cash-strapped customer couldn't settle their bill so offered to pay him in sheep. 'I'd never heard of Wensleydales before and when I saw them I thought, what have I done?'

But after buying a 'decent tup' at Skipton Market, Jim started breeding Wensleydales and then taking them to shows around the country. Things have changed a great deal in the three decades since then, especially for lambs that were considered black sheep in every sense. Jim explains that until recently Wensleydales with black fleeces were rejected by traditionalists and there was even shame if you bred one. He recalls how some owners kept their black lambs hidden in a shed or outbuilding to save face, while secretly keeping the genetic black trait in the flock. Now attitudes have improved, thanks largely to wool spinners who wanted naturally coloured yarn and drove change. 'A lot of Dales breeders have gone so there aren't so many Wensleydales in Yorkshire now – but fortunately there are plenty of others elsewhere in the UK.' Jim would know, he's from Mid-Wales, and there are others throughout England, Scotland and Northern Ireland.

All those breeders, scattered around the country, will be familiar with one particular address in the West Riding and it's a place that is crucially important to them. Wool House is the Bradford headquarters of the British Wool Marketing Board, which works to get farmers the best price for their fleeces.

Years ago, there were government-sanctioned marketing boards for milk, eggs and even potatoes, which were responsible for slogans such as 'Gotta lotta bottle', 'Go to work on an egg' and a long-forgotten cartoon character called Potato Pete. The Meat and Livestock Commission carried out a similar role for the red meat sector. Over the years the boards were all abolished or merged, but somehow the Wool Marketing Board (now renamed simply British Wool) has survived and carries on doing exactly what it was created for in 1950 – to collect, grade, sell and promote wool on behalf of 40,000 farmers. At times, it must have felt like a losing battle in the war against cheap foreign imports, man-made fibres and a market so uneconomical that the price it paid per fleece was less than the cost of shearing the sheep. Thankfully incomes are up now and we're beginning to love British wool again.

Ian Brooksbank is senior head grader in the Bradford depot, spending his days sorting the neatly rolled fleeces as they arrive, separating Swaledale from Suffolk or Cotswold from Cambridge before dividing them up by type. Asked what breed produces the best wool in Britain, Ian's answer is immediate: 'There's no such thing as "best, they all have their different characteristics.' When it comes to a personal preference though, he relents a little: 'I do like the Longwools, they look better to my eye both as a fleece and as a live animal.'

The numbers are impressive. The graders deal with wool from 60 different UK breeds and their depots around the country grade 12 million fleeces every year. And what about the consumers at the end of the process who buy wool carpets, blankets and sweaters? 'For most people, the different breeds don't register with them at all,' Ian says, 'but they're still interested.'

Ian's work is every bit as hands-on as the shearer's, back on the farm. Grading wool still uses old-school techniques with each individual fleece assessed by eye and touch for its fineness, length, colour and strength. You can't learn that in an afternoon; the graders' apprenticeship lasts five years. But selling the wool is totally hi-tech, with trading done digitally at fortnightly computerised auctions. It's unrecognisable from the days, not so very long ago, when brokers gathered in the Bradford Mechanics Institute for the seasonal open-cry auctions, where bidding was done in pennies, ha'pennies and farthings for each pound of wool.

Yorkshire is also the native land of arguably the greatest British breed of them all, one of the most distinctive of all livestock, an animal that was at the centre of a great farming revolution and one that's become a figurehead for the conservation movement. It also happens to be one of those breeds whose name tells you all you need to know about its most outstanding feature. It is the Longhorn cattle. They're big, straight-backed browsers with thick yet soft hides. What surprises most people is that they're quiet and docile, despite having an almost medieval air about them. The classic look is a pair of large, forward sweeping horns like giant prongs, but in fact these days you're more likely to see 'bonnet' horns which curve down around the face.

Originally they were called Old English Longhorns, although in the north of England people knew them as Craven Longhorns after the area where they developed. This wasn't the Craven district most people think of today – that's a government administrative area based in Skipton and created by Whitehall in 1974. The historic Craven, or Cravenshire, was a large area covering most of the Yorkshire Dales and parts of what we'd recognise as Lancashire and Westmorland. The territory dates back to at least the Anglo-Saxons and was established enough to be a tax-raising district well before the Domesday Book. In the early 1700s, Craven Longhorns were a large, lean breed which were used across the north as trained draught oxen, doing the bulk of the heavy agricultural work from clearing and ploughing fields to transporting the heaviest loads.

But destiny beckoned and the Longhorn's great legacy in the history of British farming came about thanks to the livestock breeder and animal improver,

Robert Bakewell. Yes, him again! He saw the Longhorn as having the potential to be England's foremost meat providing breed, summed up in his famous phrase 'all is useless that is not beef'. He used the Craven with other strains in a strict programme of inbreeding to turn long-legged, coarse-boned cattle into a short-legged, neatly-boned breed which became famous as the Dishley Longhorn, named after his home village in the Midlands.

The story of the Longhorn is a riches to rags tale. At one time, there were more Longhorns in Britain than any other cattle, but it was their dominant feature that proved to be their downfall. Their oversized horns were, and are, impressive, but when farming started to become intensified, owners realised they couldn't fit as many Longhorns in a yard or in front of a trough as animals with smaller horns (or no horns at all). So they lost their place in the herdsman's heart and were replaced by polled cattle and the Shorthorn. What saved them from complete extinction was their beauty, because while they weren't practical to keep anymore, they were striking to look at, and a few wealthy land-owners kept them as ornamental cattle to decorate their parkland. In the 1970s there were just five herds left, numbering fewer than 300 cattle. That was enough of a wake-up call to enthusiasts to step up.

One of the people with undimmed faith in the Longhorn, past and present, is Pat Quinn. She's now in her nineties but still unstoppable on her quad bike as she does the rounds on her Cotswold valley farm. Pat's belief in the Longhorn at a time when it was unfashionable and her obvious passion for the breed is inspiring. Unlike some farmers who have long family associations with certain breeds or well-established herds, Pat started out as a complete novice but knew she wanted to do something to help a rare breed.

Her devotion began on a Saturday morning in November 1976 when my dad took her to a dispersal sale on a farm in North Essex. One of the Longhorns she bought that day, a four-year-old cow called Essex Ernestine, was sold for £577, a record at the time. Pat went on to have one of the finest herds in the entire UK. Through sheer grit and hard graft she got the numbers up and encouraged other enthusiasts, until the Longhorn was able to come off the rare breeds danger list. Pat feels the Longhorn ticks two important boxes: it has the romantic appeal of our past heritage while also proving its worth in a modern world. I couldn't put it better myself and it's an approach that could still help other once-forgotten breeds to find new favour with butchers, restaurants and discerning diners.

Centuries after Bakewell's great vision, the Longhorn is at the heart of rural innovation and experiment once again. This time it's not about biology but ecology. The Knepp Castle Estate on the Sussex Weald near Horsham used to include a traditional arable and dairy farm until a large part of the land was given over to nature in a fascinating rewilding project. Three and a half thousand acres have been left uncultivated for the last two decades and have now reverted to untamed scrub, wild grass and woodland. Almost 400 Longhorns have been introduced as free-roaming, organic grazers and I joined the estate stockman, Patrick Toe, to see these unique herds for myself. They were harder to find than I thought, but eventually we caught sight of the elusive Longhorns in a vast area of trees and undergrowth. 'The primary objective is ecology, it's about what they do with their mouth parts, their hoofs and the impact they make,' Patrick explained when I asked why the Longhorns were there, 'but beef is a very important secondary.' Animal numbers have to be controlled and every year about a hundred cattle are sold as premium quality meat.

Alongside the cattle there are Tamworth pigs and Exmoor ponies as well as Red, Fallow and Roe deer. The project is raising all sorts of questions about conservation and how we look at the British landscape in the future. The owners of the estate insist that the poor soil in that part of Sussex means that growing wheat is unproductive and unprofitable. But at a time when land is a valuable resource in providing food for a growing world population, some people are asking if giving over vast areas of farmland to nature is ever justified. It's a debate that's not going away.

Someone who would've loved to have seen the Knepp Longhorns was Gordon Beningfield. Charming, gentle and talented, he was a wonderful wildlife artist, naturalist and conservationist who became a regular and reliable contributor to a whole range of TV and radio shows in the 1970s and 80s. Gordon wasn't starry or affected though – he spoke with calm authority and whenever I saw him, on screen or off, he always wore a collar and tie, a tweed jacket and 'proper' shoes.

Despite his deep affection for the countryside, he was actually a Bermondsey boy with a background that could barely be more industrial. His father was a lighterman, handling freight barges on the Thames and overseeing the transfer of cargos at a time when the Port of London and the East End docks were the busiest in the world. Those were the days when the banks of the capital's famous old waterway were lined with Victorian brick warehouses and tall, clanking cranes.

Gordon really understood the importance of our native cattle and he felt that just looking at a Longhorn cow summed up a 'fabulous image of the past'. It was almost as if he could sense the heritage of these animals in his bones. I can remember him on the farm at Bemborough just leaning on a fence admiring them, his face beaming when we told him he could hitch a ride on the farm wagon pulled by a pair of Longhorn oxen. I was told recently that one of his paintings of a Longhorn cow stills hangs in the Hertfordshire cottage he shared with his wife, Betty.

Gordon died in 1998 at the age of just 61. But it's a mark of the man that his influence continues to be felt in the art world and in conservation circles. His paintings remain much sought-after, exhibitions of his work are still held and at West Milton in Dorset there's a secluded 20-acre beauty spot named Beningfield Wood in his honour. He was a modest bloke, but he would have felt very proud to be recognised in such a way.

On a shelf somewhere in the temperature-controlled film vaults of the University of Brighton there are some long lost Longhorns. The university houses thousands of old films, videos and even Victorian magic lantern slides, all belonging to Screen Archive South East. In among them is a little-known 15-minute 'short' filmed on Super 8mm and called 'Once Upon a Farm'. It's a snapshot of the state of rare breeds conservation in the mid-1980s and sure enough, a sequence towards the end of the film features a small herd of Longhorn cows with their calves grazing in the sunshine.

It is the work of Beryl Armstrong, who made a hundred movies throughout the 1970s and 80s, most of them with a rural theme. There was one on bee-keeping, another about heavy horse shows, which she called 'The Rally of the Giants', and a tour of the Weald and Downland Open Air Museum near Chichester (a sort of farm park for rare and threatened buildings rather than farm animals). Beryl's rare breeds movie has been categorised under 'amateur film', and it's true that even by the standards of the time, it's obvious the production didn't have the slick professionalism of a proper studio. But what shines out is a film made with love, knowledge and concern for the breeds, with Beryl not only shooting and editing the film but also providing the commentary. It's still very watchable and the British Film Institute has made it available for free on their website. It's worth 15 minutes of anyone's time.

The Longhorn should never be confused with another northern breed created by using Bakewell's selective breeding method: the Shorthorn. An old variety of short horned cattle descended from the herds of the Anglo Saxons had been bred by the Dukes of Northumberland since the 1500s, but it took another 200 years before the Shorthorn name came into its own. The new, improved type was the result of crossing two reliable dairy breeds in the north east of England, the Old Teeswater and the Durham. Once established, the Shorthorn totally overshadowed Bakewell's Longhorn, as the lack of large, awkward and often dangerous horns meant they were much easier to house, move and manage. And so they became the preferred choice of farmers, drovers, auctioneers and slaughtermen.

There are three main varieties: the quick growing meaty Beef Shorthorn, the larger long-lived Dairy Shorthorn and possibly the most controversial animal in any herd, the Northern Dairy Shorthorn. This third variety is slightly different again, and because it's a smaller, hairier type of cattle it can be left to overwinter on the snowy hills and dales. Despite the dairy name, it was developed as a dual-purpose animal in an area stretching from Durham in the east across the

Pennines to Westmorland, and in 1944 owners set up a separate breed society. The Northern Dairy Shorthorn was the subject of an enormous amount of argument and debate (sometimes quite heated) as its fans lined up to defend its diversity against others who insisted it wasn't genetically varied enough to warrant being classed as a separate breed at all.

'It looks like something from a fairy tale, "the Cow that Jumped over the Moon" even,' says Gail Sprake from the Rare Breeds Survival Trust. She's one of the Northern Dairy Shorthorn's great defenders and owns four cows. 'I believe it is a separate breed and of course they share a lot of genetics. But if the different names raise passion and interest, I'm all for that, as long as it's tempered by common sense.' A truce of sorts was called and peace was restored when the Northern Dairy Shorthorn was eventually included in the Trust's annual tally of pure native breeds alongside a white strain popular in the Scottish borders called the Whitebred Shorthorn.

Shorthorns can claim two historic firsts. They were the first breed in the world to have a pedigree herd book, published in 1822 by George Coates and containing details of 1,500 animals. To this day, the herd book is known to everyone in the business as Coates's. Secondly, a fine and famous Shorthorn called Comet became a record-breaker in 1810 as the first bull to sell for a thousand guineas. There are breeders I know whose eyes would water at that sort of auction price today! There's another notorious old Shorthorn who I simply can't avoid – because his picture is on my lounge wall at home. I've got a huge framed print of the Durham Ox, a showstopper of a Shorthorn who weighed in at almost 200 stone. He was such a fine specimen that in the early 1800s he was exhibited around the country, transported in a specially made horse-drawn carriage, with curious punters at country fairs paying for the privilege of seeing him. He was immortalised in thousands of prints and pictures (just like mine) and by having several pubs named after him, especially in the north of England. But in Australia they've really put the UK to shame. Three hours by road from Melbourne in flat, rural Victoria, a town was named Durham Ox in honour of the great beast. And he never even went there!

In Yorkshire the pig is big, in every sense. That's been the case for the last 200 years at least. Certainly back to the days of an ugly old breed called the Yorkshire and Lincolnshire, which was said to be as big as the proverbial 'Scotch Ox', and would have been a spectacle even by Victorian standards. The Yorks and Lincs gave way to a good bacon pig known as the Old Yorkshire, and after a long period of cross-breeding and improving it became a breed we know today, the Large White. This new pig on the block caused quite a stir the first time it was seen at the Royal Windsor Show in 1831 but it wasn't given official recognition as a distinct breed for another 37 years. Then, when it was discovered just how easily it coped with foreign climates and unfamiliar terrain, Large White exports took off. They're superb for crossing (especially with a Welsh or a Landrace) and so good at improving other breeds that they've become key to commercial pig production here and overseas. They're not called 'the world's favourite pig' for nothing.

But back home they have an important place in local food heritage too. York is a city famed for its Roman ruins, a magnificent minster, the National Railway Museum and for being chocoholic heaven as the traditional home of both Terry's and Rowntree's. However, there was a time when every reputable charcutier in Europe was familiar with York. Or York ham at least, and it was all down to the impressive size of the Large White pig. As the sows got bigger they put on more fat than other breeds, a trick they can still perform, to the delight of local meat dealers. York ham, the dry cured, pear-shaped king of hams, was the pride of Yorkshire's county town where it was first prepared and sold by a butcher called Atkinson from his shop on Blossom Street in the late 1800s.

The York method required the meat to sit on a bed of salt for several days in a dry, cool cellar before being hung for anything up to ten weeks. Traditionally curing began on St Martin's Day, 11 November, when the pigs were at their fattest, the weather was cooler and the summer flies had buzzed off. Today, real York ham is far rarer than the pig it comes from, but if you know where to look you can still find it on sale in the city.

God's own county hasn't just produced traditional pig, sheep and cattle breeds though. The Yorkshire Hornet wasn't an insect, a local newspaper or even an old make of British motorcycle (although with such a glorious name it should have been). Instead, it was a flamboyant breed of crested chicken. This was an alert, upright bird with a spangled plumage and a fan tail, but its signature feature was on top of its head. Its crowning glory was exactly that: a gold-coloured comb with a tuft of forward pointing feathers. Just imagine the appeal of a chicken like that strutting around the yard showing off its headgear. It probably emerged in the 1850s when foreign poultry was being crossed with domestic breeds.

Reports of its demise before the First World War may have been exaggerated, because articles and photographs of the Yorkshire Hornet were appearing in the poultry press as late as the 1930s. Some books and papers suggest it was officially extinct by 1970. But many years later there was an attempt to revive the breed by Andrew Sheppy, the livestock legend from Somerset who had done so much to restore the Oxford Sandy and Black pig and many other breeds. He discovered a male Yorkshire Hornet and had high hopes of rekindling the breed but sadly the bird was too old and infertile and, for once, Shep was foiled.

In contrast, one of the chicken breeds you'll see at many poultry shows these days is a bird with good northern roots that go back centuries. The Old English

Pheasant Fowl gets its name from its spangled pheasant-like plumage and it was once so popular in the region that it was known as the Yorkshire Pheasant Fowl, despite having followers with flocks in Lancashire, Cumberland, Westmorland and County Durham as well. The breed was revived and renamed in 1914, although diehard smallholders still called it by the Old Yorkshire name for years afterwards.

Yorkshire's north country neighbour is Lancashire and they meet in the Pennines, the backbone of England. The rivalry between the two proud counties is legendary – for some, the War of the Roses is still being fought; it's black pudding versus Yorkshire pudding in the great north-north divide.

On the face of it, the livestock story of Lancashire is overshadowed by the White Rose County to the east with its native breed big-hitters. But a closer look reveals a long heritage of farm breeds in Lancashire. There were once Lancashire cattle. Probably not a distinct breed, but one of several strains of the same breed found from Westmorland to Derbyshire and south to Staffordshire, all with similar long horns, some with a white finch back and looking more or less like plough oxen. Their identities were lost in cross breeding down the years, but their descendants influenced the Longhorn types of northern England that Robert Bakewell famously developed. So somewhere in the DNA of every Longhorn lie Lancashire genes. The county also produced a local strain of swine, but sadly the Lancashire pig is also a thing of the past.

There have been some triumphs though, and a range of breeds that are very much still with us today. The British White is a beef breed which was developed from the old white horned cattle that roamed the valleys of the Forest of Bowland hundreds of years ago. By the 1600s, now polled, the British White was established in the park at Whalley Abbey near Clitheroe. Two hundred years ago, the herd was moved across the country to Norfolk and the breed has been associated with the eastern counties ever since. It could easily have disappeared but for a group of breeders with vision and verve who found a new role for them as demand grew for grass-fed, matured beef from British herds.

The county has paid its way in the poultry world too. The Hamburgh chicken is known here as the Bolton Grey or the Lancashire Mooney while one of our rarest poultry breeds, the Marsh Daisy, was also developed in the county back in the 1880s. Much better known is another true native of Lancashire and a traditional sight on the Pennines for centuries: Lonk sheep. The name comes from the local dialect word for 'lanky', and unbelievably there's one Lonk flock in the county that can be traced back to 1740. There's an alternative name for the breed too, the Improved Haslingden, which comes from the town in the steep-sided Rossendale Valley that prospered as a centre for wool and weaving 200 years ago.

I always think this nimble mountain breed is surprisingly large for a hill sheep, yet somehow it looks just right in the beautiful, desolate mountain landscape. It has a square, bulky fleece, spiral horns and a face that's speckled black and white. And it must be more than just coincidence that the meat of this authentic Lancashire breed should make a fantastic-tasting Lancashire hotpot. Just ask Prue Leith and the other judges on TV's *Great British Menu*. They were so impressed by Lonk hotpot that they made it the main course winner of the series in 2009. The chef and restaurateur Nigel Howarth shook things up a bit by using three different Lonk cuts in his recipe: shoulder, shin and neck chops. The lightly seasoned meat, mixed with onions sweated in butter and topped with sliced potato was served with pickled red cabbage, carrots and leeks to all-round approval.

Back home at Bemborough, one of my toughest jobs normally takes an hour or two sometime in the early summer, but if I make a mistake, I'll be reminded of it for an entire year. Selecting photographs for the next Cotswold Farm Park calendar is a much harder task than it sounds. I've got to choose just 12 breeds and it's like being asked to name your favourite child! I want to ensure all the main species are represented but, if anything, that makes the job even more difficult with so many striking, photogenic characters across the board. This time there's one stand-out breed I'm determined will appear though. White Park cattle were called the 'mightiest of all the beasts' by the poet Sir Walter Scott, and I have to agree. With their large horns and long black eyelashes, these stylish-looking beef animals have a regal presence. Fifty years ago, there were so few of them that the Rare Breeds Survival Trust almost had no choice but to choose a White Park's head as its logo.

They're very special because they remind me of my first ever film shoot. I was ten and it almost ended in disaster. My sister Becca and I were extras in the Ann-Margaret movie *Joseph Andrews* and director Tony Richardson wanted to film the opening scene just down the road from us in Lower Slaughter (don't be put off by the name, it's a dreamy Cotswold village on the River Eye). Dressed as eighteenth-century farm hands, we each had to ride a White Park ox while all around us revellers were singing and dancing at a May fair and geese waddled along in front of a horse-drawn carriage. It was all going brilliantly well until something spooked the White Parks and they bolted with two little Henson children hanging on for dear life. Worse was to come, because when the oxen stopped, Becca and I were almost thrown head first into the river. I don't know who's got the outtakes but I still get nervous every time *It'll Be Alright on the Night* comes on TV.

I might not ride them now, but I occasionally buy White Parks and the qualities I look for are exactly the same characteristics I want in all my cattle – a strong head, a straight back and good legs to give it plenty of mobility. You can tell a lot by just looking at how a cow or bull moves. But in the White Park there are other traits that are crucial. Their muzzle and ears must be black, the colour of liquorice ideally, and the gently curved horns have to grow horizontally, not swept up like a Gloucester or too far forward like a Longhorn. Those smart pearly-white horns with their black tips will keep growing too, and while not quite as scientifically accurate as counting the rings in a tree trunk, the rule of thumb is that the longer the horns, the older the White Park. They're a breed that'll win your heart and even tough, bluff Winston Churchill wasn't immune to their appeal. During the war he arranged for a bull and two pregnant heifers to be sent to safety in America in case Hitler's army made it across the channel and invaded.

The White Park is a slow maturing breed, which means ideally they'll be three years old before they're ready for the table, which is twice as old as most commercial breeds. That's what the celebrated breeder John Lean does with his beef herd and although his cattle aren't earning him any money while they're growing, feasting on lush Devon grass in summer and silage in winter, he's happy to play a waiting game. It adds depth and taste which means the meat can attract a premium when it's sold and it's exactly what intensive beef production *isn't*.

To test the quality for myself, I went to see a specialist rare breeds butcher in London – in fact, it's the only whole-carcass butcher in the capital. Nathan Mills' family have been in the meat trade for three genera-tions and in 2018 he expanded his business by opening a new shop in Old Spitalfields Market, a London land-mark where 'fresh fowl and roots' were first sold nearly 400 years ago. In his cutting room, Nathan showed me a beautiful White Park rib which had been hanging in a cool room for 75 days to age the meat and intensify the flavour. It changes the colour too, so that it has a rich, dark quality which you just don't see in the bright red cuts from fast-grown beef that's sold in supermarkets. Resting the rib on a large wooden butcher's block, Nathan cut through the meat and I was amazed at how easily the knife sliced through it. I tried a piece. It was soft, tender and flavoursome and when I closed my eyes I'm sure I could taste a hint of the grass it was raised on. I think flavour and heritage are wrapped up together when you have food like this, and the story of the breed is part of the eating experience.

We know Romans used white coloured cattle in their religious rituals and those animals may well have been the ancestors of today's White Parks. What is certain is that when the Norman barons started enclosing common grazing land, there were a handful of herds of white cattle which were rounded up and confined to deer parks. And that's where they stayed for 900 years, give or take. Over time, all those herds were improved with domestic blood added to the line, except one. It's the most notorious and probably the grumpiest herd in the north of England.

The wild white cattle of Chillingham Park near Alnwick roam freely as feral animals. They've been left to their own devices for seven centuries with no human interference and to be honest, you can't get near them if you try. They won't tolerate the scent of humans on them and if there's any contact it can prove fatal. There are horrific stories of calves becoming trapped in the park and freed by estate workers, but when the animals were returned to the herd they were gored to death by their mothers. Today there are around a hundred Chillingham cattle but the numbers have fluctuated over the years. Before the First World War there were 80, but the population crashed to just 13 in 1947 when the park suffered appalling winter blizzards with 40-foot snow drifts and a desperate shortage of food.

There's a primitive pecking order among the cattle at Chillingham which never fails to amaze. Their social hierarchy, common with many breeds, includes a 'boss' cow who goes ahead of the herd and leads the others to food or warns them if she senses danger. But the entire herd is ruled over by a 'king' bull. He's the fittest and strongest of the males and it's been known for the others to fight to the death to establish supremacy in the herd. It's the sort of primaeval behaviour that we expect from wild animals but is unlike anything we see in the milder domesticated breeds we've developed over centuries.

The 'king' fathers all the Chillingham calves that are born during his reign as the dominant bull. When it's time to calve, the mother will hide the newborn away from the herd, going back to feed it a couple of times a day before introducing it to the others. There's even an old Northumberland legend that the king bull inspects every newborn calf that's presented to him and rejects any that don't come up to scratch.

Uncompromising breeds are a feature of tough, unyielding landscapes. Among the most resilient are a couple of horse breeds; the Fell pony and the Dales pony. The Fell pony originates from the 'top' of England, on mountains and moors from the Lake District across to the Cheviot hills. It's one of those steadfast breeds of British equines with a sturdy nature and a strong will to live, and they're still used in field sports for bringing deer carcasses down off the hills and carrying wicker grouse panniers. The royal family is particularly keen on Fell ponies and the Queen still breeds them. At time of writing, in her nineties she's still occasionally seen riding her favourite pony around Windsor Great Park.

The story of the modern Dales pony is linked to the northern lead mines of the Middle Ages and later, where they worked as packhorses carrying heavy cargoes as far as the ports on the north-east coast. They were used in a wide swathe of the country from the Derbyshire Peaks right up to the Scottish border but their stronghold was always the upper dales of the Tyne, Wear, Tees, Allen and Swale. Dales ponies aren't just strong, they're brave too, carrying supplies in the First and Second World Wars. An army captain inspecting ponies for the Board of Agriculture once described them as having 'the most perfect foot in the British Isles'.

Beatrix Potter is one of the best-loved children's authors of all time; her books still sell two million copies a year while her most popular invention has found a whole new audience with a recent TV and movie re-boot of Peter Rabbit. That's not bad for an old buck in a blue jacket who's been around since 1902. But while Peter, Flopsy, Mopsy and all the other creatures are Potter's literary legacy, it's her work as a sheep farmer that has contributed most to her reputation in the Lake District.

Beatrix lived on a farm at Near Sawrey, a village between world-famous Windermere and the cobbled streets of Hawkshead, where she bred her sheep and helped preserve the local landscape. Potter's breed was the Herdwick, which are a unique part of the Lakeland culture and about as hardy as any mountain sheep gets. The ewes lamb outside on their own and they're very well adapted to the wet with a fleece that dries out quicker than almost any other breed, which is a jolly good thing in a place where it rains as much as it does in the Lake District.

Potter fell in love with the area after family holidays there and bought her farm in 1905, starting a Herdwick flock the following year, just after her fortieth birthday. Photographs taken in the 1930s and early 40s show her looking every inch the northern countrywoman in felt hat, thick tweed jacket, long skirt and clogs with walking stick in hand.

There are two things about Herdwicks that make them such remarkable animals. First, they're a sheep that changes colour. The lambs are born black then as they grow their faces turn white (or 'hoar-frosted' as the farmers here call it) and the fleece takes on a beautiful mixed grey/blue colour. But it's their instinctive ability to find their ancestral fell and stay there which I find remarkable, as if they're guided by Mother Nature's very own GPS. There are no fences in a landscape like this, but instead of wandering away, getting lost or mixing with neighbouring flocks, the Herdwick stays on home turf. They're what's called hefted sheep, which means the mothers teach their offspring the territorial knowledge they need and they hold to the same part of the mountain for generation after generation. It's one of the reasons that when farms are sold the flocks are part of the deal, and why something like 99 per cent of Herdwick sheep still live in the Lake District.

Herdwicks are front and centre at one of England's oldest agricultural get-togethers, the Wasdale Head Show and Shepherds' Meet. Held on fields below England's highest mountain, Scafell Pike, Herdwicks are brought in their hundreds to be judged, admired and, let's be honest, coveted. If you ignore for a moment the manoeuvring tractors, the rows of parked cars and the commentator's voice crackling over the public address system, you can imagine that the scene hasn't altered much since the first shepherd's gathering when sheep were walked over the fells hundreds of years ago. The setting is breath-taking – the sheep are penned by wooden hurdles and surrounded by grey dry stone walls, craggy mountains, deep lakes and often, as the event is held in October, fog. But hardy sheep and even hardier shepherds don't mind a blanket of mist if honour is at stake. At the last count, there were 30 different competition classes, such as 'Best Lamb Ram' and 'Best Female', in addition to a few innovations such as the prize for the 'Best Sheep on Field that Hasn't Won Anything'. The shepherds can do battle with each other for the title of Best Beard too. Bouts of Cumberland and Westmorland wrestling, a fell running contest and terrier racing all give the event a timeless air, and so does the shepherd's crook competition. As well as being the reliable old working tool of the Lakeland hill farmers, beautifully crafted and carved crooks are considered a work of art at Wasdale with the ones fashioned from Herdwick horn the most admired of all.

If you come off the mountains and head along the Eden Valley into towns like Penrith and on to Carlisle you're in Cumberland pig territory. Or to be entirely accurate, you *would* have been in Cumberland pig territory if you were here at any time up until the late 1950s. Before then, the county breed of flat-faced, floppy eared, short-snouted porkers were a feature of the pig farms that were dotted around the area. They were well suited to the local landscape and originally grew fat on thistles before they became a backyard breed. These were large, long-backed, white pigs with silky smooth skin and long straight tails, and they did well at the big agricultural shows like the Yorkshire and the Royal Lancashire in the 1920s. A herd book from the time states clearly how any pig in the show ring with black hair, black spots or prick ears would be disqualified immediately. Cumberland ham was a local speciality and the Cumberland sausage was traditionally made from the meat of the breed, which are named after the pig not the place. Since the breed is extinct, there are people in the region who insist that the chunky, curled bangers sold in their thousands today shouldn't be labelled Cumberland sausage at all.

It was the move to intensive pig farming which left the breed, and the breeders, behind and by 1955 just three registered boars were left in the area. The last Cumberland, a sow owned by a Mr Thirwell from the village of Bothel, died in 1960 and that, tragically, was that. There was an attempt to recreate the Cumberland pig by selective breeding in the 2000s and a lot of promise in a sow called Wendy with a similar DNA match. A single pig isn't a breed of course and recreations are enormously controversial, but as it turned out Wendy was infertile and any hopes of turning the clock back were well and truly dashed. Just like the

Lincolnshire Curly-Coat, the Cumberland is a pig I would love to have seen. But let's keep talking about the breeds that we foolishly allowed to die out, because that's as good as a dig in the ribs to remind us to never let it happen again.

Beef and Ale Pie

Serves: 6

Ingredients
vegetable oil, for frying
1kg (2lb 4oz) diced braising steak
2 large white onions, chopped
3 carrots, peeled and chopped
150g (5^1/$_2$oz) bacon lardons
2 tbsp tomato purée
4 tbsp plain flour
1 bottle of Adam Henson's Rare Breed Ale
200ml (7fl oz) boiling water
1 beef stock cube
2 bay leaves
^{1}/$_2$ bunch fresh thyme, chopped

For the pie lid
1 sheet ready-rolled puff pastry, thawed if frozen
beaten egg, for glazing

To serve
mashed potato
seasonal vegetables

Method
1. Preheat the oven to 160°C/325°F/gas 3.
2. Heat 1 tablespoon of vegetable oil in a large casserole dish. Add the diced braising steak and brown all over, then remove and set aside.
3. Add the onions and carrots to the dish, adding more oil if needed, then gently fry for 5 minutes, then add the bacon and tomato purée.
4. Return the braising steak and any juices to the dish and stir well. Pour over the Rare Breed ale and boiling water. Mix the flour with a little cold water to make a paste, pour into the dish and stir well. Crumble in the stock cube, stir in the herbs and bring to a simmer.

5. Cover the dish with a lid and place in the preheated oven for about 2 hours, until the meat is tender.
6. Remove from the oven and keep warm while you make the pastry lid. Turn the oven up to 220°C/425°F/gas 7.
7. Cut the pastry to the size required to cover your casserole dish, place on a baking sheet, brush with the beaten egg and bake for 15–20 minutes or until puffed up and golden.
8. Place the pastry lid on top of the casserole dish and serve the pie with mashed potato and seasonal vegetables.

Andy Boreham
Head Chef, Cotswold Farm Park

CHAPTER 6

Scotland

The national animal of Scotland is the unicorn. It's a fact that all Scots learn at school but it's probably news for the majority of folk from the rest of the UK who have a completely different creature in mind when they think of Scotland. The big, horned, ginger-fringed Highland cow has come to symbolise the country, and with millions of postcards, whisky bottle labels and shortbread biscuit tins featuring images of them, it's no wonder the breed has become Scotland's *unofficial* national animal.

Everyone can identify the handsomely hairy Highland cattle and for many people it's probably the only bovine breed they know by name. The word icon is overused, but in the case of this shaggy-coated beauty, it's absolutely the right one. They're not a rare breed, and perhaps the universal appeal of their straggly fringe, long eye-lashes and wide-sweeping handlebar-like horns is the reason why. But any collection of British livestock would be lacking if it didn't include them, so I am duty-bound to give them an honourable mention.

Although unlike other breeds of cattle, a group of Highlands is never called a herd, instead it's described as a fold. The word comes from the tradition of keeping them in open shelters during the winter to shield them from the harshest weather. Those stone-built retreats were called folds and the term stuck.

The Highland is an ancient breed, descended from the longhorned cattle brought to Britain by Neolithic tribes at the end of the Stone Age. Later, the Iron Age Celts would have used them as working beasts in the fields and for pulling carts. The first detailed records of these cows were written in 1884 and describe the two types of Highlands which were kept at the time. The West Highland was known as the Kyloe, and the legend in the Western Isles is that they were herded to the water's edge and swum across the straits, or kyles, to the mainland to be taken to market. It's something that was tried again in an experiment for the BBC's much-loved and sorely-missed early evening magazine programme, *Nationwide*, back in 1981. The producers must have been thrilled at the very idea of being the first to capture on film the spectacle of Highland cattle free-swimming. But instead of 20 horned heads bobbing through the waves towards the opposite shore, the only footage they got was of angry herdsmen shouting, cajoling and splashing about as the fold refused to budge. In the end the animals crossed the water by ferry, like everyone else, as it was decided the swimming instinct had been lost over time and they'd just become too tame.

The other type of Highland, and one which definitely didn't need swimming lessons, was the mainland variety. They were popular in the north of Scotland and weren't quite as tough or as long-haired as the West Highland. Importantly they were able to grow bigger and beefier than their island counterparts thanks to better grazing and their more sheltered surroundings. Most Highlands we see on film or photographed now have red or gingery coats, but originally there was a whole range of colours. The West Highland was likely to be black and the mainland type was often dun or red but there were also white, yellow and tawny brown cattle in the folds, and those colour variations still come through. If you catch sight of a small fold of different coloured Highlands standing or grazing side by side, it's impossible to resist stopping the car to get a better look. They're like a living swatch book.

Highlands have even made their mark in the unlikely setting of the gentle Gloucestershire countryside. They arrived on our farm in the Cotswolds when I was four years old and their striking, colourful appearance made an instant impression on me. Hard as it is to believe now, these wonderful animals were unwanted livestock at the time and in desperate need of a new home. When

Whipsnade discontinued its rare breeds conservation work, the zoo passed the cattle on to Reading University, but within a year or two the researchers there were having second thoughts about their expanding and expensive lodgers. Luckily they found a permanent home for them with us at Bemborough Farm. Our first two cows were a blonde we called Goldie Hawn and a red called Brigitte Bardot, named after the famous actresses my Uncle Nicky had recently worked with. I'm not sure either would have been entirely flattered but to me our cows were just as beautiful.

Dad always had an eye for the perfect publicity shot and it's down to the beauty of our first Highland cows that he managed to get a superb bit of promotion shortly after the Farm Park opened in 1971. *Cotswold Life* was a relatively new magazine at that time and the editor decided to publish a four-page feature about Dad and what they called his 'noble venture' of rescuing rare breeds from extinction. The headline was 'Survival on a Cotswold Hillside' and the writer, June Lewis, explained that as she walked around looking at the animals she 'felt the same kind of awe and privilege one feels on being shown a rare and priceless Old Master'. June's glowing prose was accompanied by a lovely portrait of one of our Highland cows with her calf at foot, both helpfully looking straight down the photographer's lens. The caption read 'The parent stares protectively from inside the enclosure while the calf entertains a cheeky, quizzical expression,' and looking at the picture now, after almost half a century, I can't help thinking that these days it would be a sure-fire contender for the BBC *Countryfile* calendar.

When the article appeared Dad was delighted, not just because it set out his dream of a sustainable future for rare breeds but also because it mentioned the practical stuff like free parking, our snack bar and the fact there were toilet facilities at the farm. He was always grateful to the magazine for taking his vision seriously and helping to boost visitor numbers.

I was reminded of those early years with our old Highland cattle when I met champion breeder Michael Poland and some of his 300-strong fold. On a cold, misty morning I walked with Michael into his yard to meet his magnificent two-year-old bull, with a pretty magnificent name to match. Eoin Mhor the Eighth of Mottistone was fresh from competing successfully for the top titles at three of the biggest and most important livestock shows of the year: the Royal Highland, the Glasgow International for Highland Cattle and the Great Yorkshire. With an eye to improving my own stock, I wanted to know what it was about Eoin Mhor that made him a top-notch bull. Michael was more than happy to share his vast experience: 'As you walk up to him, his whole profile is saying "look at me I'm a bull", and it's important that you're getting the masculinity from him.' He showed me the prize-winner's noble head, its wide body and the broadness of the mouth, and when he gave the bull a friendly pat on the head, I learned a new word. The first time Michael mentioned it, I didn't quite catch what he said. So he repeated it for me. *Dossan*, I discovered, is the Highlanders' word for their cattle's distinctive fringe. They say that if it looks like a sporran then it's doing a good job of protecting the animal's eyes from the ferocious Scottish snow, sleet and rain. Like they say, every day's a school day!

Michael's bull was definitely a showstopper, but it was one of his female Highlands I really wanted to see. Her name was Tanya of Mottistone and she eyed us suspiciously as we walked up the sloping field towards her, probably wondering what I had under my arm. It was in fact Dad's old calving book, a handwritten record of all the new arrivals on our farm going back to 1974. I'd brought it especially to show Michael. As it turned out, I was holding what was in effect Tanya's birth certificate, because as we spoke, Michael pulled a piece of paper from his coat pocket and unfolded it in front of me. It was his cow's pedigree chart, essentially a diagram of her family tree, and it proved that she was the granddaughter of one of our Highlands from years ago, Tanya of Bemborough. Suddenly it all felt like a bovine episode of *Who Do You Think You Are?*

Any appearance of Highlands on *Countryfile* gets a huge, positive audience reaction and I suppose the programme helped make big, beefy Eric the best known bull in the land. In 2011, I was searching for a new bull to sire the next generation of Highlands on the farm and when I headed off to find a prime example at the Spring Highland Cattle Sale at Oban, the BBC cameras followed me. I had a tick list of the qualities I was looking for in my new animal: a strong working physique, a lively look, good upward slanting horns and straight feet. That's when I spotted Eric and he became an instant TV star.

It was a similar story a couple of years later when I needed a name for Eric's newborn son, a beautiful bull calf with a shaggy, silver coat. We broadcast an appeal for suggestions and I was astounded when 11,000 viewers got in contact with us. The winning name, suitably Scottish and perfectly Highland, was Nevis.

I'm not the only Cotswold farmer who loves this breed. There's another fold about 30 miles further south of us, in the small market town of Minchinhampton, and these cattle also attract plenty of attention. Walkers and sightseers getting their first glimpse of this wide-horned, hardy livestock in such a mellow landscape will give them a disbelieving look. They often get one back. The Minchinhampton Highlands are owned by Joyce Jones who's named the cows after her granddaughters and overwinters the cattle on a field just five hundred yards from the town centre. She always wanted to keep Highlands and eventually gave in to her heart's desire: 'I love them and they've become quite iconic, certainly people would be very upset if they ever disappeared from here.'

Every summer, her ten-strong fold is released with hundreds of other cattle of all types on to nearby common land. The livestock roam free in the sunshine on 500 acres of high limestone grassland. It's a nationally important wildlife habitat and home to a wide array of plants and insects. In spring the common is transformed into a sea of yellow cowslips, there are lovely early purple orchids and a keen eye will spot the rare Adonis blue butterfly. It's a landscape that has never been ploughed or tilled and, not surprisingly, it's a Site of Special Scientific Interest (the conservation equivalent of the Crown Jewels). The grazing Highlands help cut back the tallest, most invasive grass, allowing the precious flowers to thrive, which in turn attract pollinators and insects. Even the cowpats are good news because they attract nocturnal dung beetles which are food for the growing population of Lesser and Greater Horseshoe bats which roost nearby. This really is a conservation win-win situation. As Joyce says, 'There's a lot of grass out there, and hopefully my cattle will come back in October very fat.'

Lovely as the Highland is, it's just one of Scotland's many headline-hogging native breeds. The border country, lowlands, mountains, coast and islands are home to some of the oldest, wildest and most outstanding livestock of all. The Scottish breeds encompass a diverse and fascinating collection of cattle, sheep, horse, poultry and waterfowl. Curiously, though, there are no surviving native pig breeds north of the English border. No unicorns either.

It's a nation which has given us breeds of primitive wiry sheep which, helpfully, are all named after their places of origin. More than almost anywhere else in the British Isles, the story of these sheep is a lesson in geography as much as it is zoology: Boreray, Castlemilk Moorit, Hebridean, North Ronaldsay, Shetland and Soay. The same is true for Scottish equines: Clydesdale, Eriskay, Highland and, again, Shetland. Outside the UK, most of those place names and their local breeds will mean nothing to the vast majority of people. But if the Highland is the best-known Scottish breed within Britain, then the Aberdeen Angus is the Saltire-waving, international ambassador who takes Scotland to the world stage. Not so much a breed, more a global brand.

The Aberdeen Angus is known throughout Europe, in Russia, South Africa, Australia, New Zealand, North America, Argentina, Uruguay ... and the list goes on and on. Its reputation as a top-class meat beast here was helped, no doubt, by the famous steak house chain and the fact that there's no need for a geography lesson with this breed. Their traditional home is the fertile valleys of Aberdeenshire and the neighbouring county of Angus, where they emerged from the black hornless cattle which roamed north and eastern Scotland 900 years ago. By the 1700s, there were two local breeds, both blessed with brilliant names; the short-legged black Buchan Humlies and the hairy, hornless Angus Doddies. They formed the basis of the Aberdeen Angus we know today – black, rumpy animals with big ears set at ten-to-two and a broad face.

A hundred and fifty years ago, Aberdeenshire was the cattle capital of Scotland with more herds being raised and grazed in the county than anywhere else north of the English border. But for all that, the place that's become known as the home of the Aberdeen Angus is the grounds of a fairytale castle in neighbouring Banffshire called Ballindalloch, which sits on the flat grassland where the River Avon meets the fast-flowing waters of the Spey. The fortress was built in the 1500s on what was known then as 'the coo's haugh' or, in English, the cow's meadow. It's here that Sir George Macpherson-Grant brought his first Aberdeen Angus cattle in 1860 and the breed has never left, every subsequent generation of the family refining and improving the stock. It's now the oldest surviving herd in the world.

If you want to buy or sell the very best Aberdeen Angus cattle then there's only one place to be – the Stirling Bull Sales. The auction has a heritage that goes back more than 150 years and people come from all over the world to take part. There's a buzz at every livestock market but nothing like the level of tension and excitement I witnessed among the breeders in the collection ring at Stirling just before the start of business.

The sheer number of breeds in these isles of ours can be a bit bewildering. If you weren't brought up on rare breed farming and you don't have a photographic memory, there's a heck of a lot to learn. Even the 'experts' have been known to get caught out, mistaking a Lincoln Longwool ewe for a Cotswold. Not the worst crime in the world you might think, but embarrassing if you're a livestock judge at a big county show. A good example of how confusing it can be is Galloway cattle. Look the words up and you'll not only find information about Black Galloways but also references to Red Galloways, Dun Galloways, White Galloways and Riggit Galloways, distinguished by a white strip along their spines (an old Scottish word for back is riggit). They're all variations or strains of the original, but be warned, not all Galloways are born equal. Black cattle are often preferred over Reds and Duns for instance (although all three are registered with the Galloway Cattle Society) while the Riggit was regarded by some farmers as a genetic throwback and they went unrecognised for so long that a breed society wasn't formed until 2007.

There is one variation that does stand alone, though. Zebra cows, Oreo cattle or the livestock with the Polo mint middles – they've been called all sorts of imaginative things. But whatever name you use for them, the beautiful Belted Galloway with its black and white markings is a landmark on legs. Their heritage goes back to the 1600s, and old Scottish herdsmen and drovers preferred them simply because on dreary days these cattle were far more visible across the murky, featureless landscape than plain black or brown cows. A hundred years ago it was still possible, in a few parts of the country at least, to lean on a farm gate and see cattle with distinctive white-sandwiched coats. But after the extinction of the Somerset Sheeted and the demise of isolated herds like Lord Palmerston's curious white-bellied dairy cattle on his Broadlands estate in Hampshire, the Belted Galloway was left as the last officially recognised belted cattle breed in the UK.

The most original description of the 'Beltie' I've ever heard was when the Bishop of Ripon, the Right Reverend Dr Helen-Ann Hartley, went on TV's *Songs of Praise* to ... well, sing their praises. 'They look a little bit like clergy, they're black with this band of white round their middle and I just find them quite a satisfying cow to look at, they're fab.' I agree with her, although I'm still getting used to hearing words like 'fab' from the Church of England. 'Farming is as old as religion in some ways,' Bishop Helen-Ann explained. 'You only have to look at the Bible to get a sense that our forebears and ancestors in faith were very much people who worked the land.'

If you're particularly observant you might have spotted an entirely new variety in the breed – one I call the Green Galloway. As more effort is put into restoring ancient landscapes, encouraging native wild flowers and providing eco-friendly wildlife habitats around the UK, conservation groups have hit upon the idea of putting the Belted Galloway to work as an environmental ally. Herds are being allowed to roam freely at some of the country's most picturesque and scientifically important locations to simply do what comes naturally; eat the grass. It's a new role that until recently was entirely unforeseen but it's one which can only help keep herd numbers up by creating a use for the breed.

There are plenty of diehard Belted Galloway enthusiasts and they would never forgive me if I didn't mention Cracker. In the same way that Eric the bull became an animal celebrity after appearing with me on TV, Cracker enjoyed his own moment in the media spotlight. I bought him to run with the three belted cows we already had on the farm, but he was grumpy from the moment he arrived and almost sent me flying as he charged out of his trailer. After that his behaviour didn't improve very much to be honest, although I think viewers relished seeing the trouble he caused me, ruining fences and getting far too friendly with cows from some of the other breeds.

He came to me from the Yorkshire Dales where he was bred by my old friend and established Belted Galloway herdsman, Neil Heseltine. His cattle graze high up near Malham Cove where, just like Scotland, the scenery is beautiful but the weather can be brutal. I once helped Neil move his herd to new pasture on lower ground, when we were caught in a sudden blizzard. While the two of us were battered and blinded by howling winds and drifting snow, the cattle didn't flinch. They ploughed on with their heads up, facing into the storm as if nothing was happening. I got a strong sense that they were proving that their reputation for being a tough, strong and steady breed was totally justified.

When you talk to anyone who's in the know about 'Belties', it's not very long before Flora Stuart's name crops up. The world's leading expert on Belted Galloways, she ran the breed society for 20 years with such passion and belief that she made even the most ardent rare breeds enthusiast look laid back. It's reckoned that she knew every bull and cow in the herd book, spent much of her free time advising other breeders and helped establish herds in countries as far away as Canada, Australia and New Zealand. Without her single-mindedness, driving the breed forward and encouraging people to show their best animals in competitions around the country, it's likely that the Belted Galloway and its distinctive white belly band would have been lost to us decades ago.

Although Flora Stuart was born on the Isle of Bute in 1941 (her grandfather was the Marquis of Bute, no less) she grew up in Wigtownshire, the most south-westerly part of Scotland which sticks out awkwardly into the Irish Sea like a misshaped wing nut. It's classic home territory for all the Galloway breeds and the family estate, Mochrum, was in the midst of typically tough, isolated terrain, surrounded by moorland and bogs broken up by jagged rocks and boulders – just the sort of place that hardy, no-nonsense cattle love. Flora was a hardy, no-nonsense type too and although she had the formal title of Lady, everybody knew her as plain Miss Flora. I think the best word to use for her is unpretentious. She was a regular at the monthly meetings of the Wigtownshire Guild of Spinners, Weavers and Dyers and she was rarely seen wearing anything except her working clothes. When a reporter from the *Galloway Gazette* once asked her what the highlight of her life had been, she told him it was the day one of her cattle won the Champion of Champions title at the Wigtown Agricultural Show.

Despite her aristocratic background, Miss Flora was a modest and very private person. She was a slight, softly-spoken woman who never married and was completely devoted to her cattle and her other livestock including a small flock of rare breed Shetland sheep. So there was genuine surprise after she died when the newspapers reported that she'd left more than £6 million.

If Flora Stuart's Belted Galloways were a classic example of hard-headed, robust cattle then it's extraordinary that the same corner of Scotland also produced a dainty little sheep. The Castlemilk Moorit is a lovely, agile animal which seems to trot about on its slim legs and small feet. If I didn't know better I'd say they tiptoe everywhere. They have a similar air of antiquity about them as the primitive sheep of Shetland and the Hebrides, with the ewes as well as the rams sporting a pair of fine-looking horns. So it's a surprise to many people to discover that the Castlemilk Moorit is the youngest of Britain's rare breeds. Their roots don't go back thousands of years like the Soay, but less than a century to when Sir Jock Buchanan-Jardine looked out across the family estate near the red sandstone town of Lockerbie and decided that a new flock of grazing sheep would be just the thing to beautify the parkland.

Sir Jock was quite the old Etonian landowner; he was a former captain in the Royal Horse Guards, Master of the Dumfriesshire Hounds, a racehorse owner and at one time he was even described as 'the world's best dressed man' by the bespoke tailors of Savile Row. I imagine he was the type of person who always got what he wanted, and although his livestock collection included Dorset Horns, Wiltshire Horns and Black Welsh Mountain sheep, there were no breeds which quite suited his vision for a new park flock, so he went ahead and created his own. Using Shetlands, Manx Loaghtans and the genetics of the ancient, wild Mouflon sheep he evolved his own unique breed. Not for anything practical like producing milk, meat or commercial wool but principally as decoration to adorn the view. The fleeces weren't wasted though, because they were used on a small-scale to provide the family with 'home-spun' clothing.

For almost four decades this one-of-a-kind feral flock happily had the run of Sir Jock's Castlemilk estate, virtually unnoticed by the world outside. All that changed in 1969 when the great man died (not at home in chilly Dumfriesshire but in sunny Cannes) and within a year it was decided that his ornamental sheep were no longer needed and the flock should be dispersed, or disposed of, at the earliest opportunity. My dad got word of this, and hating the idea of any rare breeds being destroyed, he arranged to have a ram and six ewes from the Buchanan-Jardine estate brought to our farm in the Cotswolds. But what arrived at Bemborough wasn't at all what he expected.

Dad had been told that Sir Jock had developed a flock of Moorit Shetlands; moorit is a Scottish word to describe a red-brown colour. When the trailer that had carried them all the way from Lockerbie arrived, it wasn't moorit-coloured Shetlands which emerged but seven alert, short-tailed sheep with wallaby faces and the nimbleness of roe deer. Dad later called them 'a beautiful creature the like of which I'd never seen before'. Apart from a further four ewes which had been sold to another rare breeds enthusiast, the rest of this exceptional flock of more than a hundred sheep was culled. It was a tragedy which signalled the start of another Henson mercy mission, as Dad went about ensuring this extraordinary breed was brought back from the cliff edge of extinction.

The first thing he did was to find a fitting name for them, because Moorit Shetland was inaccurate as well as confusing. Eventually he settled on Castlemilk Moorit as a tribute to their Dumfriesshire heritage – they'd been raised in the shadow of Sir Jock's towered, turreted old baronial mansion on the banks of a wonderfully-named salmon fishing river called the Water of

Milk which flows into the Annan. Dad knew it was vital to start a flock book, set up a breed society and to get the sheep registered with the Rare Breeds Survival Trust, which in turn would open the door to encouraging ownership, promote breeding and safeguard the sheep's future. It took 13 years to achieve all that, but the result is a UK population of around a thousand breeding Castlemilk Moorits today, and every one of them is descended from the small handful of lucky survivors that tottered from that trailer in front of my astonished father in the autumn of 1970.

It is heritage like that which appeals to Stuart and Lynda Jarvis. They have a flock of 40 Castlemilks, if you include their latest fall of lambs, which they describe with a roll of the eyes as their 'full-time' hobby. 'We wanted to do our bit for conservation,' says Lynda. 'But they have a character and spirit about them, so although you can halter train them to appear in competitions, the more shows you go to, the more badly behaved they become.'

Life for Stuart as a breeder of rare British sheep couldn't be more different from his old job as a miner in the Yorkshire coalfields, and he admits to being the one responsible for the couple's love affair with Castlemilk Moorits. In 2011 he decided to spend a day visiting the annual Rare Breeds Sale and Show at Melton Mowbray, the biggest event of its kind in the entire UK, and he went with some strict instructions from Lynda ringing in his ears: 'don't buy anything!' He came back home that night with three ewes, a pair of lambs and a wallet that was £200 lighter. The attraction was partly what Stuart calls the breed's 'wildness' – a trait that can cause problems in the field: 'They'll often boss the dog, so when you pen them up you need to use something that takes charge of them, like a border collie. You just can't do it if you've got a dog that dilly-dallies.'

While the Jarvises don't need telling how special the Castlemilk is, there are other people who apparently do. Perhaps it's their relative obscurity, their low numbers (fewer than 1,500) or the fact that they don't have a centuries-old history like many of the other native breeds, but the Castlemilk Moorit could certainly benefit from a publicity campaign. Stuart and Lynda are often met with puzzled looks and backhanded compliments when they show off their flock. They talk about the time they won first prize at a livestock show in the Yorkshire Dales. A dedicated Swaledale sheep breeder ran after them pointing at their champion ewe: 'I'll tell yer what, it's a hell of a thing – but what is it?' When they told him, he replied with a frown, 'Castlemilk Moorit yer say? Never 'eard of it.' Then there was the interbreed judge at the Driffield Show who was full of blunt admiration. 'I don't know what it is,' he bravely admitted, 'but it's in bloody good nick.'

Scotland can proudly boast the oldest British breed and our longest living link with the past. It's not a rough, tough cattle breed like the Highland or the Belted Galloway though, and it doesn't come from the mainland. Instead we have to go offshore to a remote chain of islands and sea stacks in the stormy North Atlantic.

Forty miles further out to sea than the main isles of the Outer Hebrides, the St Kilda archipelago is heaven for natural history buffs. Together the islands of Hirta, Dùn, Soay and Boreray have the highest sea cliffs anywhere in the UK. The islands are home to a million seabirds, including the UK's largest colonies of Fulmars and Atlantic puffins and one of the world's biggest gatherings of gannets, as well as a unique species of wren and their own type of mouse. That's before we even get to the dolphins and minke whales which regularly visit the seas around the islands. David Attenborough would have a field day and enough material for a whole new TV series. But the islands have held a life-long fascination for me because they are the home of the very first breed we find in Britain and the most ancient sheep of them all. When you look a Soay ram in the eye, you're gazing back 5,000 years. They're descended from the ancestors of all our native sheep, the first kind to evolve from hair to fleece and what's left of the primitive breed that was once spread all over Northern Europe. Soay sheep have managed to remain unchanged since Iron Age times by being isolated from other breeds, so far off the north-west coast of Scotland. Fittingly the word Soay comes from the Old Norse for 'island of sheep' and from the Scottish Gaelic, Sòthaigh.

They're very small sheep with white bellies and white patches round their short tails, just like deer. Both sexes sport great curved horns which dominate the slender heads of these very canny little animals. They're much more like wild animals than domestic sheep. The Soay comes in two different shades of brown with the wool only growing two or three inches long in winter and it's then shed in the spring, when they look very mangy with long strands hanging off them. It doesn't sound as if it would be much use, but Soay wool is becoming quite popular with hand-knitters, and if you like the taste of gamey-flavoured mutton, it's worth giving Soay meat a try.

On the island, their main predators were seabirds, which were bold enough to take the newborn lambs, so just like a primitive population of deer or even the enormous herds of wildebeest on the great plains of Africa, it was vital that all the females gave birth at the same time. This was all about creating safety in numbers and an example of Charles Darwin's great theory of natural selection in practice with the Soay ewes all lambing within a few days of each other to lessen the chance of a kill from above.

The Soay has a close cousin on a nearby island in St Kilda, the Boreray sheep, which is similar in shape and size to the Soay but has a different ancestry. Their speckled, black or tan-coloured faces peer out from a fleece that's mostly creamy white and they developed from an old breed called the Scottish Dunface which died out completely in the 1880s. If you want to know why the Boreray is so appealing, just ask the Duke of Rothesay, the Earl of Carrick, Baron of Renfrew and Lord of the Isles – or as he's better known when he's not in Scotland, the Prince of Wales. In the summer of 2018 he was presented with a two-month old Boreray lamb named Bryher to recognise his work as the patron of the Rare Breeds Survival Trust.

I'm aware that members of the Royal family are given thousands of gifts every year, many of them as a formality or out of courtesy and I'm sure after the official handover some are never seen again. But I know for a fact that Prince Charles has taken a personal interest in his Boreray sheep, in the same spirit that has led him to hand-pick Shetland geese, Scots Grey and Scots Dumpy chickens to help save them.

Shetland geese are small, meaty, white and grey-coloured wildfowl, which make good guard-geese if you can't afford a dog. The Scots Grey is a tall, upright bird that looks as if it's standing to attention, and from the 1500s onwards it was the hen of choice for cottagers and farmers' wives. The Scots Dumpy lives up to its name – its short legs means it waddles rather than struts, and it makes an excellent alarm clock (if you like to be woken by a cockerel crowing at the first hint of sun rise). Those three Scottish birds are just a few of the many native and rare breeds on HRH's conservation farm at Dumfries House, the country estate in Ayrshire he rescued and restored for the nation.

If you want to see the free-roaming feral sheep of St Kilda but don't have the stomach for a sea crossing, head instead for Somerset and set the sat nav for Cheddar Gorge. The Soay sheep population on the West Country's famous craggy limestone cliffs is thought to be at least a hundred and is probably more. No one knows for sure, because although the National Trust organises a sheep count every year, it's impossible to be accurate when your subject moves around or hides out of view.

Have the Soays been clinging to the rock in England's largest gorge for thousands of years? Not quite. The story villagers in Cheddar love to tell is that two rams and five ewes started the feral flock when they were abandoned there in 1992. The tale begins with a skint gambler who put the sheep up as his stake in a game of poker and when he lost, the winner took them home at the end of the night. But when the man's wife opened the bedroom curtains in the morning and saw seven woolly vandals eating their way through the garden, he was told in words of one syllable to get rid of them fast. So in desperation he secretly gave them their freedom in the gorge and they've multiplied happily ever since.

There's a 400-foot drop to the floor of the gorge, so I wouldn't recommend trying to capture one of Cheddar's wild Soays. But anyone curious about how they taste ought to know that you need to be familiar with eating game or venison to really appreciate Soay mutton. It has that same strong smell and flavour, so it's ideal if you like a dish that's big, rich and powerful on the palate. I've noticed that online butchers and meat box companies are beginning to do a decent trade in Soay lamb too, appealing to buyers watching what they eat and opting for something tender, lean and low in cholesterol.

Another isolated island breed, the North Ronaldsay sheep, also has a reputation for great-tasting meat and that's all down to their own peculiar eating habits. Whatever is said or written about them, the North Ronaldsay will forever be known as the seaweed-eating sheep. It's an evolutionary marvel and a unique trait that anyone used to seeing lambs nibbling on spring grass in gentle green meadows finds hard to believe. Yet they're almost taken for granted on the island in the Orkney archipelago which shares their name, as they roam along the shoreline, seeking out seaweed washed up by the powerful winds and strong tides. They live all year round on the narrow strip of stony beach around the island, blocked from straying inland by a 13-mile long, 6-foot high dry stone wall, or sheep dyke, which surrounds the island.

The breed's taste for seaweed came about more by necessity than by choice. The dyke was built in 1832 after the island's profitable kelp industry waned. Potash and soda from burning kelp had been a valuable commodity, with soap-factories and glass-makers willing to pay good money to fishermen and crofters for harvesting and preparing it. The laird of the island decided that the future lay in farming beef cattle and bigger, more profitable breeds of sheep. So the stone barrier went up to keep the North Ronaldsay flock away from the crofts and to protect the islanders' livelihoods.

Away from the more fertile grazing, large parts of the island are rocky rather than grassy and where there is greenery it can be sandy, while the rest could never be called lush. Banished to the beach, it was a case of 'needs must when the devil drives' for the native breed. The sheeps' odd diet has given them a digestive system and metabolism not seen in other sheep, but the down side is that they're incredibly sensitive to copper and if they're moved to unfamiliar grazing they are at risk of copper poisoning, which can kill them. There's another unusual characteristic which marks out the North Ronaldsay. The rams all have a fringe of coarse hair under their necks, the straggly strands resting on their chests in true hipster style. If it wasn't for their head-line-grabbing love of seaweed they'd almost certainly be famous for being Britain's weirdy beardy sheep.

These slender, primitive animals are part of the same family of ancient northern European sheep as the Soay, the Shetland and similar breeds from Finland, Sweden and Iceland; perhaps that's not surprising when you check out a map and see that the Orkney Islands are further north than the southern tip of Norway. The rams have curved horns, the fleece can be just about any colour from white through to black and the wool is shed naturally (although it can and does get plucked by hand and trimmed with shears). The sheep have survived in Orkney more or less unchanged since the days of their Bronze Age ancestors. They're an antique on legs for certain.

For me, though, the North Ronaldsay will always be associated in my mind with a wonderful adventure I shared with my dad when I was a little boy. Years later, he put his memories of the trip in writing for a magazine article:

The first major project of the Rare Breeds Survival Trust was to buy the Island of Linga Holm as an alternative sanctuary for the Orkney sheep of North Ronaldsay. I flew up to Orkney in 1974 and bought the Island for the Trust together with a ruined house on the shore of Stronsay overlooking Linga Holm. I returned the following year with my eight-year-old son Adam and we moved a hundred and twenty-five sheep to the island and brought a hundred sheep home to found flocks in England. Also twenty-five sheep went to the Island of Lihou off Guernsey. In 1997 I returned to North Ronaldsay for the first time and it brought back many happy memories.

They're happy memories for me too. The flickering home-movie footage of that trip has been shown on *Countryfile* several times and while it's lovely to see moving images of Dad in the prime of life, I hardly recognise the cheeky little ginger-haired boy beside him. In most of the footage I'm being buffeted by the bitterly cold winds that I remember whipped across the island constantly.

In 1974 we stayed with a well-known local couple, Tommy and Christine Muir, who are proud islanders and between them they probably know more about the place and its long, long history than anyone. Almost 40 years after that father and son mercy mission, Dad and I went back to make a TV film and we called in on the Muirs at their home to reminisce.

Christine isn't an Orcadian by birth, although you'd never know it from her love for and knowledge of her adoptive home. She's really a Leith lass but moved here when she married and then made a name for herself with exquisite word portraits of 'life as a farmer's wife on North Ronaldsay' which were published in the *Scotsman* newspaper. After all these years of watching and writing about them, Christine has worked out who's boss: 'The sheep are so ancient that you can tell by the way they stare at you that *they* own the place, not people.'

My return to North Ronaldsay wasn't just a nostalgia trip though. I got my hands dirty helping the islanders with an annual tradition. It's called punding. Along the sheep dyke there are large loops in the construction which form stone pens, or punds. The sheep only leave the shoreline for lambing and shearing, but herding them into the punds to do it takes a heck of a lot of effort. So the locals form a line right across the beach and walk forward, driving the sheep towards the pens. Once they were in, I sat down with a pair of hand shears and joined the others in giving the flock a swift check and a short back and sides.

The whole order of livestock management on the island, and the purity of the North Ronaldsay's genes, relies on that sheep dyke doing its job at keeping the flock in its place. It was a system put at serious risk in the terrible winter of 2012/13 by a succession of fierce storms and rip tides which brought large sections of the dry stone wall crashing down. I was shocked at the devastation wrought by the sheer power of Mother Nature as I stepped through long stretches of the wall that had been smashed by huge waves, scattering the heavy stones like toy bricks.

Finding willing volunteers with the required muscle-power to repair the dyke was easy in the days when 500 or 600 people lived on the island. Not so now, when the population is nearer 50. I did what little I could, joining a small working party of helpers piecing several yards of the dyke back together like a giant, never-ending jigsaw. On one side of me was a gentleman celebrating his seventy-ninth birthday that day and on the other, the great-great-great granddaughter of the laird who'd originally ordered the building of the wall. You'll be relieved to know that the mammoth rebuilding job wasn't just down to me. After years of hard graft by people from all over Scotland and beyond, the dyke is looking more like it should once again. What's more, a new tradition has been created. Every year the North

Ronaldsay Sheep Festival brings people from all over the world to the island to help rebuild and maintain the wall while they enjoy a fortnight of music, dancing, food and even football.

The North Ronaldsay sheep might be the pride of the most northerly of the Orkney Islands, but as Dad recalled, they also gained a foothold 900 miles away in our most southerly isles too. Lihou is a rocky tidal outcrop off the west coast of Guernsey which can only be reached on foot for about two weeks every month by way of a stone causeway which is exposed at low water. It's a stunningly tranquil spot and the only signs of human interference are an old farmhouse and the ruins of a 900-year-old Benedictine priory, which are surrounded by oystercatchers, peregrine falcons and visiting grey herons.

My dad's dedicated and loyal shepherd, Robert Boodle, remembers that relocating the North Ronaldsay flock here didn't go exactly to plan: 'Unfortunately these sheep were so used to paddling in the sea that when the tide was low they decided to head for the main island and they got into the famous Guernsey tomato crop.' This feral flock of trespassing North Ronaldsays caused a huge fuss at the time and, after the tomato fiasco had died down, there were demands for the flock to be banned. Anybody else would have been left thoroughly embarrassed, but Robert recalls the incident actually worked in Dad's favour: 'It gave him publicity, because he was one of those people who could bring the newspapers on board, so people would get interested in rare breeds and that achieved his great aim.' That was Dad all over – the master craftsman at turning a negative into an undeniable positive. It helped that he was a man who knew exactly what he thought on any subject, and clarity like that was evident when he went on TV in the 1970s to talk about the North Ronaldsays: 'Who is to say that in the hungry, overcrowded world of tomorrow a breed of sheep which can turn seaweed into mutton and wool might not be very useful?'

Mutton that's very tasty, as it happens. The meat of the North Ronaldsay is lean, gamey and delicious. It tastes similar to wild duck and comes with the sort of gourmet reputation normally reserved for caviar or truffles. It's such a treat that it's been given the celebrity chef seal of approval by Gary Rhodes, the Hairy Bikers and my old friend Cyrus Todiwala, who have all gone public with their love for cooking with North Ronaldsay lamb, hogget and mutton. Cyrus went even further and put North Ronaldsay mutton at the heart of a specially created dish which he cooked for the Queen to celebrate her Diamond Jubilee. As only he can, Cyrus gave a spicy twist to the classic shepherd's pie and presented Her Majesty with his cumin, coriander and chilli infused version of a slow-cooked favourite called The Country Captain. Feeding the monarch is a special privilege that would put anybody under intense pressure but I do know that Cyrus had nothing to worry about because the Queen and Prince Phillip loved what he'd done with that North Ronaldsay mutton. After getting the royal thumbs-up, the recipe was featured on BBC One's *Saturday Kitchen* and was added to the menu at Mr Todiwala's Café Spice Namaste restaurant in London. That's not bad for a breed that is little-known outside Scotland and one which could so easily have been left to wither away and die.

I don't know for sure if my love for the island of North Ronaldsay is because its native sheep played such an important role in my formative years. Perhaps my fondness for the sheep came about because of the pull of the island. Whatever was first, there's certainly a magical draw to the place which calls you back. In Orkney they have a saying; 'You will return. It is a sweet compulsion.'

If you want to win Rare Breeds top trumps, then you must have hold of the Shetland card. It would be hard to find a place that betters it. The hundred sub-arctic islands and outcrops that sit halfway between Scotland and Scandinavia are the most remote, and most northerly, part of the UK. Twelve hours by boat from Aberdeen, Shetland is much more than just knitwear, the Northern Lights and the backdrop for a tense TV crime series. It's a hotbed of farm breeds with a remarkable number of species, past and present. The most famous is the Shetland pony. But there's also Shetland sheep, cattle, duck, geese and even the Shetland sheepdog (a small herding dog that's known by everyone as the Sheltie). Although, the list is only truly complete if you include the breeds that are now extinct. They are two local sheep varieties – the Papa Stour and the St Rona's Hill – and lastly the most mysterious beast of them all, a fearsome pig called the Grice. It was the size of a large dog, covered in black bristles with curved tusks and a bad habit of killing lambs. It sounds like a charmer. But no one alive today has ever seen one; it died out in the 1800s.

The array of Shetland breeds past and present shows a wonderful diversity of livestock unique in the British Isles, but what they all have in common is a natural toughness. It's in the genes of all the natives (human and animal), because while the landscape here is utterly beautiful it's also rugged and harsh, battered by the elements and often gloomy during the long, dark days of winter.

At first glance, though, the Shetland pony doesn't look much like a robust, hard-nosed, all-weather sort of animal. For a start, they remind you too much of the 'fat little ponies' in Norman Thelwell's horsey cartoons: short and squat with an unruly, hairy mane. But closer inspection reveals a coat that adapts to the weather. In the summer it's soft and silky with a lovely sheen, but in the winter it becomes a double layer of thick insulation. That long mane and a generous tail also helps protect them from the toughest, bleakest conditions. Bones from the Bronze Age, identical to those of the Shetland pony, have been discovered during archaeological digs on the islands. It was around this point in history when the ponies would have been first tamed by our ancestors.

A Shetland can only be called a Shetland if it stands at 42 inches or less, but what they lack in height they make up for in strength. They have immense power, and, for their size, they're the strongest horse in the world. When you consider they have an inbred ability to survive on sparse, poor quality grazing, you get an idea of just what a phenomenal little creature this is. No wonder they were the nifty little shifters of Shetland and played such a vital role in island life into the Victorian era – pulling ploughs and carts, harrowing the fields and bringing fuel home to the crofts. Fishermen even used the pony's tail hairs to attach the hooks to their lines.

But dark times were around the corner. Literally. When children were banned from working in coal mines in 1847, they were replaced by Shetlands which were rounded up and taken off the islands by boat before starting new lives underground as pit ponies. The knock-on effect back in Shetland was a severe drop in the number of quality stallions, until the 1880s when studs were set up to breed new stock. Now in the modern world they have a new job as the children's pony of choice, not just in the UK but all round the globe, and that role has secured the Shetland pony's future. Not a rare breed but definitely a remarkable one.

You could have a long and heated pub discussion over which Scottish equine breed is the most famous. I'd happily bet my beer money on the Shetland pony but there are several others. The next best known is probably the Highland pony. This is the mountain and moorland breed, known for its stamina and sturdiness, and used for everything from carriage driving to logging in British woodland. Tracing its ancestry isn't easy though. The modern Highland is a genetic jumble. It starts straightforwardly enough, derived from the same basic group of equines as the Shetland. Then later on, Spanish and French blood was introduced from breeds like the mighty draught horse, the Percheron. There's a theory that Arab, Norwegian and the now-extinct Norfolk Trotter influenced the Highland at some point, along with suggestions of nineteenth-century breeding involving the Fell and Dales ponies. Got all that? Thankfully there's a footnote in the Highland's history which is much easier to fathom. If you've ever been pony trekking, on whatever type of mount, you've got the Highland to thank.

The pastime was invented in Inverness-shire in 1952 when a string of ponies belonging to Ewan Ormiston set off from the Balavil Arms Hotel at Newtonmore. Ewan's family had been breeding Highlands since the mid-1800s and the first treks took the riders and their ponies out of the town to the woodland edges, across the still, shallow river and along the lower slopes of the Monadhliath mountains with views of the Cairngorms off in the distance. With a start like that, it wasn't going to be long before 'Holidays on Horseback' caught on nationwide.

All the horse breeds of Scotland have been put to good use and earned their keep down the centuries, but only one is known as the working-class hero. Two hundred years ago, farmers in Lanarkshire realised that to do their job effectively they needed a helping hand – or to be strictly accurate, four helping hoofs. The industrial boom in Glasgow brought many more mouths to feed, which in turn meant farms had to grow more food and move it more quickly. The answer was a draught animal fit for the task. The Clydesdale is a big, elegant-looking horse with a straight nose, finely-feathered legs and a high step which makes them look almost theatrical. But there's strength beneath the showiness. They became the power behind Victorian agriculture and industry, pulling ploughs, carts, grocery vans and brewery drays; working in quarries, docks and forests, seen everywhere from hay fields and towpaths to coal yards and dairies.

Then came the First World War and an unimaginable role. Heavy horses were desperately needed for transporting supplies and ammunition in France and Belgium to support the British forces. In total, about a million horses were bought, borrowed or requisitioned by the War Office and ended up amid the bombs, blood, mud and madness of the trenches along the Western Front and in the other battle zones. Most never came home.

After the peace, another killer blow was the mechanisation of British farming as tractors gradually replaced teams of working horses. There wasn't much room for sentiment and, as farmers were being reminded, 'tractors don't need feeding or mucking out'.

There have been good times too and plenty of them. When prohibition ended in the United States in 1933, it was a team of Clydesdales who helped mark the occasion for the American nation. The first crates of post-prohibition Budweiser beer were delivered to President Franklin D. Roosevelt at the White House on a large wagon pulled by six beautiful Clydesdales, the horses belonging to the brewing magnet August A. Busch Snr. The great Scottish work horse has also taken part in two presidential inauguration parades in Washington, first for Harry S. Truman in 1949 and again for Bill Clinton in 1993. Back in Scotland there's evidence of what could be an even greater honour. Serious enthusiasts claim that the comic book hero of *The Dandy*, Desperate Dan, canters around Cactusville on what looks remarkably like a cartoon Clydesdale horse. The character is published by a Dundee-based company, DC Thomson, so they may well be right.

The last of the Scottish equines is the placid little Eriskay pony. It's last only because it's the least known of them all. The island of Eriskay is in the Outer Hebrides and it's where Bonnie Prince Charlie first set foot on Scottish soil in his failed attempt to seize the British throne in 1745, getting a beating at the Battle of Culloden. The Eriskay ponies are small, nearly always grey in colour with a thick, waterproof coat to protect them from the worst that the Hebridean weather can throw their way. They were used as pack animals by generations of crofters who slung large wicker baskets over their backs to carry home peat or seaweed and they even ferried small children to and from school. Then the motor engine came along, and by the 1970s there were just twenty Eriskays left, which spurred the local priest and the island's doctor to rally local people into promoting the pony and setting up a breeding programme. Things have improved in the decades since, but there are still fewer than 300 females, so a world without the enigmatic Eriskay pony remains a possibility.

In the *Countryfile* office in Bristol arrangements had been made for me to meet a couple of exceptional young people on Shetland, Kirsty and Aimee Budge, who had made it to the finals of the BBC Food and Farming Awards. I love the Scottish islands, the atmosphere is so different from the landlocked Cotswolds of home, so I didn't need asking twice. This time I had a companion. Joining me on the long journey north was my fellow awards judge, good friend and *Countryfile* co-presenter, Charlotte Smith. We've known each other since my early days on the programme. In fact, she helped me get the job in the first place, giving me lots of tips about camera technique on the day all the finalists for the new presenter were put through our paces for selection. She's a phenomenal journalist and for a long time she's been the voice that wakes up the nation as one of the presenters of *Farming Today* on BBC Radio 4. Charlotte and I have become a bit of a double act, making three or four films together every year as we go around the country meeting the contenders for the *Countryfile* Farming Hero Award.

Kirsty and Aimee are sisters and had been nominated after they successfully took on the running of the family farm after their dad was tragically killed in an accident. At the time Kirsty was 21 and Aimee was only 17. It was truly humbling to see what they had both achieved, when it would have been so much easier to walk away from the responsibility. Their grit and sense of duty moved so many people and a few weeks after our visit they very deservedly won the award.

Wherever I go I've always got half an eye on the livestock nearby, and I noticed that the Budge sisters used the little native Shetland sheep to cross with Cheviots, a breed from the border country. Their flock of almost 250 ewes graze on the stunning little island of St Ninian's which is linked to the farm on South Mainland by a sandy causeway. If my ewes back home could see it, they would be incredibly jealous.

A little known fact: not only is the Shetland Britain's smallest sheep, it's the only one with a criminal record for homicide in the US. I don't know how Shetland sheep ended up grazing in front of the White House in Washington D.C., but there are plenty of people who'll insist that they were a favourite with the author of the American Declaration of Independence and the third US President, Thomas Jefferson. He was a farmer and plantation owner in Virginia but after his election to the White House in 1801, it sounds as if he was struck by a bout of chronic homesickness for the Blue Ridge Mountains and his life in the country. He brought 40 Shetlands to the capital and kept them on the President's Square within sight of his window. It must have been a very rustic and peaceful scene, except for the fact that the flock included an unusual four-horned ram with some serious anger management issues. Jefferson was impressed by 'this round and beautiful animal' but its handsome looks disguised a terrible temper. The ram was fiercely territorial and caused mayhem, attacking and injuring several passers-by who strayed too close. The final straw came when the Shetland charged at a small boy who wandered near the lawn. The child was killed in the attack and the ram was swiftly exiled to the President's Virginia estate where it carried on its vendetta by fatally wounding other sheep until it had to be put down.

Unlike Thomas Jefferson, Tony Bennett wasn't the least bit interested in Shetland sheep. He was originally a keeper of chickens, up in Ramsbottom on the West Pennine Moors. Then one fateful day in 1989 he went to buy a Shetland duck. He was intrigued by these busy little black birds and especially their reputation for laying large eggs – and lots of them. But the duck breeder he met also had a small flock of Shetland sheep and Tony was immediately smitten. 'I just couldn't get over the fact they were all different colours.' His face breaks into a broad smile as he shares his theory that the multi-coloured Fair Isle jumper came about because the crofters weren't able to catch the same sheep two days running, so made a virtue of their sackful of mix 'n' match fleeces. Though there's a growing appreciation of the Shetland as a meat sheep, it's all about the wool for Tony. 'I think Shetland is the finest wool in Britain and it could be as popular and as good as alpaca or merino,' he tells me, before explaining that for every ball of wool he sells from his flock of 30 Shetlands, he makes about two pounds in profit. To me it doesn't seem much return for all the effort involved, but if there's one thing I've worked out about Tony, it's that he's a fair man. 'When it comes to the wool we only play at it, but we like to play properly.'

The best advert for this beautiful, natural fibre is the often-heard claim that a four-foot-square Shetland wool shawl can be pulled through a wedding ring. For a moment I thought about asking Tony to show me if it's true, but instead I asked him how he feels about breeding a primitive Scottish sheep when he lives in England. 'Shetland is dull, damp and dark,' he says with a twinkle, 'and so is Lancashire, it's very similar.'

As we're about to say goodbye, Tony hands me a gift. It's a Shetland Breed Society memento which I can tell fills him with pride. Rolled up in a cardboard tube is a poster showing row after row of identical outlines of the same Shetland sheep. But that's the only thing the little sketches have in common, because the colours and markings on each picture are all different, illustrating the 603 recorded variations in the breed. It truly is a work of art and a symbol of dedication to the cause. The markings have evocative and mysterious Viking-sounding names, from Bersugget (random patches of different colours) all the way to Yuglet (a separate colour around the eyes). It's a diversity which must surely make the breed unique and, as someone who has campaigned to promote British wool, seeing all this variety on one chart really appeals to me. Looking at this I can really appreciate how Tony's head was turned on the day he brought home a Shetland sheep instead of a Shetland duck.

There's a similar fascination with markings for fans of the small, hardy and horned Shetland cattle. Especially for Mary Knibbs who has been breeding them for the last 15 years. 'I love the different colours,' she tells me, almost as if it's a secret. 'When they calve you never quite know what you're going to get.' These small, slender good-natured cattle are usually black or black and white, but they can also be dun, grey, red and blue-necked, or any combination of those colours. So you can see why Mary enjoys the lottery of calving time. Historically isolated on the islands from all other cattle they become the crofters' cow, with families owning two or three to supply them with meat, milk, butter and cheese. Mary tells me a tale of Shetland cattle that I've never heard before. Apparently when the old crofters sold one, they would tear off a piece of their apron which went with the cow to its new home to pacify it, like a comfort blanket. By all accounts it's a custom that worked a treat at calming them down and made milking far easier.

Being so far from the mainland, Shetland cattle became working animals too, and in the early 1800s there were around 15,000 pure-bred cattle in Shetland. Of course, it couldn't last. By the 1950s a shrinking human population and the arrival of tractors to do the heaviest work on the land meant there were only about 40 pure Shetlands left on the islands. Now, thanks to some great work to promote them for cross-breeding, as beef animals and as conservation grazers, the national herd of pure Shetlands is up to 1,500, with about half of them on the mainland.

The breed is now truly transatlantic too. A milestone was achieved in 2018 when a red bull calf named Magnus became the first Shetland to be born in America, from embryos created in the UK and implanted into surrogate cows. Two heifer calves, Athena and Anabella, followed soon afterwards and hopes are high that after years of planning, this little foundation herd in Texas will flourish.

A Black Wensleydale. Britain's rare and native breeds have diverse and unique characteristics.

The Longhorn has been called 'pure beef on the hoof' and 'the perfect example of a British breed.'

A Highland cow and calf in a heart-warming display of motherly love.

In the age of the cattle drovers, highly visible Belted Galloways were used to pinpoint a herd's progress on dark and gloomy days.

My sister Libby with a Henson family success story – the Castlemilk Moorit sheep.

The Soay sheep is history on legs. It's our most primitive breed with a direct link back to the Stone Age.

Every spring hundreds of rare and native breed lambs are born at Bemborough including the cute Borerays.

Dad with one of the first North Ronaldsay sheep introduced to the Cotswold Farm Park from the Orkney Islands.

Shetland sheep produce the finest wool of any British breed – as soft as silk but as strong as cotton.

The brown Manx Loaghtan and black Hebridean are impressive, multi-horned breeds.

Dexter cattle are usually black but sometimes red.

The living plough – Dad's business partner, John Neave, training White Park and Gloucester oxen, which we used for films and shows.

The pride of Staffordshire. The Tamworth is the pig which it's thought most resembles the old English forest swine.

Joe Henson – the animal 'anorak' who became a conservation pioneer, with Old English Goats.

Britain's newest 'old' breed. Albion cattle at home on the Cotswold Farm Park.

Simple Soay

Serves: 4

2–3 onions, sliced
1 whole leg of Soay lamb, 1.25kg (2Ib 12oz)
olive oil, for brushing
4–5 tomatoes, sliced
good handful of roughly chopped parsley
salt and black pepper

To serve
new potatoes
mint sauce

1. Preheat the oven to 230°C/450°F/gas 8.
2. Place a layer of sliced onions in a large roasting pan as a bed for the lamb. The bed should be sufficient for the leg to lie on.
3. Place the leg on the bed of onions and brush the top and sides with olive oil.
4. Season well with salt and black pepper and then place slices of tomato over the lamb, overlapping to provide a good covering. Sprinkle over the chopped parsley.
5. Place in the preheated oven and cook for 10 minutes, then lower the oven temperature to 180°C/350°F/gas 4 and then cook for a further 60 minutes or until cooked to your liking.

Tips: To work out the cooking time for a bigger or smaller leg of lamb, the cooking time equates to 26 minutes per 450g (1lb) plus 15 minutes over. You can serve the onions with the lamb or add them to a soup stock or casserole, if you prefer.

Iain Forbes, Bradford on Avon
The Rare Breeds Survival Trust

CHAPTER 7

An Island and Two Irelands

M eet a living, breathing hat stand. The Manx Loaghtan is a true island survivor, a primitive lean sheep from the Isle of Man and one of the most striking native breeds you'll ever see. They're small animals with long legs and naturally short tails and they can boast some truly impressive headwear – a set of two, four or even six horns. Both the males and the females sport these fearsome looking horns but of course it's the rams which use them as a weapon of attack and defence in the battle of supremacy over a mate. Although having four horns, or more, is actually a bit of a hindrance if you're an aggressive ram; males that are up for a fight will often do more damage to themselves than to their rivals.

The four horned characteristic is thought to be a Viking trait making the Manx at least 1,200 years old and probably much older. The Norsemen were famously keen on using horn for making all sorts of instruments and drinking vessels and one theory is that they'd have wanted livestock that gave them a ready supply of the raw material. Although, the one thing we were all taught about the Viking invaders, that they wore horned helmets, is apparently completely untrue and a story invented later to make them sound more bloodthirsty and terrifying. It seems that Noggin the Nog got it wrong.

In North America the Navajo people also have a breed of multi-horned sheep which play an important spiritual role in their culture. Four is considered to be a sacred number; there are four directions, four winds, four seasons, four original clans and four sacred mountains. So another, more likely reason for the Manx Loaghtan's impressive horns is that they also had some sort of religious significance for the Scandinavian seafarers.

Manx wool is short, self-shedding and rich in the naturally waxy lanolin that makes it so soft to touch. The colours of the fleece used to include black, grey and white until it was realised that clothing made from one shade of wool was valued more highly than the rest. So brown sheep won out and that's the colour that was selected to satisfy local spinners and weavers. The Manx Loaghtan has a literal, descriptive name, just like White Park Cattle (white cattle in parks) and Gloucestershire Old Spots pigs (old spotted pigs from Gloucestershire). Manx refers to the Isle of Man and Loaghtan describes their colour, made up of two local words – 'lugh' meaning mouse and 'dhoan' which means brown.

The mouse brown Manx sheep are nothing like their domesticated cousins on the mainland, such as the gentle, lazy breeds that thrive in England's southern counties. No, Manx Loaghtans are canny and bright-eyed; they live feral on the Calf of Man and deal with the wild winter storms with little or no shepherding from one end of the year to the next. They're also surprisingly fast and athletic with a flair for scurrying up steep slopes and leaping over fences. Speaking as someone who has to catch Manx Loaghtans on a regular basis, I've had a few bruises that can vouch for their nimbleness.

Until the eighteenth century they roamed the hills of the Isle of Man in their thousands, but numbers dwindled as more profitable, commercial breeds were favoured and several times in the last couple of centuries they've faced being wiped out completely. In the 1950s there was just a handful left. Salvation for these unique sheep came in 1973 with the creation of the Rare Breeds Survival Trust. The charity raised the profile of the Manx Loaghtan and the peril they were in, and set about encouraging their conservation and stepping up breeding programmes among a handful of owners. Their dedication paid off so that today, while the Manx Loaghtan is still classed as an 'at risk' breed, there are up to 1,500 breeding ewes in flocks both on the Isle of Man and throughout the UK.

Mad motorcyclists burning rubber around the TT race course is the global image of the Isle of Man, but on the island itself, the native horned herbivores are an important symbol of local identity, and as if to prove the point one of the most talked about attractions of the last few years has been an enormous wooden sculpture of a Manx Loaghtan.

Before I landed at the capital, Douglas, I'd been told to make time for a pilgrimage to the Snaefell mountain road, overlooking a stretch of the TT course, to see this unusual new landmark. Rare breeds don't often inspire gigantic public works of art, so I wasn't going to miss the spectacle, and I wasn't disappointed. Anchored into the ground by thick carved legs, it must have been 25 feet tall. Standing beside it and looking up at the Loaghtan's big wooden features, its strong head slightly turned with four long horns, made me feel pint-sized by comparison. The artists, Darren Jackson and Stephanie Quayle, used a steel frame for the main body of the sculpture and covered it in greenery which hung down just like a fleece.

Not as tall as the sheep sculpture but just as memorable is a character called Loki the Loaghtan. Most football teams have a club mascot; it's usually a man dressed in a bird, bear or lion costume (depending on the squad's nickname) whose job is to play the fool in front of the home crowd before kick-off. The Isle of Man's capital, Douglas, has an official town mascot. Loki is soft and brown with an extremely short Manx tartan waistcoat and a pair of curly horns, which short changes him a bit in the headwear stakes but probably keeps him on the right side of mascot health and safety rules. Loki's first outing was on St Valentine's Day in 2017, giving red roses to shoppers in the town centre, and he's been part of parades and PR events of all descriptions. Loki the Manx Loaghtan has certainly become a talking point in the island's capital, and many years ago the real thing got tongues wagging back home in the Cotswolds, too.

In the early days of the Farm Park, when Dad's dream of making his rare breeds pay had started to become a reality, his business partner John decided he had enough money to indulge in a new hobby. He started taking flying lessons from the small commercial airport at Staverton near Gloucester, about 20 miles from the farm. It didn't take him long to get his full pilot's licence, and once he was 'legal', one of his first solo flights was to the Isle of Man to collect a four-horned Manx Loaghtan ram lamb for Dad. On his return, he landed the little prop plane on a field on the edge of the farm and emerged carrying a crate containing his precious, bleating cargo. It seemed a very glamorous way of transporting livestock, and it definitely gave the neighbours and our farming friends something to talk about for years afterwards. Until the flying ram arrived we only had a little mob of decidedly non-pedigree Manx ewes, but thanks to John's excursion over the Irish Sea we were able to make a start on a flock of pure-bred Loaghtans, which are still at the heart of the Farm Park today.

'Early June in Northern Ireland. The fields are flush with new green. Warm air moves across the land. And through it all, rivers glide cool and slow.' It's a pearl of a description, isn't it? Those honeyed remarks are from the opening moments of a summer edition of *Countryfile*; poetic scene-setting like that is a trademark of the show but equally it could have come straight from the publicity department at the Northern Ireland tourism board. It's a perfectly accurate picture of the north, but not one that was heard much when I was growing up in the 1970s, or around the time I was starting my working life in the 1980s. This was when the Troubles were at their height and the grim, grizzly reality of bullets and bombs seemed to be headline news every day. As a boy living in an isolated area in the west of England my only impressions of Northern Ireland were formed from grainy film footage of rifles, roadblocks and riots, and what seemed to be a political conundrum I couldn't even begin to understand. It was as if war, or something very much like it, was on the doorstep.

Not anymore. Since then, an entire generation has grown up in relative peace, never exposed to the kind of violence which their parents and grandparents witnessed, either in person or on TV night after night. Now, at long last, the Northern Ireland that's remarkable for its green glens, lofty mountain ranges, granite tors, waterfalls, woodlands and one of the most beautiful coastlines I've ever seen is getting the sort of attention it deserves. As if to prove it, the site of the notorious Maze prison near Lisburn is now a 65-acre showground that's home to the biggest and best-known rural event in Northern Ireland's tourism calendar, the Balmoral Show. Over four days in May, the event draws in a crowd of 150,000 people – visitor numbers which would be welcomed by many big agricultural shows on the UK mainland, but which seem even more impressive when you realise that Northern Ireland's entire population is below two million.

For the purposes of my study of the livestock of the British Isles I'm treating the two Irelands as one. That's partly because the border separating Northern Ireland and Eire was created long after the breeds on the island of Ireland were developed and established. There's also the fact that, over the centuries, farmers, breeders, stockmen and shepherds, like their livestock, moved from place to place.

Sometimes the grass really is greener – here that's more than simply a proverb, because mild winters, the kind Gulf Stream air and just the right amount of rain mean the grass does grow green, long and lush. Much of the country features flower-rich pastures that are perfect for grazing dairy cows that produce high quality milk. There's a reason why Irish butter sells so well. Dairy cows have long been the preferred livestock for thousands of farming families down the years, and herds still dot the fields and hillsides everywhere, north and south. When it comes to global reputation, the Republic has always punched well above its weight among the top ten dairy exporters in the world. Beef cattle too, that spend most of the year grazing in green, open fields in the fresh Irish air are famed for the full taste and fine texture of their meat. That's why Irish steak has an enviable standing across the globe.

But this island isn't solely the territory of beef and dairy herds. From the North Channel coast to the shores of the Celtic Sea, there's a long legacy of breeding sheep, horses and swine. The Ulster White was a popular bacon pig and it was easily the most common breed in the north of Ireland right up until the start of the Second World War.

Ulster is often used as an alternative term for Northern Ireland, but there's an important distinction. Ulster is a traditional Irish province that's made up of nine counties – the six counties that since 1921 have formed Northern Ireland and three which are part of the Republic of Ireland. Pigs are about as non-political as you can get, and the Ulster White was farmed right across the region, from Down to Donegal and beyond. It was a large, fatty, white-skinned pig with short, stubby legs and big pointed ears. It was an animal that paid its way too; a prolific breeder, it was useful, widespread and beloved. It's even been called the most economically efficient breed of all time, and I reckon if it had reached its peak of popularity in different times it would almost certainly have become an Ulster icon.

So the question is, if it was so favoured then why was it allowed to die out? The answer is changing tastes and changing times I'm afraid.

One problem for the breed was that they were such appalling travellers. They had notoriously thin skin so when they were loaded on to trucks or herded into railway wagons they had a tendency to bruise easily, just like a peach. Bruised meat wasn't acceptable for the Wiltshire curing process which used a 'wet' brine method and became popular in the inter-war years. The tenderness of the pig's flesh also made them totally unsuitable for live exports. Up until about the 1940s, it was common practice to slaughter pigs on the farm. But when the pork industry became more industrialised officials started frowning on home-slaughtering. In addition, the English Large White pig, originally from Yorkshire, was gaining in reputation with curers. Just before the Second World War, cash incentives were introduced to persuade Northern Ireland's farmers to raise Large White boars, and this really sounded the death knell for the Ulster breed.

The Ulster White isn't the only Irish pig we've lost over time. The Irish Greyhound pig was an unusual beast with an unusual name. Related to the wild swine which had lived in Irish forests since prehistoric times, it was first tamed by Stone Age farmers. From the Middle Ages right up until the dawn of the Victorian era, writers and travellers visiting Ireland remarked on how many pigs they saw, not just in the country but in coastal areas, town streets and even people's houses. The Greyhound name comes from their appearance: they were a grey-skinned narrow-bodied hog with sharp features and long legs that carried their slim bellies high off the ground. So they had hardly anything in common with the 'improved' pigs we're familiar with today. They were apparently ugly, bony and greedy as well with wattles hanging from their necks. It sounds like a beast that was difficult to love, and with not much to recommend the taste of their meat either, the last Irish Greyhound pig died around the beginning of the twentieth century. Nobody was shocked.

The smallest breed of cattle in the whole of the British Isles is the charming little Dexter. Originally an Irish breed, they were rare up until a recovery in their numbers gained pace in the last ten or twelve years. Less than half the size of the traditional Hereford, there's a reason why these friendly, dual purpose cattle are sometimes called dinky Dexters. And when they're standing next to the biggest, beefiest breeds in the land the difference can make for a great shot. There's newsreel footage taken at the Bath and West Show as long ago as 1933, where a tiny Dexter was filmed next to a massive champion South Devon bull, 'one of the biggest fellows in the show'.

The naming ritual for British breeds is uncomplicated and well-established. As has probably become obvious by now, they mainly take the name of their place of origin – such as in Shetland, Gloucester and

Ayrshire cattle or Orpington, Ixworth and Sussex chickens. Sometimes it's dictated by their most distinguishing feature, as with Longhorns, Shorthorns and Red Polls. Occasionally it's a combination of both, which gives us Welsh Black cattle, Greyface Dartmoor sheep and Oxford Sandy and Black pigs. But only a tiny handful of breeds are named after a person, although I don't know why pioneering farmers, livestock innovators and the nation's top breeders weren't honoured in this way more often.

The Khaki Campbell duck is a light brown bird developed by a Victorian lady called Adele Campbell in the Gloucestershire village of Uley. The Bagot goat was named in honour of Lord and Lady Bagot in the English Midlands. The one and only Biblical name to crop up belongs to Jacob sheep which are spotted and speckled, just like Jacob's flock in the Old Testament. The point I am leading up to is you can look as hard as you like on a map of Irish cattle-rearing country trying to find a place called Dexter, but you won't have any luck. The most modest-sized of all cattle breeds takes its name from a mysterious character known only as Mr Dexter.

We don't know much about him apart from the fact that he was the agent for the politician Lord Hawarden, and that he developed his little black breed with its 'roundness of form' and 'shortness of legs' from the tough cattle that lived in the hills and mountains around Tipperary. There's a suspicion that he was a man who liked to collect small livestock, specifically two types which, despite looking alike, actually have an important genetic difference – miniature cattle and dwarf cattle. Miniatures are bred to be intentionally small, and the appeal of keeping animals like them has never waned. Just look at the fashion over the last 20 years for keeping miniature horses, pygmy goats and 'micro' pigs. Mr Dexter's cows, however, were dwarf cattle – animals born with a congenital trait which caused disproportionate abnormalities, the most obvious being severely shortened legs. The logic behind Dexter's thinking was that two of his diminutive cows could be kept on the space it would usually take to rear one, and more cattle per acre made economic sense. Two of these small cattle don't eat much more than one larger cow, and by ensuring they calved at different times of the year a continuous supply of milk could be guaranteed. He was nothing if not ingenious.

We know about Dexter (the man) and the early days of Dexter (the breed) thanks to a foresighted writer called David Low. He was professor of agriculture at the University of Edinburgh and the man behind a book that's widely regarded as a sacred text in the farm animal world. When you flick through *The Breeds of the Domestic Animals of the British Isles* you're transported back to the 1840s in what can best be described as the first modern appreciation of many of our unique breeds and some of the earliest accounts of how they came about. There are glimpses of a time long past, with the cattle, sheep and ponies of Shetland referred to by their old name of 'the Zetland breeds'. Low's writing is all brought to life by finely detailed plate illustrations of everything from an Old English Cart horse and a West Highland ox to a beautifully engraved image of a 'South Down' ewe with a lamb by her side. It makes for somewhat sad reading too, when you learn about county breeds and local strains the Victorians cared for but which we've allowed to die out since. I'd have loved to have seen a Pink-nosed Somerset sheep!

The book is known colloquially simply as 'Low' and owning a copy is a matter of enormous pride for rare breeds fanatics. If you've got a first edition or you find one in an antiquarian bookshop or on an internet auction site, hold on to it. Not only are they valuable and historic but possessing one is like having access to the thoughts of the farmers of our great-great-grandparents' generation. The copy of Low that's been on the Henson bookshelf for decades is a precious family heirloom.

Low included a long section on Kerry cattle, the black dairy breed from south-west Ireland which was 'capable of subsisting on scanty fare' and has always been popular with cheese and yoghurt makers. The Kerry is related to the Dexter through genetics that according to Irish mythology go back to the ancient black cattle of the Celts.

It stands to reason that the Dexter is light on its feet. They were built nimble so they could survive on sparse mountain pasture and seek food in rocky or boggy places where heavier, modern breeds come a cropper. That thriftiness proved to be the Dexter's saving grace in the Irish fodder crisis of 2013. A long, cold winter and terrible weather the following spring saturated the ground which meant there just wasn't enough grass in the fields and valley pastures to feed every animal. Food stores emptied quickly, extra silage was in drastically short supply, some farmers were bankrupted and there were animals which literally starved to death. But the Dexter escaped the worst of the desperate situation due to that inbuilt ability to find and thrive on even the poorest grazing.

Dexters have a hardiness and a resilience about them that's probably only bettered in Ireland by the Kerry Bog pony. Originally wild animals, the moorland ponies were eventually tamed and used as pack animals to carry peat from the bogs or seaweed from the shoreline into the villages. A thick mane, a long winter coat and an impressive ability to walk on wet, unstable ground makes them fantastic all-weather survivors.

The Dexter also has something in common with a handful of other cattle breeds on the opposite side of the Irish Sea. I'm thinking in particular of the Highland and the Belted Galloway. They share with the Dexter the ability to be brilliant eco-cattle. If you need conservation grazing in Ireland and you want to keep it local then there's only one breed that will do the job.

I saw it for myself in south-west Ireland on a steep-sided nature reserve near the old walled town of Dingle.

The small fishing port has a population of a little over 2,000, but it has big town ambition and drive: Dingle not only fancies itself as the most westerly town in Europe with a lucrative tourist trade but it has also forged a new reputation as a top food destination with more than its fair portion of good restaurants and interesting eateries. The town sits on the Dingle peninsula, one of the five fingers of land that push out from the left-hand corner of Ireland as if they're offering a handshake to the North Atlantic. When you face the chill wind and look straight out to sea from here it's hard to believe that the next stop is America.

In this lush, rustic setting on the very edge of the British Isles it was equally difficult to imagine that there would be a place for anything as sophisticated as satellite technology. But sure enough, I was genuinely surprised to hear that some of the cattle used for conservation grazing here were fitted with GPS tracking collars to monitor their behaviour as they ate and the exact locations where they roamed in order to build up a picture of how and why they're so successful on such poor pasture.

Someone who's been a great ambassador for the Dexter over many years is the comedian, poet and old Henson family friend, Pam Ayres. She's joked, written, broadcast and even recited poems about her animals in the past. When Pam first became interested in keeping rare breeds she was, in her own words, 'a duffer' and did what so many novice breeders have done over the decades: turn to my dad for an encouraging word, a bit of straight-talking and some practical advice. She takes enormous delight in telling of the time she called Dad for a chat one evening, but was told by Mum on a very dodgy phone line that unfortunately he was out that night at his sewing club. Pam was taken aback at the idea that he was so actively involved in needlecraft and it was only later that she realised she'd misheard and that he'd actually been out discussing sheep at his *Soay* club. She might not have been familiar with Scottish island breeds, but Pam's own collection of animals thrived and grew to include Cotswold sheep, Old Spots and Tamworth pigs, ex-battery hens, guinea fowl, a hive of bees and Belted Galloway cattle as well as her beloved Dexters.

A pair of docile Dexters were also the innocent parties in a near catastrophe involving the Hensons on live TV. Whenever my dad's long, remarkable career is discussed there's almost always a mention of the fondly remembered children's TV programme *Animal Magic*. The show was launched in April 1962 when the *Radio Times* billed it as 'a fortnightly series in which Johnny Morris looks at Creatures Great and Small'. Over the course of the next 21 years it didn't stray an inch from its original mission to delight and enlighten youngsters of all ages about the wonders of the animal kingdom. I loved it and so did millions of others. Although describing Johnny Morris's act today to anyone under the age of about 45 is guaranteed to provoke a look of disbelief.

I'm not sure there are many TV executives now who would commission a middle-aged man to dress up as a zoo-keeper and do funny animal voices. Anthropomorphism might have fallen out of fashion in the media but old clips on the internet of 'keeper Morris' creating brilliant vocal characters for camels, gorillas and giraffes are as enchanting as ever. The great man was the king of the ad-libs and he's still revered at BBC Bristol where *Animal Magic* was produced and transmitted every week live from the legendary Studio A at Whiteladies Road.

The show gave my dad his break into television when he was 'discovered' by the show's producer, George Inger. He was a respected veteran of the BBC Natural History Unit who had heard about the Cotswold Farm Park and realised what great TV potential there was in the various rare breeds we had at Bemborough. At first the idea was that a crew would come to the farm and make a short film about us. But when the production team saw the rushes they were so impressed they wanted Dad to travel to Bristol with a couple of his animals and appear in the studio as well. But it didn't go quite as planned. My father was a great raconteur, so instead of my version of the story, here's how he recounted the tale in a radio interview years later:

We went into the Animal Magic studio early, rehearsed through the morning and I took in a little Dexter cow with a Dexter calf. The set-designers had made a make-believe farm fence so that Johnny Morris could stand on one side and I'd be on the other. I'd taken all four children with me and the producer asked if one of them could hold the calf while I held the cow, so of course I said yes. It was hot in the studio and there was that amazing feeling of nervous excitement that you only get with live TV.

The tension was building and before we knew it the gallery began counting us down. 'Five-four-three ...' and at that point my daughter Louise, who was holding the Dexter calf, turned to me and said 'Daddy, I'm going to faint.' Disaster! So just before the camera switched to us I handed the two ropes to Johnny, caught Louise in my arms and carried her behind some scenery, only just managing to get back on set in time to do the interview. But now, thinking back to how talented and versatile Johnny Morris was, it would have made much better television if I hadn't got back at all. He'd have interviewed the cow!

Thankfully that little drama didn't end Dad's TV career when it had barely begun, and it wasn't the last time he took a Dexter to the *Animal Magic* studio either.

Sadly there wasn't nearly as much interest from the media in another favourite from the Emerald Isle: Irish Moiled cattle. If you imagine a white cow splattered with reddish brown paint then you're not far off the mark. 'The small Moiled Cow for the small Irish hill farmer' was how they were described more than a hundred years ago. That phrase was heard so often that it became the motto of the breed society when it was founded in 1926 at a meeting in Belfast's imposing red-brick Old Town Hall by a group of breeders who called themselves the Irish Moiled Cattle Fanciers. It was a quaint expression even then and I think it's only homing pigeon enthusiasts and a select band of pedigree cat breeders who refer to themselves as fanciers nowadays.

The first Irish Moiled to be registered in the inaugural herd book was a bit of a veteran. It was claimed that 'Donegall Biddy' was a 23-year-old cow owned by a County Antrim farmer called John O'Neill. He reared his animals at Crumlin and there's a tantalising glimpse of his style of cattle farming in a single-line caption from volume one of the herd book: 'John likes the kind that can live among the rushes.' These cows were highly prized by owners like O'Neill and there was an old rural saying which demonstrates that special bond: 'Never buy a Moiled cow, never sell a Moiled cow and never be without a Moiled cow.'

The name is unusual, certainly to English ears, and as with so many breeds there's a difference of opinion over its exact origins. Moiled comes from *Maol* which is a Gaelic word that has been interpreted as meaning bald, hornless or domed. There's certainly no dispute about their lack of horns and the breed's outstanding characteristic is indeed the distinctive mound (or dome) on the top of their heads, just as if they were wearing school caps.

They're tough characters that live on rough pasture in boggy Irish countryside. Just by looking at them you can understand instantly why they were outclassed by continental beef breeds; they're relatively small, they haven't got much of a frame and their heritage as a milk-and-meat animal did them no favours in the face of foreign competition. Things got so desperate that in the 1970s there were fewer than 30 cows owned by just two farmers in Northern Ireland.

We didn't have Irish Moileds in our collection in Gloucestershire for many years, mainly because their colouring is very similar to the Longhorn. Although in some other important ways they couldn't be more different – Moilies are polled after all so there's no chance of horns, long or otherwise. But things changed at Bemborough when we were given a small herd to keep at the Farm Park. It marked a personal milestone for me, as they became the first rare cattle breed that I personally introduced to the farm after I took on my dad's livestock when he retired.

I know that beauty is in the eye of the beholder and all that, but there can't be many people who'd call this an attractive breed. Even the breed society agreed in a brutally honest guide to show judges in 1932: 'An Irish Moil may give one the appearance of ruggedness even to the extent of ugliness as compared with most other breeds.' But they have an appeal nonetheless and it's not just farmers or sentimentalists who have a thing about the Irish Moiled. They seem to be the livestock of choice for sculptors too, and after seeing the massive, motionless Manx Loaghtan on the Isle of Man, I'm wondering if this desire to recreate a living creature as a work of art is inspired by something in the Irish Sea breezes. Harriet Mead got to work with her angle grinder in 2012 to turn a heap of scrap metal into a life-sized Moilie for a museum at Dungannon.

Harriet is an artist who specialises in cutting and welding junk ironmongery to create life-sized models of animals, although she normally restricts herself to more manageable subjects like hares, stouts, skylarks and dragonflies. But she took on the challenge of making a full-scale cow with gusto, scooping up old scythes, sickles, lawn mower blades, prongs, beet forks and anything else she could lay her hands on. The udder was fashioned from shovels and a grocer's scales while a set of adjustable spanners were turned into teats. It's with good reason that Harriet calls these types of artwork her 'found objects' sculptures. One piece of discarded junk even gave the metal Moilie its nickname. There aren't many cows called 'Stanley' but there really wasn't any other option after she spotted that particular brand name stamped on an old blade that she'd used to make the forehead.

Harriet's love of nature may have been inherited from her famous father, the ornithologist Chris Mead. Sometimes called 'the Nightingale Man' after his affection for the loveliest songster of all woodland birds, he was kept so busy talking, writing and broadcasting about nature that for 40 years he was known as 'the voice of the British Trust for Ornithology'.

Stanley isn't the only large scale metalwork that Harriet has turned her hand to. She created Suffolk's celebrated trio of local breeds (horse, ram and bull) to stand guard at the entrance of the appropriately-named Trinity Park Showground near Ipswich and she sculpted a beautiful piece of public art called 'The Plough Horse and Man' which proudly marks the site of the old black-smith's forge in the village of Dromore, County Tyrone.

Another artist, Bob Johnston, was equally inspired to construct a life-size Irish Moiled, but for his creation he didn't need a welding torch and goggles. Bob is an award-winning craftsman and basket-maker who is well-known as one of the team of time-travellers who demonstrate the ways of the past to history-hungry visitors at the Ulster Folk and Transport Museum near Belfast. When the museum bosses were planning what to put on their exhibition stand at the annual Balmoral Show to pull in the punters, they plumped for a massive willow sculpture of an Irish Moiled bull.

The Balmoral dates back to the 1850s when, in the aftermath of the Great Famine, farmers gathered at the Belfast Corporation Markets on the banks of the River Lagan for their first ever show. The annual event holds a special importance for exhibitors and visitors alike, and it's a hugely valuable PR opportunity for everyone who takes part. So having your hard work placed as the cen-trepiece of any stand at the show is a really big deal. Bob's bull looked remarkably lifelike with the weave and flow of the willow rods looking just like a Moilie's thick winter coat. The sculpture was surrounded by blacksmithing demos and basket-making displays to give it some proper historical context, and it attracted something that would have left the visitors to that first Victorian agricultural show in Belfast town utterly mystified: a procession of people waving smartphones and holding selfie-sticks. I don't know for sure what the number one most-tweeted image from the show was, but it's a fair bet that Bob's willow handiwork was well up there.

Cattle dominate the public's image of Irish livestock farming, past and present, but there's a fascinating sheep story which deserves telling. It's time for a hero on horseback to make a return. Enter Robert Bakewell again, the 'patron saint' of selective breeding. Once his New Leicester was established in the mid 1700s, he sent large numbers of the rams to Ireland to repeat his success in England by improving the Roscommon sheep. This was a large, white-faced hornless breed and although it was officially classed as a Longwool, its fleece was finer than most and nothing like the flowing lustrous tresses of a Cotswold or a Lincoln.

Roscommon is a county that is literally built on limestone. Over the years, demand for building materials and ornamental stone meant that a profitable quarrying industry grew up. For centuries the earth gave up other treasure here too; from the early seventeenth century, mining for iron ore and later for coal employed generations, and the discovery of white clay deposits in the south east of the county led to a booming business in tobacco pipe manufacture.

At the Claypipe Visitor Centre in Knockcroghery they commemorate the time in the late 1800s when virtually the entire population of the village was involved with the pipe making trade in one way or another. In Ireland the pipes were often smoked at wakes and taken to gravesides, but at home in the Cotswolds, when the distinctive honey-coloured dry stone walls are repaired, it's not unusual to find similar old clay pipes hidden among the knappings, left like a workaday time capsule by the Victorian wallers who built them.

Roscommon's county breed was overwhelmed by Bakewell's Leicesters, with the vigour and success of the new breeding stock leading to the slow, eventual extinction of the local sheep. But from the Roscommon a smaller, neater sheep had been bred, and because it was popular with farmers in neighbouring County Galway this closely related type survived. Galway sheep are smaller than the Roscommon, they have totally white, noble-looking faces and they can be instantly identified by a bob of wool on the top of their heads. It certainly helps when you're trying to pick them out in a big mixed flock.

The Galway did well in the western counties and is now Ireland's only native sheep, but it took a long time for it to gain a following on the other side of the Irish Sea. Eventually the breed was introduced to Great Britain in 1990 and now there are flocks across a swathe of the country from Devon in the south west as far north as Derbyshire and up to Scotland, with a big cluster of breeders in Leicestershire and neighbouring Lincolnshire.

Just outside the old port town of Boston is where you'll find the most unusual Galway flock of the lot. In fact it's a contender for the most extraordinary flock anywhere. The sheep live at North Sea Camp, which might sound a bit *Hi-de-Hi*, but is, in fact, one of Her Majesty's category D men's prisons. It started out as a Borstal in 1935 to reform what were then called 'seriously delinquent youths' and, not surprisingly, the site lent itself to use as a military camp during the Second World War. But what makes HMP North Sea Camp stand out is the prison farm. Not only does it boast one of the UK's biggest flocks of Galway sheep but it's also been home to Lincoln Longwool sheep, Dexter cattle, a huge herd of pigs and even a couple of alpacas.

The Galway flock there is registered in the name of the governor but for almost 30 years the sheep were cherished and cared for by a remarkable man called John Toolan. He was the prison shepherd and something of a legend. In his office there was a meticulously updated card index detailing every lamb born over the decades, and up on the wall was a huge circular chart depicting all the bloodlines in the flock. I was told that when he took his best Galways to the rare breeds show at Melton Mowbray he'd make sure a couple of prisoners who had worked with the animals on the farm accompanied the sheep on their day out. But of course they had to leave in good time to get the inmates back by 6 p.m.!

John was a founder of the British Galway Sheep Society, which today is overseen by Pam Hall and her husband Kelly. The couple have kept Galways since 1999 when they bought a pair of ewes at the Stoneleigh Rare Breeds Show and Sale. 'I like their faces and the wool on their heads,' confides Pam. 'And of course the boys are so handsome.'

The Halls are great believers in making good use of their flock, even the ewes who fail to get pregnant and can't produce lambs for the table. That's when you'll hear them talk with passion about the great mutton revival. The meat of older sheep is rich in colour and taste but, as a nation, we lost our appetite for it in the 1950s and 60s. Not Pam and Kelly though, who will gladly share their recipe for leg or shoulder of Galway mutton with anyone who shows an interest. They recommend that it's cooked very slowly. 'The longer the better,' says Kelly, 'so that all the flavour is contained.'

The way farming was revolutionised in the twentieth century, mainly by machines like tractors and intensive methods to rapidly boost production, has dictated the fortunes of so many of the old farm breeds. That hasn't always meant struggle or extinction though and there's one quiet, classy world-beating breed whose reputation and riches were made in the post-war years. There was a time when County Galway was about the only place you'd find

Connemara ponies, named after the boggy, mountainous region that's surrounded on three sides by the Atlantic, an area described by Oscar Wilde as a place of 'savage beauty'. The ponies that thrived here were sturdy and tough, perfectly suited to the wet, windy weather brought in from the ocean (when that happens the locals call it a 'soft day'). Their hardy ponies were always kept as working horses on the small farms that spread out across the west, but from the mid-1920s onwards a gradual change began.

As breed standards were introduced, farmers started bringing their fully-grown ponies down from the hills every spring for an annual inspection. Compact animals, short in the back and legs with sloping shoulders and never taller than 14.2 hands, the Connemara began to catch the eye. Their fame soon spread, first to Great Britain, then the United States, and by the 1960s breeders across Scandinavia, continental Europe and as far away as Australia had caught the Connemara bug. They're remarkably versatile ponies when compared to Dartmoors or Exmoors, and much more athletic, so they were taken up for riding, hunting and eventing and it wasn't long before they became one of the top pony breeds in the world. Even in the 1970s a really good pure-bred Connemara could change hands for £5000.

But the international showcase for the breed isn't in Kentucky, Seville, New South Wales or any of the other equine capitals around the world – it's the annual Connemara Pony Show, traditionally held on the third

Thursday of August, in the little coastal town of Clifden. The biggest gathering of Connemaras on the planet attracts hundreds of ponies and thousands of spectators to the simple showground close to the narrow Owenglin River with the breathtaking backdrop of the sharp summits and ridges of the grey-blue Twelve Bens mountain range. It was here that one keen competitor attracted more attention than the average Connemara owner could ever expect. But then there was never much that was average about Peter O'Toole. An Oscar-nominated, RADA-trained actor with a background in Shakespearian roles, he was the man who brought Lawrence of Arabia to life for millions of cinema-goers in 1962. More than two decades later he was still turning heads, although he'd exchanged his desert head-cloth and cloak for a tweed hat and a waxed jacket when he paraded his ponies in front of the judges.

O'Toole considered Clifden as home and he said more than once that the pony show was the highlight of his year. He was certainly an enthusiastic owner but it's debatable just how skilled a horseman he was. At the 1985 event he was upstaged by his flighty two-year-old colt, Dr Slattery, who dragged O'Toole round the rain-soaked ring and twice almost threw the great actor to the ground in front of riveted onlookers.

Potted Brisket of Dexter Beef

Serves: 4–6

beef dripping, for frying
1 boned and rolled joint of brisket, approx. 500g (1lb 1oz)
1 onion, sliced
1 carrot, sliced
1 stick celery, sliced
1 small swede, chopped
1 leek, sliced
hot beef stock
2 mace blades
100g melted butter
salt and pepper

1. Preheat the oven to 140°C/325°F/gas 3.
2. Heat a little beef dripping in a large casserole dish, then sear the joint in the hot dripping until brown on all sides and remove from the dish.
3. Add all of the vegetables to the dish and cook until golden, then return the beef to the dish. Add enough stock to cover the vegetables and come halfway up the beef. Add salt and pepper and a couple of mace blades.
4. Bring to the boil, then remove from the heat, cover and place in the preheated oven for about 3 hours.
5. Remove from oven and allow to cool. Remove the joint from casserole dish and take off the strings.
6. Trim the fat off the meat, chop the meat into small pieces and mix in a little of the melted butter. Pack the mixture into a basin or mould and pour over enough melted butter to almost cover the meat. Chill in the fridge until the butter is set.
7. Depending on how small the meat is chopped, this can be served with salad or can be spread in sandwiches.

Tip: The vegetable stock can be made into a delicious soup.

Mrs Robert Geering, Woodchurch
The Rare Breeds Survival Trust

CHAPTER 8

Wales

Welsh ex-pats all over the world take enormous pride in knowing every word of their nation's anthem *Hen Wlad Fy Nhadau* (in English that's 'Land of My Fathers'), but for me Wales will always be the land of my mother, Gillie. During the war, she was evacuated from Coventry to Wales. She grew up there and went to school in the heart of coal mining country, the Rhondda Valley. I think of her whenever I drive west over the Severn Bridge and cross into the country she knew so well as a girl.

It seems rather obvious to point out that one of the things Wales is famous for is its sheep, but they are truly amazing. There are ten million of them in Wales, which is three times the number of people, and while that figure includes large commercial flocks and crosses, there remains a strong tradition of farming old and minority Welsh breeds. The types, behaviour and characteristics of the native sheep here are as fascinating and diverse as the country itself. Whether it's high up on the mountain rocks, on bleak windy hillsides or down in the deep grassy valleys, there are sheep that survive and thrive whatever the environment.

The scenery that we see today hasn't changed much in a millennium, but the flocks of the past had a lasting influence on Welsh life and culture. Our need for their wool, milk, meat and skins led to new farm skills and handicrafts, laid the foundations of early trade, altered the way fields were managed and even determined the locations of market towns. There are other places in the British Isles that can claim to be historic sheep country but nowhere are there quite so many different types in such a relatively small area. It may well be globally unique.

Sheep farming in the UK is based on a three-tier system, and the DNA of some of the Welsh breeds plays a crucial role in the wider sheep industry. It works in an extraordinary way. The Stratified System plays to the individual strengths and characteristics of each breed. In simple terms, sheep are mated with breeds that are naturally downhill of them, to exploit the best of their genetics to the next level. The tough, go-it-alone mountain and hill sheep are on the top tier. Some of those females are crossed with long wool types from the milder upland areas below to produce half-bred lambs which inherit the hill ewe's temperament and good mothering instincts along with the better growth rate of their fathers. And on it goes down the tiers, transferring the most desirable traits from those half-bred ewes and using the best-performing, meat-producing rams en route to eventually produce fast-growing, great-tasting, meaty lamb for the table.

There's a similar hierarchy that you should bear in mind if you ever want to start a new life in the country and fancy becoming a Welsh shepherd: sheep should always be sold downhill. The quality of grazing and the weather conditions gradually improve as you move from the mountain tops to the lower pastures, and sheep that are moved will only flourish if they go from poorer land to more fertile pasture. And perhaps it's also true of people. As one hill farmer in North Wales said to me as I stood in his lambing shed, 'You'll never get a lowland farmer coming up hill. Farming's a hard life up here and it's not for the faint-hearted.' Inspired by that, it makes sense to meet the breeds of Wales in order, from top to bottom; high ridge to valley floor.

The mountain breeds are the equivalent of Ray Mears in the livestock world. They're tough, uncompromising, self-reliant animals that can cope with everything their harsh environment, and even harsher weather, can throw at them. All the varieties on the mountains of Wales are quite small with white or tan faces and good strong feet for navigating across the hard terrain. Wales is notoriously wet, but the mountain flocks have all-weather wool that's snow and rain repellent. The fleece has a long hair coat to repel water and a fine undercoat to keep them warm.

In the past, the mountain breeds were never monitored and registered in the sense of having formal breed societies and flock books. That means a lot of uncertainty and conflicting accounts when it comes to getting hard facts about their history, something that's not easy even with the best-recorded breeds. Just as every Welsh mountain range is unique, so the mountain sheep that live on them all differ. What they have in common though, is that the ewes are hefted on the slopes while the rams might be brought down and exchanged at the nearest mart. So the livestock never move more than 20 or 30 miles in their entire lives. There's limited human involvement in the way they live, and in some ways it's Charles Darwin's great theory at work, as it really is a case of what survives, lives and goes on to breed to bring on the next generation. The ewes are great mothers, because they have to be; they're instinctive and the sort of sheep that can sniff the air and know when a storm's coming. That's when they'll shift to the driest side of a rocky outcrop to get the best shelter. They are remarkable creatures.

Starting at the top, the breed that's easiest to remember is the straightforwardly named Welsh Mountain sheep. It's a small, strong, shaggy-fleeced animal which seems to do best in the wettest, harshest places. The ewes have sweet, gentle faces while the rams sport wonderful curved horns. Six hundred years ago, it was their milk that was in demand, but by the nineteenth century attention had turned to the taste, quality and tenderness of their meat with Queen Victoria herself demanding that lamb from the Welsh Mountain breed was served by the royal kitchens.

Years ago, one lucky little Mountain lamb caused a great commotion and thrust Dad and my sister Libby into the media spotlight. A talented sound recordist called Ken Jackson was a good friend to the Farm Park and loved making radio programmes with us at Bemborough. But during one visit they noticed a Welsh Mountain ewe struggling to deliver her lamb. Sleeves rolled up, the Hensons went to the rescue, and not only was the poor thing breech but when they eventually got it out there was little sign of life. Its tiny lungs were full of fluid, it wasn't breathing and no matter what they did it just couldn't be revived. The minutes were ticking by, so Dad heroically gave this fast-fading newborn the kiss of life. Between gasps, his voice quavering with tension, Dad whispered the memorable line: 'Come on, please don't die on me now.' To everyone's huge relief it worked, with the whole drama captured by Ken's microphone and later broadcast on BBC Radio 4's *Woman's Hour*. The calls and letters of appreciation from emotionally drained listeners continued for a long time afterwards.

Back on the mountains, there's a South Wales breed which is sometimes called the Nelson or the Glamorgan

Welsh. It has a harsh, wiry fleece and there's a fair chance that if you've bought a British wool carpet or rug, it contained South Wales Mountain fibres. Its claim to fame is that it's the largest of all the Welsh mountain breeds.

Still on the high ground there are a handful of breeds we can call the Coloured Sheep of Wales. The first is the Badger Face Welsh Mountain sheep and everything you need to know about them is in the name. There are two types which are identical apart from having reversed colouring: the Torddu (a white sheep with a black belly) and the Torwen (a black sheep with a white belly). Side by side it's like looking at a negative.

Mid-Wales is the stronghold of the Black Welsh Mountain sheep which can be traced back to written accounts from the Middle Ages when black fleeced mountain sheep were first recorded. Their wool is short, thick and firm to handle, and it never needs to be dyed so it's perfect for making into cloth or for traditional Welsh woollens, while the ram horns can be turned into buttons, knife handles and used for walking sticks.

The Balwen is the black sheep with the white socks, developed by a small group of Victorian breeders in the Tywi Valley. They're small and boxy, but despite being a tough mountain breed the Balwen was almost wiped out in the freezing winter of 1947 when the worst snows for 50 years left just one ram surviving.

As we come down from the mountains to the lower upland slopes we find the hill breeds. They're the sensible sheep in the flock. They don't make a fuss, they just get on with being sheep. They're bigger than the mountain breeds with a heavy, less coarse fleece and they often live in large flocks. The ewes are normally polled (hornless), generally give birth to twins and produce a fair amount of milk. But they don't have anything like the grit and resilience of their mountain cousins and probably couldn't survive if they were moved to higher ground. Lower down, though, they're great grazers and as a lot of grassland conservation needs hungry animals to clear weeds and undergrowth, the hill sheep of Wales do the job handsomely (not to mention sensibly).

The Beulah Speckled Face could equally have been called the Speckled Legged sheep as their black skin, patterned with white marks, can be seen wherever they're free from wool. They're relative newcomers in the world of breeds, although they have been around on the hills of mid and west Wales for the last hundred years or so without the introduction of any new breeding females. As a livestock judge at one of the big agricultural shows once told me, 'Beulah's need good legs to walk up the hill and good teeth to eat the grass when they get there.' The Welsh Hill Speckled Face sounds as if it should be a cousin of the Beulah but in fact it was produced from crossing Kerry Hills with Welsh Mountain sheep. Their markings are the other way round, with black patches around the eyes, on the nose, ears and feet on otherwise white skin.

Brecknock Hill Cheviots are among the whitest sheep with the springiest wool you'll ever see. They were first farmed 400 years ago in Brecknockshire (the formal name for the county of Brecon) and they're descended from an early type of Border Cheviot sheep which hails from the hills between England and Scotland.

The Hill Radnor is the stay-at-home sheep because, although it's been recognised as a breed for more than a century, most of them are still found in the high country around Radnor, Monmouth and Breconshire, closest to the English border. This heavy, tan-faced sheep was particularly badly hit by the foot-and-mouth disease culls in 2001 and a lot of work has been done to spread flocks out to other parts of the UK.

Then we get to the comic book superhero. The Kerry Hill must have one of the most appealing faces of all British sheep; it's snowy white except for five deep-black patches, one round each eye, one for each ear and a fifth around its nose. It looks just like the headwear of some cartoon caped crusader. These striking sheep with their long, almost vertical ears come from the hills around the small town of Kerry, not far from the border with Shropshire. The first record of Kerry Hills in Montgomeryshire was more than 200 years ago, and they've developed into a bold, strong sheep with dense wool that's soft enough to be used for filling cushions, chairs and sofas, although as a traditional meat breed you're more likely to notice Kerry Hill lamb on sale at a farm shop or farmers' market.

'If you're going to have ten sheep in your garden, then you want something good to look at.' That's the verdict of Dean Whybrow, who has been enchanted by sheep since he was a boy and now has something more impressive than simply garden sheep – he's got one of the biggest flocks of pure-bred Kerry Hills in the country. The Whybrow farm in Hertfordshire is in fact a three-hour drive from Kerry, and as Welsh hill sheep don't have to live on Welsh hillsides to thrive, Dean is contributing to the aim of achieving a wide geographical spread with the breed. He's a bit of a rare breed himself, being a first-generation tenant farmer on a council owned farm at a time when many local authorities have sold off their agricultural land.

Dean calls it a 'picture postcard farm', pointing out where old ships' timbers were used in the roofs of the various historic wooden buildings. There's an old lean-to manger and the farm shop is housed in what was once a dairy, which still has some of the original milking equipment on show. 'I was planning on starting a pedigree flock, so decided to look at one of those sheep breeds posters – and the Kerry Hill just jumped out.' Dean describes what he does as 'commercial farming of a rare breed' and with a flock of 130 Kerry Hills, any lambs that aren't good enough for breeding or keeping go to the farm shop for sale to the public as joints. It's a philosophy which can only raise the profile and improve the fortunes of the breed. What's more, 'There are as many Kerry Hills outside

Wales as there are inside now,' Dean says with justi-
fiable pride.

Away from the hilliest terrain, there are a couple of
breeds which are equally happy to graze on slopes or in
the valley bottoms and they both sound distinctly Welsh.
Despite being around since the 1800s, the Llanwenog
only got its name in 1957. Until then it had been called
various things including the Blackface and the Shropshire
Cross – functional and factual names but hardly inspiring. Eventually, when the breed society was created,
someone had the bright idea of naming them after the
parish on the River Teifi in Cardigan where large
numbers of these soft, fleecy sheep were farmed.

Finally there's the sheep which can fly the flag for the
rare breeds movement thanks to its amazing story of
success. The Lleyn is a lovely white-faced breed which,
as the name implies, comes from the Lleyn, or Llŷn,
peninsula that arches out into the sea like a pointed
finger between Cardigan Bay and the Isle of Anglesey.
In the 1970s, not long after the Rare Breeds Survival
Trust was set up, the Lleyn was on the charity's first
list of breeds at risk. Now their circumstances couldn't
be more different. They're the most numerous pedigree
dam breed (or breeding mothers) in the UK and important in producing commercial lambs for the table. A lot
of attention is paid to the virility of rams but it's vital
to have good, productive ewes that lamb easily too.

More than 40,000 Lleyn ewe lambs are now registered every year and a lot of that progress is down to a

wonderful lady called Gwenda Roberts. For more than 25 years she's been devoted to the breed in her role as secretary of the Lleyn Sheep Society (motto: 'Behind every successful ram are hard working ewes'). It's probably no coincidence that she lives close to the tip of the Lleyn peninsula herself, and her work is all about the fine detail: maintaining pedigree records for every individual animal, helping breeders find the perfect rams, getting the word out about the Lleyn's qualities and ensuring everyone makes the very best of their flock. Gwenda is a great example of the importance of having exceptional people behind the scenes and the difference they make to give our native livestock a brighter future. You might even say that behind every successful breed there's a hard-working breed secretary.

Today we think nothing of loading a trailer or truck with sheep to take them wherever they need to go, but until relatively recently transporting stock was a very different task. Before the motor engine transformed farming life, getting your flock to market meant walking them there. A network of droving routes snaked their way through the Welsh countryside, and spread throughout England to Kent, Cornwall and all the way to Scotland. Some of the old roads have been tarmacked over now but in a few places it's still possible to see original hawthorn hedges and high banks. They're the tell-tale signs of the droving routes and were used to stop livestock drifting off and to prevent animals from adjacent farms joining the drove. Sheep were droved as meat on the hoof, sometimes for days on end over hundreds of miles, and they weren't the only animals to be corralled and herded across the landscape. Pigs, cattle, ponies and even geese were all moved from place to place this way.

To get a proper understanding of what life was like for the historic drovers I found myself in north-west Wales on a damp, foggy winter's morning a few years ago, with a lively collie and a small flock of a dozen sheep for company. Ahead of us was a section of the ancient droving route along the Vale of the River Clwyd through the Denbighshire countryside to Oswestry and my guide was a much-loved local author and droving expert, Idris Evans. He was an entertaining and incredibly well-informed walking companion and when he spoke about the heyday of the sheep drovers it was as if he'd actually been there. 'You must remember it was in the interest of farmers to get their animals to market as quickly as possible,' he told me, 'and as safely as possible too.'

Although the practice goes back more than a thousand years, droving peaked in the eighteenth and nineteenth centuries. At that time, the population boom in the rapidly expanding industrial towns and cities of Britain meant that demand for food soared. It was a good time to farm sheep and sell mutton. It wasn't unusual for flocks of hundreds of sheep to be moved at a time, and on narrow tracks the drover at the front would be out of sight of the herdsman at the back. So in the roughest, most remote terrain the only way for the drovers to communicate was by a system of whistles, which Idris was happy to demonstrate for me. Whistling with two fingers in the mouth reached a frequency that could travel for up to five miles he explained, and after hearing the sharp, shrill signal, I can well believe it.

In the nineteenth century droving was big business and large amounts of money changed hands as tens of thousands of sheep made the journey from the Welsh mountains to the English markets. It became a dangerous occupation and on remote rural tracks the drovers were at the mercy of muggers, chancers and highwaymen who were after their cash as well as sheep rustlers who were set on stealing their animals. At first the farmers started carrying flintlock pistols to ward off robbers, but a less risky solution soon emerged. The need for security on the open road had led directly to the creation of some of the country's first private banks and a system of IOUs. I was even shown a 200-year-old note from the long-forgotten Aberystwyth and Tregaron Bank, which was known throughout Cardiganshire as the Bank of the Black Sheep. The name came about because the value of the currency was marked by the corresponding number of black ewes pictured on the bank notes: one black sheep on a one-pound note, two on a two-pound note and so on.

The drovers fulfilled another important role in daily life too. At a time when people rarely travelled more than a few miles from home and before any form of mass communication (newspapers were only of use to people who could afford them and were able to read), the men of the road were often first with the news and gossip. Can it really be true that the Welsh nation first learnt of Napoleon's defeat at the Battle of Waterloo in 1815 from returning drovers who had heard about it in England? It seems plausible.

When we finally arrived at journey's end in the hamlet of Rhewl, I took a moment to look thirstily at the pub that had provided rest and refreshment for tired shepherds down the years, before turning to help get the flock safely on to their overnight pasture. Only when the gate was firmly shut did Idris finally reveal to me the secret of being a successful drover: 'Make sure you finish with the same number of sheep you started with.'

Walking livestock to market isn't the only old custom that's gone. Something else that's disappeared from the farming scene in Wales is the unbelievable spectacle of hundreds of sheep being picked up and thrown into fast flowing mountain rivers. For all sorts of reasons that just wouldn't happen now, but it was once the accepted practice to wash the fleece on every sheep before shearing time to get rid of all the tangled dirt and greasy deposits. It helped the hand-shearers do their job too by making the wool rise as the blades followed the contours of the sheep's skin.

One Monday night in the summer of 1956, film footage of an entire flock of mountain sheep being flung unceremoniously into the crashing waters of a river in North

Wales was shown on BBC television. The series was called *Away From It All,* in which life in remote rural areas was investigated by a 'townsman' in the shape of Christopher Chataway. He was the former Olympic athlete who two years earlier had been Roger Bannister's pacesetter for the first sub-four minute mile. If that wasn't enough, Chataway was the first-ever winner of the BBC Sports Personality of the Year Award, became Britain's first TV newscaster, was elected to Parliament, served as a government minister and was eventually knighted by the Queen. Quite a man! I've no idea what viewers made of his dramatic shots of bleating sheep plunging five or six feet into the drink, but no one in the film turned a hair and the flock seemed none the worse for their ordeal.

The 30-minute programme, filmed in black and white of course, was made on the lovely, lonely slopes of the Nant Gwynant Valley, in the shadow of Mount Snowdon. A lifetime later, I was curious to see the spot for myself and find out more about the annual dunking. On a dreary day with a sky full of heavy low clouds, I found it. But only with the help of a local wool expert who told me that when he was a youngster he'd been involved in sheep washing, helping his father prepare his own flock for shearing. He even revealed to me that they used to climb into the river themselves and swim with their animals to make sure they really were clean.

South west of the little village of Capel Curig we followed the line of a narrow, mossy path down to some dry stone walls that had once formed a pen and a few feet further on, at the water's edge, we could just make out the remnants of an old wooden platform. This had been the very spot where the shepherd in the old film had picked his sheep up, one by one, and dropped them into the river with an enormous splash. More than 60 years later, I noticed that the river was running high, much higher than it was in Chataway's day, and the flow was so fast that it was crashing off the banks on either side creating a mass of white water and throwing a thin spray into the air. You'd never get a mountain flock in and out of there today, I thought to myself. And you'd never want to.

It's easy to think that Wales has only ever been sheep country and I can understand why some people overlook the other heritage species which have a special place in the story of Welsh farming. Like the national cattle breed, the Welsh Black. History with horns is how I think of them. The ancestors of the modern Welsh Black were grazing the hills here before the Romans arrived and the herds were so valuable that they inspired the phrase 'black gold from the Welsh hills'. At first they were bred in the wet uplands of Wales but now their thick, coal-coloured coats are a common sight all over the country. Although a beef and dairy breed, the cows don't have the gentleness and delicate frame we sometimes think of when we picture a traditional milking herd. The Welsh Black is no Jersey! It's stout and hardy with the looks of a beef breed and short, straight legs that moor it firmly to the ground.

Fortunately the Welsh Black wasn't swept away by the introduction of highly commercial continental breeds but managed to find an interesting niche by being one of the first named traditional meats to be marketed. Butchers and restaurants began to promote and sell Welsh Black beef and that was helped along by the TV chef Rick Stein. In his first *Food Heroes* series in 2002, billed as a 'culinary romp around Britain' celebrating regional cuisine, he championed Welsh Black beef and almost immediately queues were forming in shops and farmers' markets.

There's something about traditional cattle breeding that attracts characters, or perhaps it's the animals that influence their owner's personality. Either way, one man who stands out from the crowd is Bernard Llewellyn. He's from Pembrokeshire, but for decades he's been a part of the farming scene in neighbouring Carmarthenshire, the place where he settled when he married Margaret, a farmer's daughter from the western end of the Brecon Beacons National Park. Bernard has played an important role in Welsh agriculture and countryside protection, even representing the UK's interests in Brussels, but at county shows around Britain this engaging grey-haired, white-bearded figure is known and recognised by everyone as the cattle man. He's fantastically knowledgeable about them and, alongside Welsh Blacks, he's always had a great passion for Highlands, White Parks and especially Longhorns. They're the cattle the Llewellyns used to establish a stunningly impressive mixed herd on their farm close to the tumbling, rocky River Cennen back in 1981.

He's a sheep farmer too, with a flock of Welsh Mountain, Cheviot, Glamorgan Welsh, Balwen, Exmoor Horn and Soay sheep, plus a few thoroughbred race-horses thrown in for good measure. The sheep aren't just here to look good, because this is a typical hill farm and with a hundred acres of land situated about a thousand feet above sea level, the hungry, grass-loving flock is essential to keep the pasture in check.

Bernard has achieved great things over the years: he was a proud chairman of the Longhorn Cattle Society and received an OBE for his considerable services to rural affairs and tourism. But above all other accolades, he can genuinely claim to be the king of the castle. That's because his home near Llandeilo is not only called Castle Farm, but the land also includes the magnificent ruins of one of the finest and most historic of all Welsh castles. The imposing Carreg Cennen castle is a thirteenth-century fortress on the top of a steep 300-foot cliff, the ancient monument looking as if it has been pushed up through the craggy rock beneath. The remains of the gatehouse, a round tower and the walls of the great hall completely dominate the landscape and almost demand to be admired. The castle was fought over, captured and recaptured, by the Welsh and

English countless times down the ages but it was finally occupied and destroyed by Yorkist forces in the War of the Roses. Although relics have revealed an even older history – archaeologists have unearthed a cache of Roman coins and four prehistoric skeletons at the site.

Bernard jokingly says that the castle was bought by mistake. In the 1960s, when the deeds were being drawn up, the ruins were accidentally included as part of the farm. An offer was made to buy the historic landmark back for £400, but by then it was too late.

Far below the tall, grey walls and battlements are soft, undulating fields and pasture, native oak woods and open moorland. There are views of the Black mountain with its Bronze Age burial cairns clearly visible on a fine day. Further away you can see the escarpment of the Carmarthenshire Fans, the biggest hills in the county, and then beyond in the far distance, the brooding, snow-capped Brecon Beacons. What a setting!

It's not surprising that Carreg Cennen has been called the country's most romantic castle, and for once there's a nugget of truth in what otherwise would sound like marketing spin. The castle attracts about a 100,000 visitors every year – although about half of them don't attempt the climb up to the ruins, preferring instead to have their breath taken away by the panoramic views from the footpaths lower down.

Despite the name, there are occasionally Welsh Blacks that are red and some can be born with white bellies too. But before farmers started deliberately selecting for black, the traditional herds came in every shade imaginable. These were the much-talked about Coloured Cattle of Wales, and one of the prime locations for them was the great county of huge contrasts – Glamorgan. It's a place of vales, villages, lowland farms, forest waterfalls, marshland and even unspoilt beaches, which stretch along the lengthy Gower coast. But it's also an industrialised landscape where the rich and ageless deposits of coal and iron were mined so successfully, and profitably. From the 1700s onwards, the narrow valleys became home to mine workers' cottages, terraced houses and colliery towns providing manpower for the large number of pits and a coal mining industry which literally fuelled the British Empire. For the last 50 years the area has been cut in two by the M4 motorway, taking a constant, snaking line of drivers back and forth from the Severn to Swansea Bay and beyond.

This varied land was the home territory of the Glamorgan cattle, an elegant and handsome-looking dairy breed with its roots in Norman times. Originally it was red in colour with pale markings including a famous finchback – the white stripe down the backbone which survives today in breeds like my own herd of Gloucesters. Over time, the Glamorgan was bred darker as farmers in the county started to prefer a mahogany coat and it appealed to breeders in neighbouring counties, Monmouthshire and Breconshire, too.

But there were unwritten, unspoken rules about just where a breed's boundaries were drawn and the

Glamorgan was hardly ever seen west of the River Dulais. The reason was that a similar but more localised cattle variety held court there. This was the Pembrokeshire, a large chocolatey black breed which in the 1830s was described by the agricultural writer William Youatt as the most useful cow or ox in Great Britain, and one which could 'thrive where others starve'. So useful in fact, that the Pembrokeshire was one of the black cattle of Wales which was most often seen on those old drover's routes, being walked in huge numbers to England where it was in demand from the Midlands right down to Sussex and Kent, where it was fattened on the rich grassland. In London too there was a ready market for Pembroke cows for use in dairies, supplying the growing capital and its ever-increasing population with nourishing milk.

There was also a Montgomeryshire breed, short and stocky which was coloured 'full red with smoky points'. In the late Victorian years there were just two pure herds left but it somehow managed to struggle on until extinction came in 1919.

The coloured cattle caught the eye of the rich and influential; the most high-profile Glamorgan cattle owner of all (and it was difficult to have a higher profile back then) was King George III, the monarch who 'lost' Britain her American colonies and the first king of the new United Kingdom, although he's mostly remembered now for his fits of ill health portrayed so brilliantly in the film *The Madness of King George*. The Glamorgan was His Majesty's favourite breed and he kept his herd of milking cows in the grounds of Windsor Castle using Glamorgan oxen for the farm work on the estate, pulling carts, harrows and rollers in the fields.

The county motto of Glamorgan is 'He that endureth, overcometh', which I think would make a very fitting slogan for the rare breeds movement. But it did nothing to help the poor old Glamorgan cattle. Unable to keep its bloodlines pure through decades of cross-breeding, it died out sometime in the 1920s. But not everyone is quite so convinced about their extinction. Curiously an apparently forgotten herd was discovered in Sussex in the 1970s, and they all had chestnut-coloured coats with a broad white stripe along their backs, down their tails and over their bellies. All these cattle were bought, to be taken back to South Wales and their historic county of origin. Descendants of those animals are still on show today beside the nineteenth-century Tudor Gothic mansion at Margam Country Park on the coastal plain near Port Talbot.

Livestock of legend seem to be everywhere in Wales. Among the most important breeds are some of the world's rarest cattle. The Vaynol is a wild-looking, semi-feral type of small, white cattle. They're timid, slender and angular with the air of a graceless, primitive beast. Their black ears and noses are complemented by a beautiful pair of horns which sweep gently upwards like a set of jet-coloured handlebars. That stark contrast between their clean white coats and their black points makes the newborn calves look more like lambs when you spot them from a distance, although from time to time they have completely black calves, several of which were born at Bemborough.

Their story actually starts not in Wales at all, but in Scotland, where in the distant past their ancestry is thought to have included influences from the Highland, the Ayrshire and some Indian cattle too. They roamed wild in Perthshire long before they moved south and their name comes from Vaynol Park in Caernarfonshire where a herd was established in 1872.

My family played a vital role in securing their survival in the 1980s when the herd had been transferred to the Midlands and was down to just a dozen animals which had failed to produce a live calf for three years. In desperation the stockmen had tried to remove calves from their mothers as they were born, in a failed attempt to raise them by hand. This resulted in the cows becoming extremely wild and aggressive. Their home, Shugborough Park near Stafford, was crisscrossed by footpaths and in 1982 it was decided that the herd, which by then belonged to the RBST, had to be moved urgently before someone was hurt. My sister Libby took a small team from Bemborough and spent half a day quietly walking the herd down out of the park into a carefully constructed funnel, and finally into the waiting lorry. Once she got them home, we put them into the two fields either side of the handling pens, and tied all the gates open. Then each day we fed them hay in the field the other side of the handling pens so that they gradually got used to walking through the pens and out the other side, without getting trapped.

As they calmed down and got used to us, we were able to quietly approach and close the gates while they were feeding, and then release them without them being afraid. By the time the first cow calved, we were able to gently move her away from the herd, and ensure the calf was suckling and strong before being reintroduced to the group. We didn't lose a single calf, reared two bulls that could be handled and have semen collected, and were able to move the herd on several years later in a much stronger position.

The RBST has now managed to establish a number of small satellite herds around the UK to lessen the risk of the entire population being wiped out by disease or disaster in one go. But the Vaynol has also been the subject of an embryo transfer programme (a kind of IVF for cows), with fertilised eggs removed and implanted into surrogate females. We first unsuccessfully attempted this with the Vaynols at Bemborough in 1985 but the technology is now much better understood and the first embryo transfer Vaynol calves were born in 2018. Although the host mother is from a different breed, the calf is a pedigree Vaynol. This means that instead of a cow producing just one calf a year, up to a dozen of her fertilized eggs could be collected and incubated in surrogate mothers. How successful those efforts will be is still in the balance; at the last count there were just 12 breeding Vaynol cows in existence, making it the rarest of all the rare breeds in Britain. This number is far lower than the next most critical breeds on the Danger List: the Cleveland Bay horse with 64 females, the Suffolk Punch at 80 and the 138 Landrace pigs.

Interestingly, Welsh pig farming doesn't get much attention, but that wasn't always the case. The landscape of the country suited cattle and sheep, so farmers specialised in beef and lamb. But in Arthurian tales and tenth-century Welsh writings there are references to white swine. In the last 200 years or so, pigs had a unique place in the homes and hearts of working families in rural Wales. While other livestock herds and flocks roamed and grazed, pigs were kept in small numbers at home. Fed on waste milk and whey from the dairy, brewer's grains and woodland windfalls they grew fat just like some of the other pig breeds such as the Old Spots and the Large Black. It hardly sounds like quality fare to us, but to the Welsh pig it was gourmet grub and that intoxicating mix of food and their natural layer of fat all added to the flavour of their meat.

There had been pale-skinned swine in Wales for centuries but it wasn't until the 1870s that real attention was given to them when they were being used in the busy pig-fattening trade that had taken off across the border in Cheshire. The First World War concentrated minds on just how self-sufficient the UK was when it came to producing our own food, and breeders started looking at how they could work with others who were farming similar long-bodied white pigs from the south and west of Wales, in the counties of Glamorgan, Carmarthen, Pembroke and Cardigan. As the country settled back to peacetime, expectations rose and more shoppers were asking for quality bacon and pork, so in response the Welsh Pig Society was formed in 1922.

In the 1950s the Welsh was held up as the UK's most viable pig, but its promotion alongside the Large White and the Landrace changed its fortunes. Crossing the old type of Welsh and the Landrace produced an 'improved' commercial pig. Remember, this was an era when the industry was aiming for a leaner, more saleable product for meat-eaters who were turning their backs on fatty cuts. But the drive towards ever more intensive pig farming and bigger carcasses with barely any regard for flavour meant the poor old Welsh fell out of fashion and numbers plummeted.

Today, the modern Welsh shows signs of the influence of those Landrace bloodlines. It's a long, lean, lop-eared baconer that just might be the pinkest pig with the curliest tail you'll ever see, and it also has the most remarkably unwrinkled skin. It's an animal that doesn't mind being out in cold wind and teeming rain, which is just as well because that's frequently what rolls in from the Irish Sea and the Atlantic Ocean. It also happens to be making money again as a top-class pig for cross breeding to produce cuts for the butcher, and is literally bringing home the bacon for its owners.

In Carmarthenshire, the Welsh breed is going back to its roots. The county had a long history of home producing and curing ham, with generation after generation of smallholders and farming families slaughtering their own animals and salting the meat to last through the winter. In recent years, artisan charcuterie from pedigree Welsh pigs has been produced locally and sold in the county once more – not just traditional sausages, pork pies and pâté, but also bacon and hams, prosciutto, salami and chorizo.

Before heading east and crossing back into England, I have to make time to raise my riding hat in tribute to some amazing equines who defied a royal death sentence. Wales has never been a nation to be falsely modest so it's no surprise to discover that it's home to the 'world's most beautiful pony', or at least that's the verdict of the Welsh Pony and Cob Society on the wonderful native Welsh Mountain pony. It certainly is a beauty, and the smallest of the Welsh pony breeds standing at under 12 hands. This is an animal that's quick, with plenty of power and full of spirit, a relative of the old Celtic pony and a breed that's been seen on the mountains of Wales for at least a thousand years. The four pony breeds of Wales are a group of closely-related horse types, equine cousins if you like, including cobs (a general term for a small sturdy horse that's taller than a pony). The different types are divided into four sections: A, B, C and D. Alphabetically, the Welsh Mountain pony is the first, next comes the Welsh pony, then it's a cob-type pony and finally the cob itself. It's confusing for an outsider but it makes sense to the equine world which classifies them neatly by height and type.

All our longest-lived British farm breeds have fought against the odds through disasters, disease, wars or abandonment to survive into the twenty-first century. But our ponies had to conquer a single, formidable enemy with murderous intent. King Henry VIII. It wasn't just the Pope and most of his wives he took a dislike to; he hated little horses of all types too and was set on wiping them off the map for ever. He introduced laws to improve the equine stock throughout the land, dreaming of producing a big, superior military breed to stand as a lasting legacy of his kingship, and a way of sticking two fingers up at his enemies overseas. It was bad news for ponies; there was a ban on breeding any stallion under 15 hands or mares under 13 hands and all horses which were deemed to be too small or not strong enough were rounded up and destroyed. Every autumn at Michaelmas, when farm tenants' quarterly rents were due, parties of men went out to drive ponies and 'inferior' horses from common land and grazing grounds to be culled.

Thankfully, many Welsh ponies escaped the king's clutches, probably because they lived in remote locations on difficult terrain a long way from London, out of sight and out of mind. Intelligent and sure-footed animals like these were always going to find a role and Welsh ponies were later used as cavalry horses, in the pits, carrying mail on postal rounds and working on farms. Nowadays though it's in pony trekking, jumping and racing where you'll see them at work. The business of traditional breeds conservation is, inevitably, a numbers game but it's one which favours the Welsh ponies. The four types together make them the most numerous, and sometimes most envied, of all our native equine breeds.

Dorking Cottagers' Pie

Serves: 6

1.3kg (3lb) Dorking chicken, including liver
450g (1lb) lean Tamworth pork
450g (1lb) Tamworth belly pork
4 rashers Tamworth bacon
1 shallot, finely chopped
225g (³/₄lb) puff pastry
1 Maran egg, beaten
salt and pepper

1. Preheat the oven to 230°C/450°F/gas 8.
2. Remove the chicken skin, cut the breast into long, thin slices and set aside.
3. Mince the pork, belly pork and the remaining chicken meat and liver and add to a bowl. Season with a little salt and pepper. Mix in the chopped shallot.
4. Line a casserole dish with two-thirds of the puff pastry. Lay 2 bacon rashers on the bottom, then fill the dish with alternating layers of mince and breast.
5. Cover the last layer of mince with the remaining bacon rasher, then cover with remaining pastry. Keep a little pastry for decoration, if required. Make a hole for the steam and brush the top with the beaten egg.
6. Bake in the preheated oven for 30 minutes, then turn the temperature down to 180°C/350°F/gas 4, cover the top of the pie with wet greaseproof paper and cook for a further 1 hour.

Timothy & Anne Wilson, Doncaster
The Rare Breeds Survival Trust

CHAPTER 9

The Midlands

My heart is pounding, my throat has suddenly gone dry and I'm hoping jelly-leg syndrome doesn't strike next. Nerves like this don't make any sense to me, especially when I think that something like eight million TV viewers see me on *Countryfile* every Sunday night. Yet there's something different about appearing in front of a living, breathing, flesh and blood audience. Is it because you can see the whites of their eyes, or is it the worry that they can see mine? Before I know it, the music fades, the house lights dim and it's time to emerge from the wings and head towards the spotlight. I'm relieved that it's a packed house – there's always the fear that you'll walk out on to a stage in silence and see row after row of empty seats. Not tonight, they're a great crowd and the lighting is bright enough for me to spot a few farmers I know in the audience.

'An Evening with Adam Henson' is underway at the Courtyard Theatre, an airy modern venue in the centre of Hereford. It feels somehow appropriate that I'm telling my animal anecdotes and stories of rural life here, in one of England's great market towns and a place that's retained a sense of having a strong farming community. In fact, the theatre is right next to the site of the city's old livestock auction. Hereford is the latest in a tour that sees me travelling from Worthing on the south coast to Durham in the north, taking in places big and small like Birmingham, Bury St Edmunds and Cheltenham. The show is peppered with photos from the family album projected on to an enormous screen behind me. It's always good to begin the evening with a laugh, so I start with an ancient snap of me and my three sisters as children, wincing into the lens and struggling to hold some wriggling little piglets. The Henson brood are all wearing hand-knitted jumpers and I'm sporting an embarrassing pudding-basin haircut. When I turn slightly to the right and catch a glimpse of my young freckly face up on the screen, I'm slightly apprehensive as to whether this was a good idea, but then the laughter starts to ripple through the room and I can relax.

Orchard-dotted Herefordshire is a good example of how the counties of the Midlands make up the most diverse and surprising region of England. There's no such thing as a quintessentially Midlands landscape, or a 'typical' breed, in an area of the country that encompasses high gritty peaks, soft lush flood plains and everything in between. Of course the old image of the region as 'the Workshop of the World' still lingers. It's dominated by England's second city, big bustling Birmingham, and features the factories of the Black Country, a mining legacy in Nottinghamshire and Derbyshire as well as industrial prowess in everything from motor cars and ceramics to brewing and carpet making. The manufacturing heritage is so strong here that the area's business initiative was called the Midlands Engine (perhaps not quite as catchy a name as the Northern Powerhouse, but apt). After all, this was the region where the Industrial Revolution began in the foundries and furnaces of Ironbridge.

As the farmers in my audience at the Courtyard will testify, soot and smoke feels a long way from Herefordshire and the rich, fertile soil which produces a wider variety of food than almost any other English county: apples, hops, potatoes, wheat, barley, peas, broccoli, asparagus, cherries, blackcurrants and straw-berries among them, and that's before the meat, dairy and drinks producers are taken into account. But asked what Herefordshire's best known produce is, most people will say Hereford beef.

The stocky, rich-red and cream-white coloured Hereford was originally a draught animal, developed from the small cattle that had roamed Roman Britain and the bigger Welsh breeds from across the border. The trademark characteristic is the white face. Every

Hereford is born with that trait, and it's so dominant that the bulls even pass it on to their crossbred offspring. They're loved and respected around here, but the Hereford is more than just a county breed. It's more, even, than a standard bearer for the Midlands breeds. It's a symbol of the nation and as much a British marque as a Bentley or an Aston Martin. There are more than five million pure-bred Hereford cattle in 50 countries around the globe and even world leaders are sold on them. When Theresa May held an official banquet for American President Donald Trump at Blenheim Palace in July 2018, she insisted he was served the best of British cuisine, and so the main course was, naturally, fillet of Hereford beef.

Dad worked with white-faced cattle all his life and lots of our family friends are or have been breeders of pedigree Herefords. So this is a breed that's not just close to me geographically, but also close to my heart.

One of the best ever herds was the Westwood Herefords from Mamble, producing champions at county shows for as long as anyone can remember, as well as providing breeding stock and genetics that have beefed up herds all over the world. A stockman called Ray Davies brought the first pedigree Hereford to Westwood Farm in 1945; a cow that at the age of ten cost 60 guineas! Those were the days when every herd of beef cattle in Herefordshire was of the county breed, which shows you just how much livestock farming has changed. They are supreme grazers and wherever there's grass, the stocky, short-legged Hereford will follow. When you look at such a noble and commanding beast it's impossible to imagine them ever falling out of favour but that's exactly what happened in the 1960s. When intensive systems took off and fashionable French breeds like the Charolais and the Limousin became popular, grassland was ploughed up to grow food for the new continental arrivals. There are two types of Hereford, horned and polled, but Ray knew what he liked and he stayed faithful to the horned type.

Herefordshire and Hollywood don't have an enormous amount in common, but even Tinseltown couldn't resist the macho muscle of the Hereford. The breed has been crossing the Atlantic since the first exports left England by ship in 1817, so the Herefords probably felt home-grown to most Americans by the time the James Stewart and Maureen O'Hara western *The Rare Breed* was released in the 1960s. In between the usual gun fights, brawls and stampedes the plot surrounds a Hereford bull and attempts to introduce the breed to cowboy country. To be frank, it's not the best film ever made and after a while it's impossible to ignore the way everyone calls the cattle 'Her-fuds'. But getting selective breeding into a Hollywood movie script must have been quite an achievement and, anyway, who can resist a Jimmy Stewart western?

So the world knows and loves Hereford cattle, but there's another contender for the title of Herefordshire's county breed. The Ryeland sheep might not be as grand or as famous as its bovine counterpart, but it could tell a tale or two about royalty and underwear that would make a bull blush. The Ryeland is an adorable down-land breed which comes from Ross-on-Wye and the countryside around the Gloucestershire and Monmouthshire borders. I suppose they ought to be called Herefordshire sheep, and they probably were in the distant past, but because the medieval monks of Leominster grazed them on ryegrass pastures, the con-nection was made with *rye land*.

Early on, the high quality of their crimpy fleece was making flock-masters such tidy sums of money that their Ryeland flocks were known as 'Lemster Ore' after the gold it earned them. In Tudor times, their fine wool was so highly prized by hand-spinners that when Queen Elizabeth I was given Ryeland stockings she insisted that she'd never wear a pair made from anything else. And she wasn't the only blue blood to think that way. Three hundred years later, Queen Victoria was so impressed with the soft fabric that she ordered Ryeland wool undergarments. Royal unmentionables aside, there was a practical use for the yarn. The fashion accessory everyone wanted in the fifteenth century was a piece of knitted headwear called the Monmouth cap. They were close fitting, thick and warm which explains why they were popular with soldiers and sailors. No one has heard of them now but at one time they were worn by labour-ers all over England, in the same way that flat caps were a symbol of the working class in the twentieth century. They're mentioned by Shakespeare, who described Welshmen wearing leeks in their Monmouth caps in *Henry V*. Original examples are almost impossible to come by, and there's only one existing Monmouth cap from the sixteenth century which is on display in Monmouth Museum.

Herefordshire is unusual in not having a big county agricultural show of its own. But sharing its farming showcase every summer with Gloucestershire and Worcestershire has been going on forever and it works a treat. The Royal Three Counties showground is in the most beautiful and impressive spot you could imagine. It sits as green and flat as a billiard table on firm Worcestershire soil in a plain at the foot of the steep, rounded Malvern Hills. Woods and grasslands dress the slopes and it's certainly the best backdrop to any agricultural show in England. Even on days when low cloud and mist swirls around the hill tops, the main arena and showground paddocks can be drenched in sunshine.

It's my local county show and I've been going there since I was a small boy. I've paraded my animals in the competition rings and I've been a livestock judge too, but now I'm very proud to be the Royal Three Counties Show ambassador. It means representing the show to visitors and officials from home and overseas, doing interviews to get the word out, as well as presenting silver cups and trophies to a long procession of prize-winning growers and breeders. On show days I'm criss-crossing the 100-acre site constantly to get to all the functions and events I promise to attend. My feet barely touch the ground, but it's a thrill to see British farming, my great passion and my life's work, put on a pedestal.

It's not just a case of turning up in Malvern for three days in June though. One spring morning I was on the road early to take part in an ambitious photo shoot to publicise the show. The setting was Worcester Cathedral and the star turns were a pair of Shropshire sheep and two splendid red North Devon bulls – all previous champions at the Three Counties Show. Today their job was to simply look magnificent either side of big baskets full of fresh local produce in front of a line of VIPs. There was the Agricultural Society chief executive, trustees and members of the council, prize-winning livestock breeders, the Lord-Lieutenant and the Bishop of Dudley, the Right Reverend Graham Usher, wearing his mitre and robes.

I wasn't expecting His Grace to pull a mobile phone out from under his vestments and take a selfie. At that point I thought I'd seen it all, until one of the bulls disgraced itself on the cathedral's beautifully polished floor in front of all the startled guests and dignitaries. Best shoes or not, I felt obliged to help when the mops and paper towels finally arrived. Despite the unexpected sideshow, we got our publicity photos.

Of all the marquees on the Royal Three Counties showground, the busiest is the poultry tent. It's noisy too, and not just from the 800 birds on display. There's loud chatter and earnest discussion on the various qualities of the breeds: the Dorking versus the Sussex, or Old English game compared to the exotically named Appenzeller Spitzhauben. A couple of exhibitors want to sell me some cockerels and another asks if I'm interested in bringing emus to the Farm Park. Calm among the clamour is Nick Langdon. He's the Poultry Show manager and he hatched his first chicks at the tender age of six. 'I love poultry because the eggs are your reward for keeping them,' he tells me while gently stroking a fat hen he's holding under one arm. 'Did you know the ground takes longer to recover in the poultry tent than anywhere else on the showground because of the footfall?'

I can well believe it, but I can't stay long to chat. I've got dates to keep and people to meet at the W.I. marquee, the Orchid Show, the goat pens and in the main arena, where my near neighbour Dick Roper is showing off his sheep herding skills with a little flock and four border collies. I've trained a few sheep dogs in my time and mostly under Dick's expert guidance. He's full of wisecracks on the mic today. 'Some people finger-whistle to their collies,' he says with a straight face, 'but when you spend all day outside with dogs and sheep, the last thing you want to do is put your fingers in your mouth!'

I'm back in the arena a few hours later for the highlight of the entire show and a spectacle that can only be described as a festival on four legs – the Grand Parade of Livestock. Thousands of spectators sitting in the stands and leaning against the white perimeter railings watch attentively as a splendid Aberdeen Angus leads a procession of the best of British. It's Rare Breeds Day at the show so I recognise most of the cattle and sheep farmers who walk past, looking incredibly smart in their uniform white coats and holding up placards declaring the name of their breed, just as athletes do in front of the national teams in the Olympic Games' opening ceremony. There are medals to be won at Malvern too, and I have the unenviable job of judging the Best Rare Breed in Show. Impossible! But in a three-way contest between a Saddleback gilt, a Beef Shorthorn heifer in calf and a Dorset Horn ewe lamb, it's the pig that pips the others.

North of Birmingham, where the M42 and the M6 Toll diverge to create a concrete wishbone, sits the capital of the Anglo-Saxon kingdom of Mercia. It's been a few other things since, of course. The site of one of England's finest Norman castles, a centre for cloth, brick and paper manufacturing and home of the Reliant motor company, famous for churning out the sort of three-wheelers so loved by Del Boy Trotter. For rare breeds enthusiasts though, Tamworth will always be the place that gave its name to a pig. To me they're a very special breed, and not just because I think no farm is complete without a healthy population of ginger animals. Long ago, when feral swine roamed freely in

British forests, that colouring was common, but now they're our only native breed of red pig. When the trend to cross local strains with new, trendy imported Chinese pigs took off in the 1800s, Staffordshire's native breed missed out because it wasn't thought 'improving' them would be worth the trouble and expense. So by chance the Tamworth stayed true and is now the closest to the 'Old English' breed.

In the 1970s, that direct link back to the historic hogs of the past was just what a team of archaeologists was looking for when they approached the Farm Park for our help in turning the clock back 3,000 years. They were setting up a replica Iron Age village on the Hampshire Downs and to make the scattering of thatched roundhouses, pits and field crops at Butser Ancient Farm even more realistic they wanted authentic livestock of the era.

For sheep it was easy, the primitive Soay with their ancient ancestry were perfect for the job. Long-legged Dexter cattle were chosen because they matched the size of the archaeological finds. But it wasn't so straightforward with swine, and as there were no Iron Age pigs in existence, we had to make our own. We borrowed a wild boar from London Zoo (and wild was an accurate description) and put him to a pair of our Tamworth sows. The result was a litter of feisty, striped piglets which grew to resemble the animals our farming ancestors would have reared. Some were as wild as their father but others were easier to handle. We selected hard and only kept those with a kinder temperament, so that within a few generations we had pigs that looked like wild boar but behaved like domestic pigs.

Afterwards, it was a real buzz to see our herd of new Iron Age pigs on TV in a fly-on-the-wall series called *Living in the Past*. Fifteen volunteers turned their back on the modern world to spend a year on their own in an ancient settlement. It was reality television before the phrase had even been invented. That was more than forty years ago when the headache for us was the desperate lack of unrelated Tamworths; with so few bloodlines, breeding them was getting tricky. But while he was filming his landmark BBC series *Great Alliance*, Dad stumbled across the solution. Later, he wrote down what happened:

On a world trip televising domestic animals I found myself in Australia where I met Phil Carter, owner of the Woorak stud of Tamworth pigs near Tamworth, New South Wales. I flew out to his farm where I saw more Tamworth pigs than we had in the whole of Britain. Phil arranged for the shipment of three young Tamworth boars and three Berkshires back to Britain for the Rare Breeds Survival Trust which did much for those breeds in this, their country of origin.

If bloodlines and good genes are the goal then it's the Tamworth which can claim first prize for piggy progeny. The oldest pedigree pig herd in the entire British Isles are the Tamworths owned by Caroline

Wheatley-Hubbard. She rears her 25 Tamworths out-doors on the chalky banks of Wiltshire's River Wylye. The family have been farming since the nineteenth century and Caroline's herd started in 1922 when Joshua Hirst bought his first pedigree pig, a sow called Jemima. Since then, a detailed record of every boar used for breeding and every piglet born on the farm has been kept.

Caroline is so proud of the purity in her pigs' heritage that she's listed every one of Jemima's descendants on an enormous family tree that's so long it has to be rolled up like a length of precious parchment. She also has an album full of old black and white photographs of the best breeding sows and a collection of prize cards from the Royal Show and the Bath and West dating back to the early 1930s. It's a real joy to see Caroline's commitment and it's obvious that in her hands the Tamworths, and their history, are safe.

The fiercest champion for rare breed pigs I think I've ever seen was the TV cook Clarissa Dickson Wright. And I mean fierce. The former barrister became a star in middle-age as one of the BBC's *Two Fat Ladies*, roaring around the country on a motorbike and sidecar alongside the food writer Jennifer Paterson. Clarissa was no-nonsense, plain-speaking, controversial and utterly non-PC with a voice like a duchess and a withering stare if something displeased her. I don't think anyone was the least bit surprised when it emerged that her full name was Clarissa Theresa Philomena Aileen

Mary Josephine Agnes Elsie Trilby Louise Esmerelda Dickson Wright (she claimed that her parents got drunk on the way to the christening).

In 2011, Clarissa made a TV programme about British pork and she used her 30 minutes of national air time to push the case for rare breed pigs. Actually, she did more than that, she looked straight down the barrel of the camera and demanded that her viewers stop shilly-shallying around and start buying traditional native pork. But she saved her scorn and rage for the government legislation that changed the fortunes of UK pig farming from a wide variety of breeds to just three. She was livid as she waved a copy of the Howitt Report in the air, smacking it with her fist as she read out its main recommendations before throwing it to the ground. It was a wonderful television moment.

Calmly watching her unleash her fury was the man she was meant to be interviewing, my old friend the pig historian and author Richard Lutwyche. There's not much about hogs that Richard doesn't know and he's the man credited with changing attitudes about eating rare breed meat. He set up the first scheme to promote high quality, pedigree beef, pork, lamb and mutton from rare breeds and encourage more people to buy it. His Traditional Breeds Meat Marketing Company oversees all the meat that's supplied to approved and accredited butchers with a certification for every carcass that's sold. Today, more than ever, shoppers need that reassurance to know the food they're buying is safe, traceable and really is from the breed described on the label.

Richard has a great knack for promotion and there's an entire species which would benefit from his kind of expertise. I've always thought goats could do with some decent public relations. Of all the farm breeds, they're the ones that are most overlooked – not as big as cattle, as numerous as sheep or as cute as pigs. But despite not being among the big 'box office' breeds, there's a great story with goats, if only more people knew about it. Goats were the second species to be domesticated (dogs were the first) and we've been herding them for around 9,000 years. They're great survivors, the most adaptable domesticated livestock species on the planet and they've acclimatised to every continent except the Antarctic. I've got about 80 goats on the farm including Golden Guernseys, the South African Boer breed, and two Swiss varieties that are now well established in the UK, the Toggenburg and the Saanen. But if you want a history lesson on hooves, then it's the Bagot you're after.

Black and white with long hair and a set of fine-looking curved horns, there's a famous legend that Richard the Lionheart brought Bagot goats to Britain more than 800 years ago on his return from the Crusades. It isn't a very good milking goat and it's not a great meat breed either, but they are lovely to look at which meant they were the perfect choice for the well-to-do who wanted an ornamental parkland goat. It's said a herd was given to Sir John Bagot of Blithfield Hall by

Richard II in return for a good day's hunting on his estate. Although my dad's old friend Phil Drabble, who actually looked after the goats in Blithfield Park, always insisted that the king had endured a *bad* day's hunting and the Bagots were a punishment!

Phil was a mellow, softly spoken gent who always seemed to be smiling and he's the man to thank for keeping the breed from dying out. The flat-cap wearing, wax-jacketed man from the Black Country was the very essence of the British countryside for the eight million people who watched *One Man and His Dog* on TV from the 1970s through to the early 1990s. Phil was so in touch with nature and the wildlife of the Midlands that when he was a guest on *Desert Island Discs*, two of his eight record choices weren't well-known hits or big musical numbers but recordings of a curlew and an English blackbird.

The first Bagots to arrive at the Cotswold Farm Park were part of the semi-feral herd which Phil looked after in Staffordshire. They'd been made homeless when their parkland was flooded to create a new reservoir to serve Birmingham, so Nancy, Lady Bagot rounded the goats up and we gave some of them a new home. In actual fact, stray Bagots have often found their way to Bemborough.

I can remember in the mid-2000s coming home to discover two Bagots I'd never seen before making themselves at home in one of the loose boxes in the yard. Dad had been told that their owners had bought them as pets but couldn't handle them, so in an act of compassion he'd driven all the way to Devon and brought them back. They were twins, called Rose and Rhea, and at that time there were only about 60 breeding female Bagots in the world, about a quarter of the number there is now. New populations are being established in the Channel Islands and also in Northern Ireland, at Tannaghmore Animal Farm. They fit the stereotype of the greedy goat exactly, and although tugging at coat sleeves and nibbling the shopping bags of passers-by is amusing, that keen appetite is being put to good use. Several nature reserves now set Bagots free for scrub clearance.

'Release them into a field of dock weed and they think they've been let loose in a sweetie shop,' says Sarah Pumfrett with a smile. Her Bagot goats were bought with practicality in mind. She had an invasive weed problem on her five-acre paddock but she didn't want to use sprays and digging didn't work, so she turned to something more organic. The bonus was that she found her wily little weed-destroyers to be charming, intelligent and talkative animals (she says she often holds conversations with the kids), although they can still be flighty and prone to run off. 'They're not like Golden Guernseys which will sit in a field and smile at you all day,' she sighs. 'If I need to do anything with the Bagots then it's a case of having to rugby tackle them.' Sarah doesn't subscribe to the connection with Richard the Lionheart ('it's a great story though') and looks instead to a genetic link to the traditional breeds of feral British goat – the Old English, Old Irish, Old Scottish, Old Welsh and a northern group of goats called the Cheviot.

There are clusters of primitive, unmanaged goats all over the UK, such as the Old English herd which lives in the fittingly named Valley of the Rocks high up on the sandstone cliffs near Lynton on the North Devon coast. For some people the wild population, their droppings and destructiveness, are a problem and one that's out of control. But Sarah is saddened by the opposition to them, preferring instead that the wild goats are moved and managed. 'It does need sorting out and there are people willing to take these feral goats on, but they'll need rounding up.' And that might take more than dock leaves and rugby tackles.

Back in the farm office I was pacing up and down. The news I'd been waiting years for was on its way. At least that's what I'd been told. But the promised email had been delayed more than once and the tension was unbearable. Months earlier I'd invested money in a herd of cattle that officially didn't exist. It sounds bonkers I know, but sometimes you have to take a gamble. Now I just needed to know if it was going to pay off.

The animals I'd bought were Albion cattle, a lost breed that virtually everyone considered extinct. They were a blue-grey dual purpose animal that was developed in the 1920s to graze the hills of west Derbyshire.

They were sometimes called Blue Albions or Bakewell Blues, after the lovely spa town in the valley of the River Wye that's the birthplace of the famous Bakewell pudding. It's thought Derbyshire breeders looking to develop a good, local dual dairy and beef animal crossed Welsh Blacks with white Dairy Shorthorns. I'd heard stories about these cattle for decades and knew about the old saying among Midland herdsmen, 'You'll never see a bad blue 'un.'

My newly acquired Albions were a young bull and seven cows, along with three crossbred calves. But the star of the herd, and the oldest of the group, was a lovely cow with a brown marking on her head in the shape of a heart. So she was immediately christened Valentine of course. Almost as soon as they'd arrived, the vet dropped by to give them a full health check.

It's vital that as early as possible all new arrivals on the farm are tested for the five main cattle diseases: a potentially fatal respiratory condition called Infectious Bovine Rhinotracheitis, Leptospirosis and Neosporosis which can both cause unborn calves to die, a horrible wasting disease called Johne's, and Bovine Viral Diarrhoea which is just as nasty as it sounds. All we need to do is take a single sample of blood from the tail of each animal which the vet sends away for analysis. It's not just about the health of those individual cattle, it's for the good of the entire herd. Sadly we lost the bull when we discovered he was suffering from a respiratory disease. Then came the final obstacle in getting the herd passed fit – the compulsory TB test. It's never easy for any farmer and even tougher when TV cameras are recording every nerve-wracking moment as you wait for the vet's verdict. I never complain about the filming though, I know that's what I signed up for! Thankfully all the cows were clear and I could smile for the first time that day.

Back in the office I opened the laptop for a final check on my emails and there, at last, was the confirmation I'd been counting on. 'Rare Albion officially recognised for the first time since 1960' was the headline on a draft press release from the Rare Breeds Survival Trust. As I'd hoped they would, after months of diligently check-ing the genetic makeup and the characteristics of several generations of these animals, the charity had declared that the 170 Albion cattle that had been located around the UK really were a true native breed after all. Tremendous news!

It was a decision with huge significance. For a start, it's incredibly difficult to get recognition for a seem-ingly 'dead' breed and as a result it's something that has happened very infrequently in the past 50 years. It's a massive detective job for the RBST to investigate the bloodlines and make sure there's concrete proof they've got genes that go back to the historic herds. Being an officially declared rare breed means that the number of productive females is properly checked, the purity of new calves can be monitored and the breed can appear on the annual Danger List.

'We can really start shouting about them,' Ruth Dalton from the RBST said as we chatted about the months of hard slog it had taken to establish this new status for the Albions. 'Now the breed society can effectively promote them, it'll make all the difference,' she added as we looked across the farm with pride (and relief) at my little herd. I think she might even have been more excited than I was.

It all begs the question, how can a British breed disappear from view so spectacularly? Well the poor old Albion was the victim of terrible bad luck. First there were devastating outbreaks of foot-and-mouth disease in 1922 and 1924, just as the breed was getting established, made worse by the great agricultural depression and the Wall Street Crash. Then, when the Ministry of Agriculture insisted that only inspected and licensed bulls could be used for breeding, there were no Albions found or put forward by their owners. So although calves were being born, no one in authority knew about it.

Over time, with no paperwork to prove their existence, the breed officially disappeared in the 1960s, which also meant they didn't crop up when the first British rare breeds census was carried out a decade later. Another outbreak of foot-and-mouth in 1967 didn't help, and as they were already scarce many people assumed the Albion was done for. But in reality there were a few tiny herds on isolated hill farms which were completely under the radar. In the 1970s, proving the progeny of these pale-skinned cattle became impossible and one of the biggest drawbacks for the Albion was its lack of a champion. As we've seen, every breed needs someone who fights for their status and pushes owners to club together, register their animals and improve the quality of their herds.

We've recently found out that the arrival of my new herd wasn't the first time Albion cattle had been at Bemborough Farm. Back in the 1980s, Dad was foresighted enough to bring one of these disputed Albion bulls home, a prime example of the breed by the name of Blue Mink. Dad even took a sample of semen from him to be put into storage, just in case it was ever needed. Regrettably he never managed to find any Albion cows to bring to the farm and join Blue Mink. History may have been very different if he had. But with official recognition, I think the breed has got a bright future now. Like so many old livestock, the Albion is great at converting rough grass into good quality milk and meat, which is so important at a time when we're looking for less intensive systems of food production. They could soon come into their own as a source of affordable, nutritious food.

Derbyshire can be really proud of its new found farm heritage and the Albion now joins the county's other local breeds: the Dales pony, the Derbyshire Redcap chicken and two tough varieties of sheep. The first, the

Derbyshire Gritstone, is as hard as its name suggests. It's one of our speckled-face sheep with black and white features and comes from the rugged High Peak country where it grew strong, robust and with a natural resistance to disease. It's in the same camp as other great hardy hill sheep like the Swaledale and the Scottish Blackface which used to 'harvest the mountains' and provide all the right genetics for crossbreeding in the Stratified System.

The second Derbyshire sheep breed is the Whitefaced Woodland and it's named after the Woodland Dale on the Pennines where they evolved. It's just as solid as the Gritstone except it has wonderful spiral horns. As well as being one of the largest mountain sheep in Britain, the Whitefaced Woodland also produces the finest hill wool. That's thanks to the influence of Spanish Merino genes, introduced by the Duke of Devonshire when he put them to his Whitefaced flock on the Chatsworth House estate at the turn of the nineteenth century. In the 1980s, before I went off to agricultural college, I spent a very memorable year on work experience at Chatsworth. Though long, long after the Merinos had had their day.

Maureen Johnson has been in love with Whitefaced Woodlands since she first saw them at an agricultural show in the 1990s and immediately vowed that one day she'd have her own. Now she's got 30 of them in her flock at home along with some free-range Derbyshire Redcaps. 'I don't care that they're not fashionable, they're beautiful, and as I'm from Derbyshire I think it's important to keep them going.' Maureen is a lawyer and a university lecturer in criminal law, so doesn't fit most people's image of a rare breeds farmer. But law and livestock chime along perfectly. 'The sheep are the balance to my professional life, the yin and yang. I'm an academic not a creative, but when the lambs are born, and I know I've chosen the genes and cared for the ewe through her pregnancy, then that's the sort of creative I can do.'

It's amazing where you find Whitefaced Woodlands. Some of these extraordinary sheep happen to live in one of Britain's most extraordinary habitats – a long, bleak shingle spit on the east coast called Orford Ness. It's low-lying so it often floods in winter and for decades it wasn't just the North Sea that made it a no go area. Its remoteness meant it was ideal as a military testing site and through both World Wars and the Cold War that followed, the exact nature of the experiments carried out by the Ministry of Defence at Orford Ness was shrouded in mystery. Now it's a coastal nature reserve where Andrew Capell looks after his Whitefaced Woodlands in a mixed flock which also includes a few other tough characters – Herdwicks, Hebrideans and Manx Loaghtans. Andrew is a National Trust ranger, but he much prefers to be called a shepherd and when he's not tending to his flock on the marshes, he'll be giving a talk to visitors or pitching up at a village hall somewhere to spread the word about his livestock and conservation grazing: 'Part of the site was a secret location so I like the theme of discovery – the discovery of sheep breeds.'

The great clay county of Leicestershire is the final destination before I turn for home. Appropriately, it's a shire famed for its sheep and it's the very heart of England; as the most central of our patchwork quilt of historic counties there are very few farms, towns and villages here that are less than a hundred miles from the sea. I'm here for two special appointments. One is a pilgrimage, the other is purely for pleasure.

When people ask me if I have a hero, I don't hesitate for a second. It was my dad. He guided me, inspired me and influenced my careers, in farming and television, more than he ever realised. In the 1970s he jokingly called himself 'the BBC's tame farmer' and I like to think that I play the same role all these years later. But if the hero question is about famous (or infamous) historical figures then I have to pick a genes genius. Today I'm on an excursion to see the final resting place of Robert Bakewell, the great livestock improver, the pioneer of selective breeding and the man it's impossible to avoid mentioning if you spend more than just a few minutes discussing farm animals. So I'm going to church. But there are no polished wooden pews here, no solid brass eagle lectern and not a single elaborately patterned stained glass window. This church is a ruined shell without a roof or a front wall. The last time a service was held at All Saints' Church in the village of Dishley near Loughborough was in 1845, but it's an important spot because it's Bakewell's final resting place. The great agriculturalist's plain grey tombstone, made of local Swithland slate, lies flat in the abandoned chancel. The simple inscription reads:

Robert Bakewell
Who departed this life
on the 1ˢᵗ of October
1795
Aged 70 Years

A grand memorial plaque in Westminster Abbey it isn't. He certainly would have deserved that honour, but then again this little parish was his home and it witnessed his great achievements.

How much of this area he'd still recognise – well that's a different issue. The original Dishley Grange where he lived has gone, rebuilt in the 1800s, and today the A6 Derby Road cuts noisily past the farm entrance and the M1 isn't far away either. But his memory lives on in the breed that changed farming for ever; the Leicester Longwool.

Bakewell wanted to develop a sheep that had the maximum meat, grew in the minimum amount of time and with the minimum expense. He began with old-fashioned Leicester and Old Lincoln sheep, and with careful selective breeding created a new, improved animal he called the Dishley Leicester – the first designer sheep in the world. In the years afterwards the Dishley became known as the Leicester Longwool and its genetics influenced many British breeds including the large, classy Border Leicester and the lustrously woolly Bluefaced Leicester.

One thing that's not so well known about Robert Bakewell is that he was a nosey neighbour. Usually that's an annoying habit, but in his case it worked to everybody's benefit. His techniques were improved by simply looking over the fence. While he was selecting the best animals in his own flocks and herds he was also inventing progeny testing, or assessing the worth of the offspring. It was simple to do. He rented out his rams to his farming neighbours and then he rode around on his horse, gazing from on high, to spot which farmer had got the best crop of lambs that spring. He'd then knock on the door and take back the ram responsible to use in his own flock. That way he did more to improve the Dishley Leicester than anybody else had ever done with any other breed in history.

Today Bakewell's legacy exists in my own flocks, but with the added advantage of new technology. In the familiar yellow ear tags worn by every sheep there's an electronic chip which links to all the information I could ever hope to know about that animal's breeding, genetics and health – when and where it was born, who its parents were, its height and weight – it's medical history and more. I can download it, even when I'm out in the field, and make informed decisions about what rams and ewes to mate for the best results. It's the twenty-first century way of constantly improving the flock – and Bakewell would approve of that.

One man who knew Leicester Longwools better than anyone I've ever met was Chris Coleman. He was the seventh generation of his family to breed them and, remarkably, could trace the bloodline of the flock further back to the very first new Leicesters and to Robert Bakewell himself. After 178 years devoted to the breed, it was officially the oldest flock of Leicester Longwools in the country and the second oldest of any sheep breed (just beaten to the record by a flock of Romneys).

When I called in on him in 2013, Chris was kind enough to show me the family heirlooms and together we pored over photos of his father and grandfather preparing ewes and lambs for competition. He remembered that when he was young, the family would send their top prize-winning animals to buyers in New Zealand, Australia, South Africa and even the United States. This was the 1940s and 50s when most British families had never been abroad for their holidays, and yet the Coleman's Leicester Longwools were off around the world. On the table in front of us a beautifully crafted silver trophy caught my eye. It was an intricately carved figure of a sheep, perfect in every detail, on top of a highly polished wooden plinth. The engraved plaque on the side revealed that this was the prize for the

Champion pen of Longwool lambs at the Royal Smithfield Show, and underneath this was a list of the 13 years between 1950 and 1974 when the prize had been won by the Colemans.

Chris was an extraordinary man, and not just because of his devotion to his breed. During his entire life, all 86 years of it, he only ever lived in two houses, and they were just a hundred yards apart. When the Rare Breeds Survival Trust was established Chris was right there from the start, and for more than 40 years he was a sheep steward at the Great Yorkshire Show. But my visit to Chris was tinged with sadness because he was just about to retire and, with no one able to carry it on, the flock was being dispersed. His last five ewes were up for sale. To me it felt like a dynasty was ending, though Chris was characteristically philosophical about the reality of the situation. 'It's alright some people saying it's just about putting a few sheep in a paddock but Adam, you and I both know that farming is a lot of work.'

In typical Longwool country, east of Leicester where the River Eye becomes the Wreake, is a town with the tastiest boundary signs in England. On all the roads into the centre there are huge boards informing you that you're entering 'the Rural Capital of Food'. Then, just as you're wondering what that actually means, there's a reminder that this is 'the home of Stilton Cheese', and another big hint 'Melton Mowbray Pork Pies'. To finish the job, that sign is topped by an image of a bottle of wine, a wedge of cheese and a half-started pork pie.

I like this place enormously and not just because it always feels like suppertime. For hundreds of people, the words Melton Mowbray mean an annual outing to the little Leicestershire town for a unique get together of breeds, breeders and bidders at what is the biggest event of its kind in the country. The Traditional and Native Breeds National Show and Sale is like Christmas Day, the Last Night of the Proms and the F.A. Cup Final all rolled into one. Since 2002 it's been the national event dedicated solely to Britain's indigenous farm breeds, where they're displayed, paraded, judged, auctioned but above all celebrated. The setting couldn't be more appropriate either. Melton Mowbray's livestock market is the biggest town centre auction in the country, and it's been in existence for a thousand years, which means there were animal sales taking place here even before William the Conqueror sent shudders round England with his great survey, the Domesday Book, in 1086. The weekly livestock auctions take place on Tuesdays and even that routine detail is imbued with historic importance: Tuesday has been sale day since at least 1324 when a market charter was granted by Edward II.

The yearly rare breeds show is so big it takes place over two days. Arriving early at the marketplace, I walk through the old stone gateposts standing like a couple of guards on sentry duty and head for the concrete steps up into the wide, open-sided modern live-stock buildings. 'I hope you like sheep, mate,' I hear a cloth-capped man say as we pass each other. He nods in the direction of the main animal pens, 'There's thousands of 'em in there.' And he's not wrong. A thousand ewes, rams and lambs of every conceivable shape, size and colour fill the entire floor space of a building that's as big as a double aircraft hangar. In the next shed there are cattle, pigs and goats. In total more than 50 different breeds are represented, and that's not counting the enormous variety of poultry and waterfowl on show. It's a wonderful, atmospheric way of 'meeting the breeds' as well as the people who are dedicated to rearing them.

There are serious breeders and seasoned old-timers everywhere you look, but it's a show that welcomes anyone with an interest and among the first-timers at Melton is Gill Marshall. A semi-retired secretary, she's brought her Lincoln Longwools here from her small-holding in Newark, where she also keeps turkeys and three Gypsy Cob horses. 'My place looks just like the farm in *The Darling Buds of May*,' she admits, 'I call myself a hobby breeder, the sheep are pets really.' Yet Gill is just as passionate about the breeds, and focused on their prospects, as any exhibitor. 'The future is touch-and-go for the Lincolns,' she says, while outside farming circles she worries that 'few people know and even fewer people care.' A bigger presence for traditional breeds at county shows is needed, she thinks, and anything that can capture the mood of the Melton Mowbray sale would definitely help.

That'll please Hugh Brown. He's the market's chief executive, and regards the event as an annual highlight. 'It's like the Crufts of livestock. Hundreds of people, literally from North Ronaldsay to the Isles of Scilly are here, and for many of them it's the only time during the year that they'll meet.' He's very open about the financial side of the Show and Sale – an event that's not as commercial as the weekly auction but more expensive to run. 'Normally we get a small number of dealers with a lot of livestock. At this event we get a large number of dealers each with a small number of animals.' Although Hugh is more than aware of the positive profile it gives the market and the town in general.

Getting the livestock on and off the site, providing feed, bedding straw and safeguarding animals' health and welfare is a logistical jigsaw which makes the weekend a triumph of planning and organisation. The person behind it all is someone I can say, with total sincerity, I've known all my life: my elder sister Libby. She's a pivotal figure in the British rare breeds movement and has been all her adult life. She went to Oxford University to study animal behaviour and while she was still in her twenties she moved to the United States to be the first chief executive of their equivalent of the RBST, the American Livestock Breeds Conservancy. She's been a UN consultant and has sat on an important parliamentary committee advising the government.

She also looks after the herd and flock books for 130 UK breeds. That's most of the breeds that appear on the RBST Danger List. The individual breed societies keep on top of the various records, registrations, births and bloodlines by using a specialist computer system that Libby created more than 20 years ago. The rare breeds sale's success is Libby's success.

As the crowds start to thin and the livestock trailers are lined up for loading at the end of another successful Melton Show and Sale, I leave Leicestershire feeling incredibly pleased for my sister, and very proud. Her long-held view is that in rearing these fascinating animals we're all simply guardians of their heritage and our job is to pass the breeds on to the next generation in a better state than we found them. It's a pretty good philosophy, certainly one which would have saved dozens of breeds in the past.

Tamworth Pork Fillets

Serves: 6

700g–900g (1^1/$_2$–2lb) pork fillet
^{1}/$_4$ tsp potato flour, arrowroot or cornflower
150ml (^{1}/$_4$ pint) mixed yoghurt and cream
1 tbsp olive oil
55g (2oz) butter
3 tbsp apple juice
2 tbsp apple jelly
2–3 tsp pink or green peppercorns or a mixture of both
salt and pepper

1. Trim the fillets, then cut on the slant into 2.5cm (1in) wide slices, then bat out gently under cling film
2. Stir the potato flour, arrowroot or cornflour into the yoghurt and cream mixture (this is so that it won't curdle when boiled).
3. Season the pork. Heat the butter and oil in a large frying pan. When the frothing subsides, sauté the medallions of pork briskly for 1–2 minutes on each side, then remove to a serving dish.
4. Add the apple juice and jelly to the pan and stir in any bits, then take off the heat to cool the pan before adding the yoghurt mixture and the peppercorns. Return the pan to heat and bring the mixture to the boil, whisking well. Then simmer a moment, taste for seasoning and pour over the pork.

Ann Wheatley-Hubbard, Boyton
The Rare Breeds Survival Trust

CHAPTER 10

The Future

J ust before Christmas in 1980, a primetime BBC Two
programme was devoted to the conservation work
that was going on at the Cotswold Farm Park. Footage
of my Dad going from paddock to paddock introducing
presenter Angela Rippon to his Highland cattle,
Longhorn oxen, Manx Loaghtan sheep and
Gloucestershire Old Spots pigs was very welcome
national exposure. But there was more to it than that.
The TV billings for the show outlined the situation
faced by traditional breeds perfectly: 'Once the basic
livestock of the countryman, they have now been super-
seded by mass-produced breeds that satisfy the demands
of today's housewife.' (It was a long time ago, so perhaps
we can forgive the casual sexism.) The listings then
went to the very heart of the issue that had occupied my
dad for years: 'Could these old-timers of the farmyard

make a comeback, or are they destined to be nostalgic reminders of our rural past?' Four decades later we could just as easily be asking ourselves the same question, but with one important modification, as we've now proved that reversing the fate of a threatened breed is possible.

Despite tales of disaster and fears of extinction, this is actually a story of hope and opportunity. I'm an optimist and take great encouragement from the remarkable about-turns we've seen in the fortunes of some of our breeds. Longhorn cattle were seriously endangered when the first survey of breeding numbers was compiled in 1976 but now they're safely out of danger and are classed as a native, rather than a rare breed. It's a similar situation for Hebridean, Kerry Hill, Shropshire and Wiltshire Horn sheep as well as Beef Shorthorn, Belted Galloway and Red Poll cattle. All of them have seen numbers of breeding stock go up, and sustainable herds and flocks created. Every time I walk through the paddocks on our farm at home, with the high wold and open skies around me, there are living, bleating reminders that their heritage is in our hands. Just looking across at the Bagot goats and Golden Guernseys, or pouring out some rations for a hungry Castlemilk Moorit or Norfolk Horn sheep, is proof that falling off the cliff of existence is not inevitable.

Time and time again I've heard people say that the only way to secure a long-term future for rare and traditional breeds is to capture the interest of young people and encourage them to take on a flock or herd of their own. It's true that a large proportion of the people who keep these livestock are middle-aged or retired and they mostly agree on the need to bring in new, young blood. It's an issue that's not unique to farming, so is anything being done? Well quite a lot actually.

It's reassuring to know that the UK's agricultural colleges and universities have been experiencing a boom in the last few years and many have courses that are oversubscribed. It's a world away from the old, out-dated image of a stuffy school for the sons of rich farmers. It helps that places like Harper Adams in Shropshire, SRUC in Scotland and the Royal Agricultural University in Cirencester are attractive, progressive and brilliantly equipped seats of learning for bright, enterprising young people. Now, I'm realistic enough to know that almost all the graduates will go on to careers somewhere within commercial agriculture, equestrianism or land management, but the important thing is that every year there are hundreds of twenty-somethings with the right skills and knowledge looking for jobs in farming and an industry eager for new blood.

But it would be wrong to think that only a university can steep you in the know-how needed to farm native breeds. In the West Country some extraordinary talent is being nurtured early, on a plot between the wild Quantock hills and the low-lying rhynes and ditches of the Somerset Levels. In the village of Cannington, children as young as 11 help run their own rare breeds farm and grow crops on 90 acres of land at Brymore Academy. It's a state school for boys, what used to be called an Agricultural Technical School, and it's something of a survivor itself having adapted over seven decades of educational reform and changing fashions in schooling. Yet it may be more relevant now than ever.

It's important to say that Brymore isn't a mock farm, it's a fully functioning operation. The pupils are taught to industry standards, the milk is sold through one of the national processors while the eggs and meat go on sale at the school's own farm shop. Every summer, the gates of Brymore are thrown open to the public for an annual country fair with blacksmithing demos and livestock parades drawing in the crowds alongside the more usual attractions like a tug of war and classic cars. It also happens to be one of the busiest days of the year at the farm shop, so if the sun shines and it's barbeque weather, the British Lop sausages and Suffolk cross lamb burgers will almost certainly be sold out.

The late Sula Gibbard attended the fair for years and always set up a stand to promote the Somerset rare breeds support group which she ran single-handedly. At the 2018 event she told me: 'To see a boy of 13 shearing a sheep is wonderful. Lots of people ask about rare breeds here because there's a general appreciation of conservation issues and traceability.' In the cattle shed at the end of the yard Sula was particularly keen to show visitors a little herd of four pure Dairy Shorthorns, owned by the Rare Breeds Survival Trust, but reared by the school. She was confident that interest in minority breeds would increase in the years to come, especially among young people with aspirations. 'There should be more schools like this. Not everyone's going to be a doctor, a dentist or an architect.'

In Gloucestershire, even younger children get a chance to look after native farm animals and learn where their food comes from at an almost legendary farm called Wick Court. It's on the Arlingham peninsula where a horse-shoe bend in the River Severn has created a tranquil, isolated island with tidal waters on three sides and the Gloucester–Sharpness Canal cutting through the landscape on the fourth.

Fifty years ago, the farm was home to the last surviving herd of pure Gloucester cattle, which had been preserved by a pair of elderly sisters known respectfully to everyone as the Miss Dowdeswells. The lonely location certainly added to the 'time capsule' they'd created. The date of their farm dispersal sale, Wednesday 25 October 1972, has gone down in local folklore as the day the county woke up to the charm and the benefits of the Gloucester breed. The buyers at that auction, including my dad, cooperated to keep the blood flowing through their herds and within months the breed society was restarted.

Today, Wick Court is run by a charity created in the 1970s by the children's author Michael Morpurgo and his wife Clare. It's called 'Farms for City Children' and it does exactly what it says on the tin. Throughout the year, classes of junior school children from inner city areas come to Arlingham for a week at a time to experience life on a farm. They discover how to sow, grow and harvest as well as tend to cattle, horses and a herd of Gloucestershire Old Spots pigs. The philosophy here, and at the other two farms the charity runs in Devon and Wales, is 'learning through doing', and after just a few days the children all understand that the livestock get their breakfast before anyone else. As one school teacher tweeted halfway through their stay: 'Another day of moving beyond the national curriculum.'

Meanwhile, in East Anglia, there's a rare breeds farmer who caught the conservation bug much, much earlier. Jordan Stone could name all the breeds of British sheep at the age of four. He went to his first rare breeds sale at five, was winning rosettes at the Royal Norfolk Show at 11 and by the time he was 18 he'd become the youngest ever committee member of the Eastern rare breeds support group. 'I just like all things Norfolk,' he explains before adding thoughtfully, 'and rare things.' The proof of his joint passions is in the list of East Anglian breeds he's displayed at the Wayland Agricultural Show. Not just Norfolk Horn sheep and Red Poll cattle but also Norfolk Black turkeys, a pair of Norfolk Grey chickens and even a Norwich canary and a Norfolk terrier. The rare breeds marquee at the show can be quite an eye-opener for the public in a region dominated by arable farming and where it's claimed people aren't 'livestock-minded' – the East is the bread-basket of England and every year farmers there grow enough wheat to make about six thousand million loaves and sufficient barley to brew two and a half million pints of beer. So Jordan's mission is to make local livestock impossible to ignore: 'Linking breeds to places has an important role to play and people are surprised when they discover their county breeds.' Although he accepts that it's never a case of 'job done' because the fortunes of some breeds 'seem to go round in circles'.

It's a view that's shared by another farmer in the Eastern region, Gail Sprake from the Rare Breeds Survival Trust. She thinks of sheep in particular as 'the victims of fashion' and singles out the slim, primitive Boreray as one breed that's currently in favour, with numbers showing encouraging signs. But for how long? 'The breeds have to be part of British agriculture in the future. 70 per cent of UK farmland is grassland and the breeds are superb at grazing with all the conservation benefits that follow.' Her aim is for these loved and lovely animals to be officially recognised as part of Britain's heritage, for retailers to do more to acknow-ledge rare breeds products and perhaps for a new symbol or logo to highlight traditional meats, similar to the Red Tractor scheme. 'I want everyone talking about our heritage breeds and how *they* played a part in ensuring their survival.'

I wonder if the key to the breeds becoming a national talking point lies in something that already exists? Every year the charity publishes a census of how each of the 116 native sheep, cattle, horse, pig and goat breeds are doing. From Aberdeen Angus cattle right through to Wiltshire Horn sheep, the annual Watchlist is a crucial piece of work because it's a 'State of the Nation' document that tells us if a rare breed really is rare. It's based on the estimated numbers of registered breeding females producing pure-bred offspring, and importantly it puts them into one of five categories from 'critical' (the worst scenario) down to 'minority'. I'd love the list to be better known outside the livestock world though, and it certainly needs to be if the issue of saving the breeds is ever going to 'cut through' to the British public in general.

On the whole, its publication goes unnoticed by the news media, but in 2018 there was a very welcome flurry of interest and some timely national press coverage, particularly of the plight of Vaynol cattle, the Cleveland Bay horse and British Lop pigs. I don't think it's a co-incidence that it was the year the document was released under a new, more direct and user-friendly name: the Danger List.

The rare breeds data isn't preserved in aspic though. Breeds doing well drop off the list, others that are struggling are added. We've had no extinctions since 1972 but some breeds that were considered dead, like the Albion cattle, have been reinstated. So Guy Baxter at the Museum of English Rural Life in Reading is already looking ahead to what might qualify as a traditional native breed in another generation or two. 'If the way we farm changes, then what we regard as commercial breeds now may themselves not be suitable in the future. If that happens *their* numbers will dwindle and someone will start a campaign to conserve them.' Could Cambridge sheep appear on the Danger List one day? Now that really could get a debate going.

What we can say for certain is that a secure future for the breeds, one that ensures they're disaster-proof, is all in the genes. It's not enough just to care for the animals that are walking around now, it's essential to preserve their DNA for generations ahead. A complete National Gene Bank is a priceless, living insurance policy for tomorrow, future-proofing for a time when dwindling herds, infertility or a deadly disease outbreak risk wiping out an historic breed. Semen from bulls has been collected, stored and used to inseminate cows for decades. It's a practice that's been familiar since the 1950s with the genetic material stored in straws (small plastic phials) then frozen in liquid nitrogen and placed for safe-keeping in large metal containers. We're talking unimaginably low temperatures of minus 196 Celsius (that's minus 320 Fahrenheit) which makes the contents of the tanks a hazardous material. Seeing them in storage is as futuristic as it sounds, with technicians in lab coats and goggles lifting stainless steel canisters through a mass of swirling white vapour, like something from a sci-fi film.

It's standard practice to keep reserves of semen from rare breed bulls and rams, but now scientific advances mean the genetic net has been cast wider. The task is underway to collect semen from the remaining rare breeds of equine, sheep, goat and pig as well as embryos from cattle, goats and sheep. It's true that some donations attract more fuss than others and there was a gang of press photographers snapping away when one of the Queen's Highland ponies, a fine chap called Balmoral Lord, gave his gift to the gene bank! The long-term aim is for horse and pig embryos to be harvested and then the far more complex job of collecting genetic material from rare breed poultry. It's not easy and it's certainly expensive: the average cost of harvesting a single embryo is around £900. But it's vital work for providing access to new blood lines when and if breed populations sink to just a few related animals, and to avoid harmful inbreeding in British herds and flocks.

Knowing the gene bank is collecting material doesn't mean we can be complacent. I know that I'm in a privileged position to be able to showcase my own animals, and the admirable work of other breeders around the UK, in front of millions of TV viewers on *Countryfile*. Of course I'd love it if the show's producers allowed me to make films about rare and native breeds every single week, but they indulge me most of the time and I never take the opportunity I'm given for granted. In TV terms, am I on my own though? It often feels like it. Apart from occasional series like *Lambing Live* and *The Farmers' Country Showdown* which have helped get the rare breeds message across to a general audience, the TV schedules don't offer much if you're wanting to know about Britain's heritage livestock.

Could celebrity chefs and the vast number of cookery programmes do more? I think so. Cyrus Todiwala is an enthusiastic advocate for rare breed meat, and there are others, but are they on television enough to make a big enough difference? Especially when everyone who eats it raves about traditional breeds meat. 'We've got a hell of a good product,' is the verdict of Davina Stanhope. She's a Cotswold sheep breeder, and a very successful one; her Tingewick flock has won plenty of cups, trophies and rosettes at competitions around the country. 'I think people *do* care, especially younger people who want to buy meat from a butcher not a supermarket,' she tells me, before adding, 'We've got to do more education though.'

She's right. We have a long way to go. A few years ago, my sister Libby went for Sunday lunch at a pub carvery and underneath a row of copper heat lamps at the counter she saw an enormous joint marked 'Tudor Beef'. This instantly raised Libby's curiosity, eyebrows and hackles all at once. She quizzed the restaurant manager, 'What is this Tudor Beef you're serving?' He answered, 'Oh it's a rare old English breed, madam.'

She replied that it wasn't, he insisted it was. Deciding not to let a disagreement ruin her weekend off, Libby let the matter lie but when she returned the next day the owner reluctantly agreed that there was no such thing as 'Tudor Beef' and it had been a regular roasting joint after all. Was Libby the only person to query it? Probably. But it's a warning for all of us to be on our guard.

There is one factor which none of us can control though, and it's the topic that dominates every discussion about farming, conservation and animal welfare. Actually, it's currently overshadowing discussion in every industry. Brexit of course. During the seemingly never-ending referendum campaign I said publicly that I was supporting Remain – a decision I based on the fact that there was so little real information available about what agriculture and the nation as a whole would look like outside the EU. I suppose I was being a typical risk-averse farmer. But unlike a lot of people (and as it turned out, some politicians) I accepted the result of the referendum. Once the voters had spoken then I was all for the negotiators getting the best possible deal for British farming.

In many important ways the true effects of Brexit won't be known for years, possibly even a decade or more. But there are two things we know about the British which are impossible to deny. First, we're a nation of animal lovers. The number of charities dedicated to helping, homing or saving animals is proof of that, and you only have to skim through the TV schedules to see the popularity of programmes about pets, vets, zoos and safari parks. Secondly, we love supporting the underdog. There's something about backing a longshot that marks us out as Brits. Can you imagine any other country that would have made a national hero of Eddie 'the Eagle' Edwards? I rest my case. Those two British characteristics should be good news in the fight to bring our rarest breeds back from the brink and keep the ones we've already saved.

You may have already taken the first small step in that process. If you've bought this book and made it as far as the final chapter, then I'm delighted. It indicates an interest and inquisitiveness about the breeds of the British Isles which is the launching pad for some great discoveries. Perhaps you're more than just interested, in which case never be embarrassed about your passions. Unashamed enthusiasm should be encouraged much more than it is. I'm reminded of a radio interview my dad gave in 2011 to mark the fortieth anniversary of the Cotswold Farm Park. In his deep, chocolatey voice he reminisced about days out when he was driven around in the family car by Mum and how he'd demand she stop and reverse if he saw an interesting cow in a field or spotted a rare breed he recognised. 'Look, look, there's a Belted Galloway!' Asked if he'd been an animal anorak, my dad replied in an instant with his trademark chuckle, 'I still am.' I love that.

The way I feel about the future of the breeds was summed up brilliantly by the unlikeliest of people. It wasn't a fellow farmer, a university professor or an expert in genetics, but the TV archaeologist, historian and BBC *Coast* presenter Neil Oliver. He's probably one of the most engaging people on the box and his passion for his topic is infectious. I caught him talking on break-fast television about his fascination with the British Isles, when he said: 'Britain's an extraordinary place, it's the best place, it's got the richest story that I know ... our islands have been here for hundreds of millions of years and they will be here long after we've gone.' That gets to the core of the rare breeds story. The oldest of the old primitive sheep have been grazing the Scottish islands for thousands of years, White Parkland herds graced the great estates for centuries and the improved cattle and pig breeds have been changing our market places, and dinner plates, for the last 200 years. It is extraordinary that some of the animals that were rec-ognised by the Vikings were still being reared by the Victorians. They survived natural disasters, war, famine, the industrial age and the workforce shift from the countryside to the cities. Yes, there have been extinctions, but for the breeds that have made it through it's a remarkable tale of endurance, often against enor-mous odds.

These unique, characterful native breeds make you look at the British Isles in an entirely new way. Travelling from place to place by rail or road isn't merely a humdrum commute when you know that Berkshire, Derbyshire, Suffolk and Hampshire are more than just county names. Places like Romney, Radnor, Wensleydale and the Lleyn peninsula take on a new meaning when you're aware of the breeds that earned local folk a living there. On a hike or a holiday even the rock and stone beneath your feet, whether it's Cotswold, Portland or Gritstone, isn't just geology, it's part of a living local identity.

If you love the landscape where you live, have pride in your county, enjoy a sense of history, concern yourself about conservation and want to eat well, then the rare, traditional and minority breeds are for you. Who wouldn't want to save something that's so important, traditional, iconic and uniquely British with a job to do today and a role to play in the future? Old-timers of the farmyard? Don't you believe it!

Lonk Lamb Lancashire Hotpot and Roast Loin

Serves: 4

450g (1lb) equal quantities shoulder, neck and shin of Lonk lamb,
cut into 2.5cm (1in) pieces
1 rack of under-shoulder chops, trimmed and cut into 4 neck chops
25g (1oz) golden granulated sugar
15g (1/2oz) plain flour
700g (11/2lb) Tarleton Onions, thinly sliced
450g (1lb) Maris Piper potatoes, peeled
55g (2 oz) salted butter, melted
1 boneless best end of lamb
olive oil, white pepper and fine sea salt

1. Preheat the oven/gas 1 to 140°C/285°F.
2. Season the lamb and the lamb chops with the sugar, salt and a good pinch of pepper. Dust with flour, then put the lamb into the base of an earthenware hotpot.
3. Cook the onions, covered, over a moderate to hot temperature in 15g (1/2oz) of the melted butter with half a teaspoon of salt for 2–3 minutes and spread evenly on top of the lamb.
4. Put the 4 neck chops evenly around the perimeter of the hotpot dish, pushing them firmly into the onions (make sure the clean bones are sticking prominently out of the hotpot dish).
5. Thinly slice the potatoes. Place in a bowl, add 30g (1oz) of the melted butter, season with 1 teaspoon of salt and a pinch of white pepper, and mix well. Put the sliced potatoes evenly on top of the onions.
6. Place the hotpot in the preheated oven and cook for 21/2 hours.
7. Seal the loin of lamb with a little olive oil, until golden in colour. Place the seared lamb loin on a trivet above the hotpot during the last 12–15 minutes, or until the lamb is cooked to your liking. Then remove the loin and allow it to set for 5 minutes on a cooling rack.
8. Brush the golden potatoes on top of the hotpot with the remaining melted butter. Carve the lamb loin and place it in the centre of the hotpot.

Northcote Hotel, Lancashire

Acknowledgments

I'm indebted to everyone who took time to share their experiences, opinions or anecdotes for this book and who are subsequently quoted or mentioned in the text. A huge thank you is owed to my sister Libby, for her expertise and rare breed knowledge, in helping to put this book together. In addition, I'm very grateful to the following for their unsung help in gathering or confirming facts and stories on my behalf; Stephanie Belcher at the Malvern Showground, Richard Broad from the Rare Breeds Survival Trust, Jim and Wanda Dale, Megan Dennis and her dedicated team at Gressenhall Farm & Workhouse in Norfolk, Peter Gibbard, Guernsey farmer and tour guide Dave Gorvel, Jonathan Hall, Sarah Laine from the Little Guernsey Donkey Factory, Simon Morgan from the Ruislip, Northwood & Eastcote Local History Society, Jo Papworth at the Royal County of Berkshire Show, Keith & Sue Stone, Heather Tarplee, Diana Walton at the Royal Three Counties Show, Lorraine Warren and Kate Whyte. Research for this book would have been impossible without assistance from Gloucestershire Libraries and the county archives, the Museum of English Rural Life, Norfolk

Museums Service, the Priaulx Library in St Peter Port and Reading University. While invaluable information was gleaned from the extensive archives and online collections of the BBC, the British Film Institute, British Pathé, *Cotswold Life*, *Country Matters*, the *Listener*, *RTÈ* and the *Radio Times* as well as countless local newspapers and numerous individual breed societies & breeders' clubs.

Index

Aberdeen Angus cattle 193–4
Ace of Spades, Berkshire pig 92
African swine fever 112
agricultural colleges and universities 325
agricultural shows
  Balmoral Show, Northern Ireland 235, 250–1
  Royal Bath and West Show 19–20, 21, 24, 25–6, 238
  Royal County of Berkshire Show 91–5, 98–9
  Royal Smithfield Show, London 51, 316–17
  Royal Three Counties Show 295–8
  Tan Hill Sheep Show, Yorkshire 153–4
  Traditional and Native Breeds National Show and Sale, Melton Mowbray 318–21
  Wasdale Head Show and Shepherds' Meet 179–80
  Wayland Agricultural Show, Norfolk 328–9
Albion cattle 306–10, 330
Alderney, Channel Islands 78
Alderney cattle 77–9
All the Queen's Horses, television programme 145
ancestors of domestic breeds xiv–xix
Andrews, Duncan x–xi
Animal Magic, television series 244–6
Anne, Princess Royal 5
Appleyard, Reginald 104–5
arable farming, East Anglia 328–9
Arlingham, Gloucestershire 327
Armstrong, Beryl 164–5
attacks, Shetland ram 223
Aurochs xiv–xv
Austen, Jane 79

Away From It All, television programme 273
Aylesbury, Buckinghamshire 103, 106
Aylesbury duck 103, 106–8
Ayres, Pam 243–4
Ayrshire, cattle 64

Badger Face Welsh Mountain sheep 264
Bagot goat 239, 303–6
Bakewell, Robert xxii–xxiv, 143–4, 160, 251, 313–15
Bakewell Blue cattle 306–10, 330
Ballindalloch castle, Banffshire 194
Balmoral Show, Northern Ireland 235, 250–1
Balwen sheep 264
Barber's, cheddar cheese makers 22–3
Bartlett, Tom 103–4
Bath and West Show 19–20, 21, 24, 25–6, 238
Baxter, Guy 97–8, 330–1
beef 333–4
  cattle 21–2
  Gloucester 19
  Guernsey 71
  Hereford 292
  Welsh Black 275
  White Park 174–5
  Beef and Ale Pie 183
  Potted Brisket of Dexter Beef 257
Beef and Ale Pie 183
Belted Galloway cattle 195–9, 324
Bemborough Farm, Gloucestershire *see* Cotswold Farm Park, Gloucestershire
Beningfield, Gordon 162–4
Bennett, Tony 223–5
Berkeley, vale of, Gloucestershire 4, 13